More Than Meets the Eye

Studies in
Interpretation

Melanie Metzger and Earl Fleetwood, General Editors

VOLUME 1 *From Topic Boundaries to Omission: New Research on Interpretation*
Melanie Metzger, Steven Collins, Valerie Dively, and Risa Shaw, Editors

VOLUME 2 *Attitudes, Innuendo, and Regulators: Challenges of Interpretation*
Melanie Metzger and Earl Fleetwood, Editors

VOLUME 3 *Translation, Sociolinguistic, and Consumer Issues in Interpreting*
Melanie Metzger and Earl Fleetwood, Editors

VOLUME 4 *Interpreting in Legal Settings*
Debra Russell and Sandra Hale, Editors

VOLUME 5 *Prosodic Markers and Utterance Boundaries in American Sign Language Interpretation*
Brenda Nicodemus

VOLUME 6 *Toward a Deaf Translation Norm*
Christopher Stone

VOLUME 7 *Interpreting in Multilingual, Multicultural Contexts*
Rachel Locker McKee and Jeffrey E. Davis, Editors

VOLUME 8 *Video Relay Service Interpreters: Intricacies of Sign Language Access*
Jeremy L. Brunson

VOLUME 9 *Signed Language Interpreting in Brazil*
Ronice Müller de Quadros, Earl Fleetwood, and Melanie Metzger, Editors

VOLUME 10 *More than Meets the Eye: Revealing the Complexities of an Interpreted Education*
Melissa B. Smith

More Than Meets the Eye

Revealing the Complexities of an Interpreted Education

Melissa B. Smith

GALLAUDET UNIVERSITY PRESS

Washington, DC

KH

Studies in Interpretation
A Series Edited by Melanie Metzger and Earl Fleetwood

Gallaudet University Press
Washington, DC 20002
http://gupress.gallaudet.edu

© 2013 by Gallaudet University
All rights reserved. Published 2013
Printed in the United States of America

ISBN 1-56368-579-5; 978-1-56368-579-8
ISSN 1545-7613

9/30/15

This work is dedicated to you, Momma,
for teaching me that one person can make a difference
and always believing that I would.

Annette, Patrick, and Hunter,
you can and do make a difference.
I believe in you.

Contents

Acknowledgments, vii

List of Figures, ix

List of Tables, x

CHAPTER 1: At First Glance: Taking a Look at Deaf Education and Interpreting in K–12 Classrooms, 1

CHAPTER 2: As Previously Seen: Interpreting in Schools, 13

CHAPTER 3: Examining the Work of Interpreters Through Multiple Lenses, 26

CHAPTER 4: Scenes and Subjects, 49

CHAPTER 5: Opening Our Eyes: Discovering What Interpreters Do and Why, 63

CHAPTER 6: What Remains to Be Seen, 164

APPENDIX A: List of Categories and Definitions for Coding Video Data, 175

APPENDIX B: Expanded List and Definitions of What and Why Categories, 178

APPENDIX C: Overarching Themes From Interview and Video Data, 183

References, 187

Index, 197

Acknowledgments

I am grateful to the many people who made this work possible. I especially want to thank the interpreters, teachers, and Deaf and hard of hearing students and their parents who welcomed me into their classrooms (with three video cameras, no less). Your courage and commitment are admirable. I hope that my telling of your stories honors your experiences and heightens appreciation of and respect for the work of educational interpreters while making a difference in the lives of Deaf and hard of hearing students. I would also like to thank PInES students for opening my clouded eyes to how hard K–12 interpreters are willing to work.

I have been fortunate to work with outstanding University of California, San Diego, faculty and committee members. I would like to thank my chair, Claire Ramsey, for believing this work is important and for thoughtful guidance, Tom Humphries for reminding me to look toward the possibilities, Rachel Mayberry for high expectations and insightful feedback, Jerry Balzano for stepping in, Jim Levin for willingness to answer questions, and Paula Levin for being an inspiring teacher. I will always be grateful for the education I received at UCSD. I hope that publishing my dissertation research in the form of this book will lead toward better education for Deaf and hard of hearing students.

Thank you to Ron Jacobs and Kathee Christensen for opening doors and for your unwavering belief in my potential, even as I was beginning my academic and professional career. Part of Chapter 5 of this volume was published in a chapter called "Opening Our Eyes: The Complexity of Competing Visual Demands in Interpreted Classrooms" in *Ethical Considerations in Educating Children Who Are Deaf or Hard of Hearing* (Gallaudet University Press, 2010), edited by Kathee Christensen. I was the sole investigator and author of the submitted chapter. Thank you, Kathee, for the opportunity.

One hundred grams and a donut to Stephanie Latkovski for being an inquisitive, responsive, and encouraging dissertation coach. Thank you for restoring my confidence as a writer when I needed it most.

I learned so much from my cohort and my writing colleagues, especially Pam Long and Cheryl Forbes, who made it bearable (and sometimes almost fun) to write and who cheered for me to write one more paragraph when I didn't think I had it in me. Pam, thank you for helping me figure out what needed to be said and for teaching me more about writing than I learned in my entire advanced academic career. Cheryl, when it seemed there was nobody who really understood the challenges of "extreme parenting," you were there. Thanks for your strength and compassion. UG hugs to you both!

I am deeply grateful for the support, input, love, and encouragement of my family through the years and tears of my graduate studies and dissertation writing. I will forever appreciate my mom for teaching me to love learning and for setting an example of living that I admire, my dad for weed-whacking so I could spend time working, and both of my parents for financial support, hugs, and unconditional love. Thank you for being such phenomenal parents and grandparents. Thanks to my sister, Holly, for coming to San Diego to help watch our four kids so I could write. To my in-laws, Fred and Barb, thank you for both financial and family support. Patrick, Julio, and Josie, you have opened my eyes forever to the truth of how important it is to give Deaf children the opportunity to see. Thank you for teaching me and sharing your love, hugs, and unbridled giggles.

My deepest gratitude and heartfelt thanks go to my wife and kids. Annette, I know how hard this was for you. Thank you for letting me go write even when you wanted me to stay home, for countless discussions to help me clarify my thoughts, for knowing this is important, and for sticking with me through the ups and downs. You are my love of a lifetime. To my beautiful boys, Patrick and Hunter, thoughts of laughing, hugs and kisses, bedtime stories, and days at the beach carried me through some of the toughest times. I can't wait to make up for the many long days I spent writing rather than being with you. I love you so very much.

Figures

Figure 1: Example of Code Input Window used to assign codes to video instances

Figure 2: Mural of student celebrating the school's trilingual learning opportunities

Figure 3: Life-sized mural of students signing at the water fountain

Figure 4: Marina clarifying instructions for Miguel, Kristie, and a hearing classmate

Figure 5: Camie looking back over her shoulder to view the map

Figure 6: Laser beam on back of Camie's hand

Figure 7: Final position next to tall bookshelf (left) with laser beam on map (near Camie's elbow)

Figure 8: Camie making sure she is not blocking hearing students' view of the board

Figure 9: Camie leaning forward to see demonstration of a magma plume under oceanic plates

Figure 10: Camie points to a location on the left as the teacher moves on and points the laser at a location on the right

Figure 11: Camie looking at and touching the drawing of the magma chamber

Figure 12: Camie incorporating teacher's gestures to show change in slope

Figure 13: Marina interpreting math questions for Miguel

Figure 14: AJ clapping her hands in a silent cheer for Angelina

Figure 15: AJ prompting Angelina to raise her hand if she knows the answer

Figure 16: AJ signing ONE and A

Figure 17: AJ emphasizing that *beware* ends with an *e*

Tables

Table 1: Corpus of data collected at each school site

Table 2: Comparison of competing visual demands as determined by principal investigator and Rater 1

Table 3: Comparison of competing visual demands as determined by principal investigator and Rater 2

Table 4: Comparison of competing visual demands as determined by principal investigator and external raters

Table 5: Description of schools, teachers, and subjects

Table 6: Demographic characteristics of Deaf and hard of hearing students

Table 7: Characteristics of focal interpreters

Table 8: Characteristics of informant interpreters from Via Portal

Table 9: Characteristics of informant interpreters from Meadowbrook

Table 10: Common sources of competing visual input

Chapter 1

At First Glance: Taking a Look at

Deaf Education and Interpreting in

K–12 Classrooms

Sign language interpreters are the channel through which many Deaf and hard of hearing students access and participate in academic and social interactions in public schools.[1] Yet, "educating children with the use of an interpreter is an educational experiment" (Schick, 2004). To complicate matters further, research has shown that interpreters perform multiple roles in the classroom (Antia & Kreimeyer, 2001; Jones, 1993, 1994, 2004), yet very little is known about what K–12 interpreters actually do. Moreover, there has been no research on the factors that inform their moment-to-moment decisions. This volume presents the results of a study that was designed to discover the range of activities and responsibilities performed by educational interpreters and to illuminate the factors they consider when making decisions.

Signed languages are visual languages. The importance of this quality was emphasized almost 100 years ago by George Veditz, a prominent leader in the Deaf community and former president of the National Association of the Deaf. Veditz (1912) delivered a passionate argument in support of American Sign Language, even in the face of intense political pressures, punctuated by the 1880 decision in Milan, Italy, to ban the use of sign language in schools for Deaf children. In this address, he characterized Deaf people as "first, last, and of all time the people of the eye." The fundamentally visual nature of American Sign Language

---

1. The term *Deaf*, with a capital *D*, is used to denote affiliation with and value of American Sign Language and Deaf cultural norms. Throughout this volume, students who use the services of sign language interpreters in public schools will be referred to as *Deaf and hard of hearing students.*

and the people who use it validated his case for the preservation of this language at a time when it seemed on the verge of eradication. Nearly a century later, some Deaf leaders are celebrating the process of discovering what it truly means to be Deaf (Ladd, 2003) and championing the essential aspect of vision as being at its core (Bahan, 2004, 2008; Lentz, 2007).

INTERPRETERS AND ACCESS LEGISLATION: EDUCATIONAL PLACEMENT OF DEAF AND HARD OF HEARING STUDENTS

Some Deaf and hard of hearing students attend special state residential schools, but the passage of legislation requiring that children with special needs be integrated into public schools dramatically increased the demand for educational interpreters. Since the implementation of Public Law 94-142, the Education for All Handicapped Children Act (1975), renamed the Individuals with Disabilities Education Act in 1990 and now called the Individuals with Disabilities Education Improvement Act of 2004 (IDEA), most Deaf and hard of hearing students go to schools with students who can hear rather than to segregated schools for Deaf children. Some of these students are placed in self-contained classrooms with all Deaf and hard of hearing students. Many others are mainstreamed in classes with hearing teachers, hearing peers, and a sign language interpreter.

In mainstream contexts, Deaf and hard of hearing students rely on interpreters for primary access to communication within the academic environment, including access to curriculum and instruction as well as social interactions. The IDEA legislation mandates a free and appropriate public education (FAPE) to all children. If specified in an Individualized Education Program (IEP), Deaf and hard of hearing students must have qualified sign language interpreters who interpret between the spoken English and the signed communication that takes place in the classroom. The definition of *qualified* varies from state to state, and some states have not yet established clear and specific standards of qualification for sign language interpreters in public schools.

The Gallaudet Research Institute's 2002–2003 *Annual Survey of Deaf and Hard of Hearing Children and Youth* reported that 23.4% of approximately 40,000 Deaf children in U.S. elementary and secondary settings used sign language interpreters. Another 16.5% had instructional aides in the classroom. In the 2003–2004 survey, there was little change: 23.1% reported working with sign language interpreters and

17.8% reported working with instructional aides. Since employees who interpret as part of their daily job duties may sometimes be classified as instructional aides, the actual percentage of Deaf students who rely on interpreting in the classroom may be even higher than reported. According to the same report, approximately 60% of Deaf and hard of hearing students were identified as being integrated with hearing students for at least part of the day. Over 35% of Deaf and hard of hearing students in California were at least partially integrated with hearing students. In the 2007–2008 national survey, 22.9% of students receiving instructional support services reported accessing instruction through sign language interpreters (Gallaudet Research Institute, 2003, 2004, 2008).

ACADEMIC PERFORMANCE OF DEAF AND HARD OF HEARING STUDENTS

Some students who are Deaf and hard of hearing do not perform as well academically as their hearing peers. Several factors potentially influence academic outcomes, including use of sign language in the home, age of intervention, amount of hearing loss, and quality of education and support structures.

Most Deaf and hard of hearing children have parents who are not Deaf or hard of hearing. According to Mitchell and Karchmer (2004), 92% of Deaf children are from families with two hearing parents, and 8% have at least one Deaf or hard of hearing parent. Only 4% of children have two Deaf parents. The high percentage of Deaf children with hearing parents is significant for several reasons. Although a signed language may be the most logical choice for a student who cannot hear a spoken language, most hearing parents with a Deaf child do not know sign language. Some researchers suggest that "young deaf children of hearing parents frequently do not have any truly accessible and competent language models, either for sign language or for spoken language" (Marschark, Lang, & Albertini, 2002, p. 12).

Although hearing parents typically serve as fluent language models for their hearing children, they are less prepared to make language accessible to children who cannot hear. Even if parents decide to learn sign language, they will often be less than proficient models of sign language since they are learning sign language along with their children. In addition, hearing parents are often uninformed about effective strategies for communicating visually with their Deaf or hard of hearing children.

This can have a profound impact not only on the language acquisition and cognitive-academic achievement of these children, but also on their socioemotional development.

Studies indicate that Deaf children who are exposed to signing at an early age perform better academically than those who are not (Calderon & Greenberg, 1997; Mayberry & Eichen, 1991; Moores, 1996; Moores & Meadow-Orlans, 1990). The most accurate predictor of academic achievement appears to be early intervention (Marschark et al., 2002; Moeller, 2000; Yoshinaga-Itano, Sedey, Coulter, & Mehl, 1998), regardless of whether parents choose sign language or favor another approach to making communication accessible to their children. Parents must seek and evaluate medical advice to make decisions about communication options as well as education for their Deaf or hard of hearing child. Critical time passes while hearing parents try to determine how best to provide access to language, and to learn to communicate effectively with their child. As a result, Deaf and hard of hearing children may not be exposed to sign language and other interventions during the most critical years for language acquisition. Even if parents begin to learn sign language along with their children, the children typically are not exposed to fluent sign language during all of their waking hours. In contrast, of course, hearing children have the obvious advantage of constant and consistent exposure to spoken language.

Like U.S. students who are native speakers of languages other than English, Deaf and hard of hearing students' English literacy skills often peak at about the fourth grade level, with the consequence that Deaf and hard of hearing students do not perform as well academically as their hearing peers (Allen, 1986; Holt, 1993; Marschark et al., 2002; Schildroth & Hotto, 1994). Academic success for Deaf and hard of hearing students is compromised by the challenge of reading and writing English, which in turn inhibits entry into postsecondary institutions. One study found that only 3% of Deaf 18-year-olds read as well as their hearing peers (Traxler, 2000). Other research provides further validation of the problem, reporting that about 83% of students admitted to the National Technical Institute for the Deaf (NTID) at the Rochester Institute of Technology (RIT) in 2001 and 2002 did not have "the requisite reading and language skills to enter a baccalaureate program in their first year" (Cuculick & Kelly, 2003, p. 279).

Besides age of intervention and signing in the home, another significant factor contributing to academic underachievement among Deaf and hard of hearing students is the communication policies within K–12 schools. Oddly, clear, accessible communication is often not provided at school.

Not even teachers who are credentialed to teach Deaf and hard of hearing children are held to rigorous sign language proficiency standards. What is more, since Marschark et al. (2005a, p. 57) "estimates that over 75% of deaf children are mainstreamed, receiving the bulk of their academic experience in circumstances mediated by sign language interpreters" (Peterson & Monikowski, 2010, p.129), one factor worthy of consideration is the impact educational interpreters are likely to have on the learning outcomes and school experiences of Deaf and hard of hearing students.

SCHOOL COMMUNICATION POLICIES

Historically, there has been much controversy about the language of instruction appropriate for the education of Deaf and hard of hearing children and youth. Heated debates continue to rage about whether students should be taught using American Sign Language (ASL), which is a language distinct from English with its own grammatical rules and vocabulary, or through a form of contact signing in which signs are used following rules for English syntax. Some educators and administrators promote the use of a signing system developed to map modified signs onto English vocabulary and grammar in the hopes of teaching English to Deaf and hard of hearing children. A few of these systems persist in spite of questionable outcomes in improving literacy among Deaf and hard of hearing students. Still others advocate that sign language should not be used at all, providing as rationale that students who are allowed to sign will not develop the ability to speak and lipread English, since sign language will take less effort for Deaf and hard of hearing students. Controversy among scholars and researchers has led many schools to establish language policies to mandate whether interpreters should "interpret" into ASL or "transliterate," which means to produce a more literal rendition of the spoken English, using ASL signs while emphasizing the vocabulary, syntax, and pronunciation (e.g., lip movements) of spoken English words. These language policies often become directives for sign language interpreters.

GOALS OF INCLUSION

The premise of mainstreaming lies in the belief that Deaf and hard of hearing students who use sign language interpreters in K–12 settings have access to and can participate fully in K–12 school activities. While Deaf and hard of hearing students deserve the same quality education that is afforded to hearing students, studies show that although Deaf and hard of hearing students may be integrated in classes with hearing peers, they are not truly included (Kurz & Langer, 2004; Komesaroff & McLean, 2006; La Bue, 1998; Lane, 1995; Power & Hyde, 2002; Ramsey, 1997; Russell, 2006).

Research clearly shows there is still a long way to go before Deaf and hard of hearing children and adolescents truly have access to the resources and support that will allow them to achieve their fullest potential. These children have long been denied the opportunity to access, let alone fully participate in academic and social activities leading to school success. Like English-language learners, students in impoverished or rural areas, students with special needs, and other children who do not have access to the cultural capital of mainstream American society, they have been systematically excluded from rich opportunities for learning.

The premise of inclusion is that Deaf and hard of hearing students will be provided the same quality of instruction and opportunity for learning as their hearing peers (Schick, 2004). Along with academic, linguistic, and cognitive development, socioemotional development through participation and peer interaction is another schooling outcome that deserves attention. School environments are structured "communities of learners" (Lave & Wenger, 1991)[2] in which Deaf and hard of hearing students must be afforded full membership. If Deaf and hard of hearing students are relegated to mere bystander status, then the promise of inclusion is hollow.

IMPACT OF INTERPRETERS ON THE SCHOOL EXPERIENCES OF DEAF STUDENTS

Although very few studies have been conducted in K–12 classrooms with working interpreters, the extant literature indicates the urgency of research in this area. Because most Deaf and hard of hearing children

---

2. Wenger and Lave coined the term *community of practice* to describe an apprenticeship model of learning, in which the community acts as a living curriculum for the apprentice. "Communities of practice are groups of people who share a concern or a passion for something they do and learn how to do it better as they interact regularly" (Wenger, 2006).

are born to parents who are not fluent in sign language, these children may not be not proficient users of any language, including sign language, when they reach school age. Even if the children have limited language proficiencies, do not know sign language, or do not know how to use interpreters to navigate the school system, they may still be assigned an interpreter for all or part of the day. This means that interpreters in public schools may very well be the children's first adult language models. Along with the tremendous responsibility of being a competent language model, interpreters often provide the primary, if not the exclusive, avenue of students' access to academic content and social discourse.

It is important to carefully examine what interpreters do in the course of their work with Deaf and hard of hearing students in mainstream K–12 classrooms and what needs arise from the interactions taking place among interpreters, students, and teachers, as well as the strategies, knowledge, and skills interpreters employ when making decisions about their work. This knowledge will provide a starting point for examining the degree to which access and inclusion are possible via an interpreted education. In addition, it will provide a better understanding of the potential effects interpreters have on the educational experiences of Deaf and hard of hearing students in public schools. Improved practice alone cannot guarantee enhanced learning outcomes, but exploring the pitfalls and possibilities of an interpreter-mediated education is a step in that direction: Empirical investigation of the work of interpreters in mainstream settings is vital to gain a clearer picture of ways in which to improve the state of Deaf education. Only through a better understanding of the work of K–12 interpreters can we begin to acknowledge their influence on the school experiences of Deaf and hard of hearing students. A deeper understanding of the responsibilities of the job is necessary to improve both the education of interpreters and practice of interpreting in educational settings.

ADEQUACY OF PREPARATION AND CONFUSION OF ROLES AND EXPECTATIONS

A substantial number of K–12 interpreters report not having been adequately prepared for employment when they were hired (Jones, 1993, 2004; Togioka, 1990). One area of confusion is the distinction between the roles and responsibilities that should be taken on by interpreters in K–12 settings and those that should remain with the classroom teacher or other members of the educational team. My own observations are consistent with these reports.

As the director and full-time faculty member of the American Sign Language-English interpreting program at Palomar College, I often hear from graduates regarding the challenge of interpreting in K–12 settings. More than half of the students who graduate from our interpreting program find employment in educational settings,[3] and many former students have informed me that they did not feel prepared for the jobs they obtained after graduating with an associate's degree in interpreting. The lack of preparation that has been reported continually for the past 20 years (since, e.g., Gustason, 1985; Stuckless, Avery, & Hurwitz, 1989) is of grave concern. Of equal concern is the fact that due to the time constraints imposed by a 2-year program, the curricular requirements are extremely demanding and the program so time consuming that it is quite common for less than half of the students who enter our interpreting program to complete it successfully. Clearly, a 50% retention rate does not provide evidence of effective teaching and scaffolding, nor is it a sign of reasonable expectations for students. It is, however, a statistic that must be acknowledged. Half of interpreting graduates will likely serve at some point in their early careers as language models for Deaf and hard of hearing students, significantly affecting those students' learning experiences and therefore their post–high school career and higher education options. As an educator of interpreters who often gain employment in K–12 settings, I have an acute interest in the role that interpreters play in the education of Deaf children and hard of hearing children, and I am committed to high standards in the education of interpreters.

One student who graduated with an associate's degree in interpreting from Palomar College and then went on to get a baccalaureate degree in Deaf Studies with an Emphasis in Interpreting from a university with a program that is well respected by the Deaf community contacted me to request information and resources about educational interpreting. She was certified by the only national organization in the United States of sign language interpreters, the Registry of Interpreters for the Deaf (RID), and she had worked as an interpreter for 1 year each at two different high schools.

---

3. In the Palomar College interpreting program, students must complete four 4-unit semester-length ASL classes before they can enroll in two years of interpreting coursework, for a total of four academic years of coursework.

After working for 2 years as an educational interpreter, she began working as a freelance interpreter. However, she often found herself back in the schools. When she contacted me looking for good references related to educational interpreting, I asked her why she was looking. She replied, "To be honest, the reason I am looking for more info on educational interpreting is just for more clarity. I think that it can be a sticky area to interpret. A lot of different ethical issues come up weekly, most of the time dealing with your role in the classroom. It seems like everyone I talk to has a varying opinion of answers to sticky situations." This interpreter went on to say that she had been disheartened by an article (Corwin, 2007) in the January 2007 issue of the *RID Views* (RID's monthly newsletter) and the subsequent editorial response (T. Smith, 2007) to the article, both of which, she felt, reflected a clear lack of consensus regarding the role of K–12 interpreters. (The article discussed historical perceptions of educational interpreters and the controversy about the RID board's decision to accept interpreters who had passed the Educational Interpreter Performance Assessment (EIPA) at a level 4.0 or above as certified members of the organization.)

Other nationally certified interpreters have expressed to me in conversation their discomfort and/or uncertainty about what is expected of interpreters working in mainstream classrooms, stating that educational interpreting has different requirements than interpreting in other settings. In spite of the fact that many interpreters are underprepared for employment in K–12 schools, I have noticed that upon entering the interpreting program some of my students mistakenly assume that interpreting at the elementary level would be easy or boring. My own experiences interpreting in elementary school settings have led me to a different conclusion.

INTERPRETING IN PRIMARY GRADES DURING MY EARLY INTERPRETING YEARS

I am a nationally certified interpreter. I hold a Certificate of Interpretation and a Certificate of Transliteration (CI and CT) from RID and a Level V: Master from the National Association of the Deaf (NAD).[4] I worked for a short time as an interpreter at the high school level, passing

---

4. After 2006, these tests were no longer offered. NAD and the RID instead jointly developed a certification instrument called the NAD-RID National Interpreting Certificate (NIC).

the ASL-to-spoken-English segment of the district's in-house evaluation at their highest level, in spite of the fact that I incorrectly interpreted several facts from the story told in ASL by an elementary-school-aged Deaf boy. Overlooking time indicators, my interpretation (as I recall) had him pull out his loose tooth at least four times before he actually pulled it out. Prior to that evaluation, I had never seen a signer under the age of 18.

I also faced an unfamiliar set of challenges when I had occasion to interpret for several long field trips at the elementary level. Roberto was in fourth grade when I first met him. I was the interpreter for a week-long field trip to an historical area of town. Students went out to different buildings and settings to observe and learn about the ways of life of people who used to occupy the region. I had been the interpreter for Roberto's group throughout the week. Roberto and several of his classmates, including some in his group, were profoundly Deaf. I had worked as an interpreter in postsecondary settings for several years, but I was completely unprepared for this light-hearted, fun-filled, fourth-grade field trip.

Every morning, 50 to 60 children filled a room in preparation for the daily activities. Sometimes the teachers would introduce the children to vocabulary or content that might be encountered later in the day. Sometimes they would just play games or sing songs until all the school buses had arrived from the various schools. One of my first challenges was trying to interpret a children's song designed to increase awareness of the phonology of vowels. The lyrics of the song are simple:

> I like to eat
> I like to eat
> I like to eat
> Eat apples and bananas.

The song is sung several times in a row, and each time, all of the vowels are replaced with the long vowel sound of a targeted vowel. For example, if the vowel *a* were specified, the task would be to replace the vowel sound in all of the words with the long *a* (/ā/) sound:

> Ā lāke tā āte
> Ā lāke tā āte
> Ā lāke tā āte
> Āte āpples ānd bānānās

The song continues with each successive long vowel sound and ends by singing the verse again with the correct pronunciation of the lyrics.

I had no idea how to interpret a song that was almost entirely based on sounds in a way that would be accessible to children who had never heard a spoken language. I remember being horrified, because all I could think to do was repeatedly sign the lyrics in their original form, without the phonetic variations. In spite of my incompetence, the Deaf students laughed and had a good time, and they happily copied my signs as the other children sang along. All of the children and staff were smiling and laughing, while I tried to keep breathing until the torture stopped.

The second challenge came when I realized that Roberto, and a few of his classmates, were recent immigrants from Mexico. Like many Deaf children in Mexico, he had not had formal schooling through any form of signed language. According to staff members who had worked with him on occasion, he had no formal language skills. He could not speak or lipread Spanish or English. He could not read or write. He did not use either Mexican or American Sign Language. He could not fingerspell or write his own name independently.

When I was assigned to Roberto's group, I learned a lot about sign language, and a whole lot more about learning. In retrospect, I recognize that I was completely ineffective in meeting Roberto's language needs. He was an easygoing kid, and we all had a great time that week. Roberto smiled just as much as the rest of us. From his reaction, an observer might not have realized just how often he was left out. There were two things working in his favor: He and his classmates had developed their own means of communicating; and most of the experiences were highly visual and interactive, so he was able to enjoy the daily activities even if he didn't fully understand what a particular lesson was about.

At the end of the week, I learned my own great lesson from Roberto. Sometimes the most effective communication does not rely on formal vocabulary. Earlier in the day, we had gone to an old stable that was still in operation. He loved seeing the horses, and we spent a long time there before moving on to the next activity. When we got back to the main classroom at the end of the day, Roberto ran up to an interpreter who was on staff at his regular school and went into an elaborate representation of what he had seen. Roberto became the horse, mimicking head movements and eating hay so vividly that he re-created the scene for those who had not been there. Although he did not use any formal signs, neither from ASL nor from Mexican Sign Language, his message was clear to signers and nonsigners alike.

During my own interpreting education, I had learned that I should assess the students' language needs, but my understanding was that we would need to decide whether to interpret or transliterate. I did not recall any mention of assessment of language needs beyond that, especially in a school setting. However, when I was out in the field, I found myself wondering how to interpret effectively for these students with such diverse linguistic needs. At the end of the day, all of the groups reconvened in one room to recap the day's events before they boarded the buses that returned them to their respective schools. During this time, all of the interpreters and students gathered in one large room, so we took turns interpreting for the whole group. From my perspective, one of the interpreters made the information so visually clear that I made a vow to emulate her approach when interpreting with Deaf elementary school students or others who had not yet developed solid language proficiencies.

Several years later, when Roberto was in middle school, I saw him again. This time, he was using ASL to describe an occurrence that had taken place at school. I couldn't help but be amazed by the development of his sign language skills, even though nobody in his family used sign language. He had acquired at least some level of language competency through exposure to sign language at school. Deaf students like Roberto and other students from cultural and linguistic backgrounds that differ from the dominant language of a society often struggle in academic environments, both with school discourse (Heath, 1983) and with cultural identity and self-esteem (Cummins, 2001). If it is true that even Deaf children who were severely language deprived during the critical years of language acquisition may still be able to acquire communicative competency when exposed to sign language as late as fourth or fifth grade, we cannot overlook the impact interpreters have on the school experiences of mainstreamed Deaf and hard of hearing children.

Because the literature confirmed my own observations and experience that interpreters were not well prepared for interpreting in K–12 settings, I wanted to explore the ways in which K–12 interpreters might facilitate or hinder optimal learning and social opportunities for mainstreamed Deaf and hard of hearing children. Furthermore, I wanted more information than I could find in the literature about the skills and knowledge that educational interpreters need to do their jobs effectively. I set out to learn more about Deaf education and interpreting in K–12 settings so that I could do a better job of preparing students for employment.

Chapter 2

As Previously Seen: Interpreting in Schools

The context and framework of my research on interpreting in public school settings focused on three areas: the accessibility of an interpreted education, the qualifications and roles of K–12 interpreters, and interpreters and decision making.

ACCESSIBILITY OF AN INTERPRETED EDUCATION

Research on what interpreters do in the classroom is scarce, resulting in a lack of knowledge about how to prepare educational interpreters to effectively meet the needs of Deaf and hard of hearing students in academic contexts. One study shines a spotlight on several types of situations that would be problematic for interpreters working with Deaf and hard of hearing students in mainstream K–12 settings. Winston (1994, 2004) analyzed videotaped classroom interactions and identified six key issues affecting the accessibility of an interpreted education. I view three of these as potentially problematic: (a) multiple channels of input, (b) processing time, and (c) visual accessibility. Winston argued that because interpreters can sign only one spoken message at a time, multiple channels of input, such as overlapping dialogue, may inhibit opportunities for Deaf and hard of hearing students to actively participate in class discussions.

Winston further reported that an essential feature of interpreting known as lag time, processing time, or *decalage* (to refer to the amount of time that elapses between the source message and the interpretation) inhibits the ability of Deaf and hard of hearing students to participate in inclusive settings. However, interpreters cannot interpret effectively into a target language until they have analyzed an incoming message, or *source message,* for its meaning. In fact, as processing time decreases, the number of errors in an interpretation increase (Cokely, 1986).

Timing issues result from this necessary delay and are perhaps most salient in the classroom context, which emphasizes question-and-answer discourse structures. By the time the interpreter has a chance to process the question for meaning and can begin to sign the question, the students who hear the question as it is spoken may have already called out their responses. Research suggests that this timing delay results in frustration and a belief among many Deaf and hard of students that they are unable to participate fully when accessing group and class discussions via an interpreter (Johnson, 1991).

Kurz and Langer (2004) interviewed 20 Deaf and hard of hearing students ranging from elementary-school-aged children to college graduates about their experiences using interpreters in educational settings. The students expressed recurring concerns about the ability to participate fully in classroom environments, primarily due to self-consciousness that their participation would be perceived as inappropriate because of the processing time inherent to interpretation. They also reported lacking confidence that their interpreters could understand them well enough to interpret signed questions accurately and appropriately into spoken English, which added to their reluctance to participate. Students explained that they would adjust their language use by being diligent about signing more slowly, fingerspelling words they would normally sign, planning carefully when to participate based on perceptions of what the interpreter could handle, and even avoiding participation altogether.

In yet another study, a Deaf high school student reported following up with his teacher after class when he did not understand class content, rather than trying to ask questions through the interpreter (La Bue, 1998). The sophisticated skills necessary to manage such additional responsibility and the cognitive burden this would impose on a student are areas worthy of further study.

Several researchers have expressed concerns about visual accessibility in interpreted classrooms (Seal, 2004; Marschark, Schick, & Spencer, 2006). When a teacher gives a spoken explanation and a visual demonstration simultaneously, the students who can look directly at the visual demonstration while listening to the teacher's explanation have a significant advantage over those students who must watch an interpreter to access the explanation. The Deaf and hard of hearing students must watch either the demonstration or the interpreter. As Winston (2004) described:

> Many barriers block seeing an interpretation: the need to write notes, the need to read from a homework paper, the need to watch a movie or

demonstration, the need to read information from the board while the teacher is writing and talking at the same time. Each time the student is forced to look away from the information to see the other required visual input, the interpreting becomes inaccessible. And, each time the deaf student looks at the interpretation, the other required visual input is lost. (p. 138)

Even university students may have trouble managing the demands for their visual attention, of necessity having to choose either to look at the board or other visual input and risk losing access to the interpretation of important information, or to maintain focus on the interpretation and risk missing critical visual information (Johnson, 1991). Although research indicates that Deaf and hard of hearing college students are able to regulate their visual attention effectively (Marschark et al., 2005), at least one study indicates even graduate students have difficulty figuring out who is speaking at a given time during group discussions (Kurz & Langer, 2004). This information is often valuable when forming social relationships and choosing study partners. The significance of visual access in K–12 settings must be explored further. To date, there have been no studies that look at what interpreters do to promote visual access.

Winston (2004) suggests that teachers must be willing to adjust their teaching style so that all instruction and communication in the classroom is sequential rather than simultaneous. However, since this is not a commonly accepted classroom practice, and because sequential presentation of visual display may not be advantageous (Marschark, et al., 2005), further research is needed to see how interpreters actually deal with challenges presented by the need for visual access.

QUALIFICATIONS AND ROLES OF K–12 INTERPRETERS

The exponential increase in demand for interpreters nationwide as a result of legislative mandates for inclusion and access in educational, government, and business sectors has far exceeded the supply of working interpreters. Only in the past two decades has the field of interpreting begun to critically examine and legitimize the work of interpreters in K–12 settings. RID, "after an exhaustive two-year investigation . . . recently announced its findings and decision to accept educational interpreters who score an Educational Interpreter Performance Assessment (EIPA) of 4.0 and above as certified members of the association" (Corwin, 2007). The decision was controversial, and some well-respected members believed that the national professional organization of sign language interpreters watered down its professional standards to make room for this lesser qualified sector of the interpreting workforce, stating that "our poor opinion of the skills of public school interpreters is a generalization, not a stereotype" (T. Smith, 2007). Outrage and discontent flared again in the summer of 2008 when the RID board made a decision to recognize educational interpreters who scored a 4.0 or higher on the EIPA and passed its written test as RID Certified: K–12 interpreters.

Many interpreting program graduates and aspiring interpreters (many of whom find work in schools) do not have the linguistic expertise in both ASL and English to interpret effectively (Patrie, 1994; Stauffer, 1994; Taylor, 1993). A growing literature shows that interpreters are exceptionally unprepared for the realities of interpreting in educational settings (Jones, 1993, 1994; Russell, 2008; Schein, 1992; Schick, Williams, & Bolster, 1999; Schick, Williams, & Kupermintz, 2006; Stewart & Kluwin, 1996; Togioka, 1990). In fact, until recently, schools were required only to provide a "qualified" interpreter, with no guidelines as to what skills and knowledge must be demonstrated. While some states are establishing legislative mandates of qualification for interpreters employed in K–12 schools (a long-awaited recognition that K–12 schools must be held accountable for hiring interpreters with the skills and knowledge that are fundamental to their jobs), as recently as 2004, only 13 states required interpreters working in public schools to achieve at least a 3.5 on the five-point EIPA scale in order to meet minimum qualification standards. Only one state, Nevada, mandated a 4.0, and one state specified a 3.0 (Schick & Williams, 2004). By 2009, six states required a 3.0, 10 required a 3.5, and California and Alaska joined Nevada in requiring a 4.0 or higher. As of 2010, 12 states mandated a 3.5 or better, and Alabama joined the other three states requiring a 4.0 (EIPA Diagnostic Center, 2004, 2009, 2010). According to the test developers, an individual scoring a 3.5 would have "frequent errors in grammar, vocabulary, and rhythm and prosody, which could lead to misunderstandings, lack of knowledge, and misinformation in the student's education" (Schick, Williams, & Bolster, 1999, p. 148). Schick further cautions that interpreters who "produce a message that is missing parts of the original message are not typically making principled omissions. That is, many interpreters are not making decisions that will preserve the most important information for the lesson. In addition, information is not just missing; it is also distorted, confused, and sometimes just wrong" (Schick & Williams, 2004, p. 82).

Although minimum standards for educational interpreters are finally beginning to be established, many states are out of compliance with their own legislative mandates or have had to revise the educational code in order to avoid a statewide loss of the workforce. In one study (Schick, Williams, & Bolster, 1999), the interpreting skills of more than half of 59 employed educational interpreters working in public schools in Colorado were below 3.5 on the 5.0 EIPA scale, even though a 3.5 EIPA score was their states' minimum entry level standard. In 2007, the California Department of Education implemented a transitional plan to join Nevada in requiring K–12 interpreters to achieve a score of at least 4.0 on the EIPA in order to maintain or obtain employment as educational interpreters. Initially, California planned to require a 4.0 by July 1, 2007, but since it was determined that too many interpreters were well below the proposed standards, California's legislation developed a three-step process to bring the public school interpreting workforce up to speed. By July 2007, all K–12 interpreters were to hold certification from the RID or the NAD-RID or score at least a 3.0 on the EIPA, the Educational Sign Skills Evaluation (ESSE), or a cued-speech testing instrument. By July 2008, K–12 interpreters had to have obtained a 3.5 or above if using the EIPA or ESSE to meet minimum qualification standards. Not until July 2009 were K–12 interpreters in California required to demonstrate the level of interpreting proficiency that the state has already defined as meeting minimum standards of qualification, 4.0 or higher on the above-mentioned assessments. As of January 2010, only Nevada, Alaska, and California required K–12 interpreters to achieve a 4.0 or higher on the EIPA, NAD-RID National Interpreter Certification, or equivalent. States are rapidly defining and raising qualification standards. In 2012, a national project funded by the U.S. Department of Education's Office of Special Education Programs (OSEP) reported that four states required K–12 interpreters to achieve at least a 3.0 on the EIPA, 13 states a 3.5 (with one more state giving its workforce until January 2014 to achieve this level), and 10 states a 4.0 or above (Johnson, Bolster, Taylor, Sieberlich, & Brown, 2012).

Although many researchers have lamented the number of educational interpreters who are not adequately prepared for employment as interpreters, K–12 interpreters themselves provide further evidence that schools have not been held accountable to any measure of qualification for their employees working as interpreters. An Oregon survey reported that 87% of interpreters in public schools did not hold any type of certification (Togioka, 1990). Jones (1993, 1994) surveyed 217 interpreters working in public schools in Kansas, Missouri, and Nebraska (74.2% of whom had worked for two or more years in their current positions). Over 63% of the respondents indicated that they held no interpreting certification of any kind. More than 25% reported that their sign language skills had never been evaluated. Alarmingly, more than 61% of these interpreters reported their sign proficiency prior to being hired as *not proficient* or *somewhat proficient,* and only 38.2% rated their sign language skills as *very proficient.* More than half reported no education beyond high school, and 94.9% expressed a need for continued interpreter training.

In a 1998 study of an interpreter working in a high school English class, La Bue found that "the linguistic or instructional integrity of the spoken message was rarely retained in the interpretation." (p. xi). She documented consistent patterns of lexical and grammatical deletions, including pronouns and spatial referencing that indicate the subject and object of many ASL sentences. The result was an "often ungrammatical and incomprehensible" interpretation (p. xi). Inadequate standards for educational interpreters have undoubtedly resulted in unsatisfactory communication access between Deaf and hard of hearing students and their classmates and teachers who do not sign.

Ample evidence exists that interpretation in the classroom is not always clear or optimal (Foster, 1988; Hurwitz, 1991; Johnson, 1991; Mertens, 1990; Schein, 1992). Consistent with earlier findings, Kurz and Langer (2004) found that Deaf and hard of hearing students did not fully comprehend classroom interpreters. Middle school students felt they completely understood interpreters an average of 94% of the time over the course of their schooling, high school students reported an average of 80.5% complete understanding, and college students (and above) reported an average of 72.9% complete understanding. Elementary school students were not asked to give a percentage-based estimate. It is interesting to note that the older the students, the lower the reports of comprehension. Since students indicated that they had more highly skilled interpreters in the higher grades, the researchers presented three possibilities to explain this trend: "that students become more discriminating about the interpreting process as they age; that interpretations suffer as content becomes more complex and specialized; or that students become more proficient language users . . . and take more serious note of miscommunications" (p. 21).

Complicating matters further has been the ongoing controversy about language modes. This debate about the best way for Deaf and hard of hearing students to succeed academically has been prolonged and intense, beginning as early as 1880 at the Second International Congress on Education of the Deaf in Milan, Italy. Arguments continue about whether students should be instructed using an oral approach through the use of lipreading and speech or through some form of signed communication, whether an English-based signing system or ASL.[5] According to Marschark, Schick, and Spencer (2006), "Today, ASL and other natural sign languages are again being used in schools, but still without widespread acceptance in the education community, which continues to favor manual versions of spoken language." The effects of interpreters' use of manual codes of spoken languages on the linguistic and cognitive development of Deaf and hard of hearing children has recently been explored (Davis, 2005; Stack, 2004) and needs further study. Educational interpreters must often demonstrate a level of proficiency in either interpretation or transliteration, but not both. *Transliterating* refers to the process of changing a message from spoken English to a signed form of English—using ASL vocabulary or lexicon while adhering to English syntax (word order). "Transliteration is the label used to account for the way interpreters attempt to visually represent English words and grammar" (Davis, 2005, p. 123), using sign language that is sign-driven, speech-driven, or some combination of both (Sofinski, Yesbeck, Gerhold, & Bach-Hansen, 2001). In contrast, *interpreting* refers to the process of interpreting between English and ASL, each of which has a distinct grammar and syntax of its own.

Research suggests that there is no significant difference in comprehension when information is presented in either ASL or a signed form of English to postsecondary Deaf students who are competent adult signers (Cokely, 1990; Hatfield, Caccamise, & Siple, 1978). These studies determined that college students who are proficient in sign language and accustomed to using interpreters in educational settings and are provided with

---

5. American Sign Language has a distinct grammar and syntax of its own. For this reason, English-based sign systems are referred to as "systems," whereas ASL is a natural language.

the most highly qualified interpreters were able to comprehend interpreted and transliterated lectures. However, Marschark et al. (2005b) reported that "deaf students in these experiments scored between 60% and 75% on multiple-choice tests of learning, as compared with scores of 85% to 90% obtained by their hearing peers." They suggest the possibility that the cumulative academic experiences of Deaf and hard of hearing students in K–12 settings may provide some insight toward understanding this discrepancy. Moreover, we know little about how language policies and interpreters' decisions about language impact the learning outcomes of Deaf and hard of hearing students.

Complicating matters further, Moores (1996) reported that "the lack of research on effective interpreting provides no base on which to build a model [curriculum for educational interpreters] for implementation with children who themselves may not have developed fluency in either ASL or an English-based sign system" (p. 306). According to Stinson and Lang (1994), "In regard to elementary and middle school students, there is virtually no reliable, data-based information on whether young deaf children can receive the same educational benefits from using an interpreter as from direct instruction" (p. 37). Winston (2004) argued that there may be an additional cognitive burden placed on Deaf and hard of hearing students who are not linguistically ready to participate in a mainstream class, explaining that when they use interpreters to access classroom content, "deaf students who do not already have a language must attempt to acquire one through less than ideal means. In addition, they are expected to acquire that language while also learning class content" (p. 56). To date, no study has explored what K–12 interpreters do when they encounter Deaf and hard of hearing students with such diverse linguistic and academic competencies. Furthermore, no study has indicated what K–12 interpreters should do to create optimal opportunities for Deaf and hard of hearing students in mainstream schools to learn, participate, and interact socially with peers.

Salient research concerning students who are not Deaf has been conducted on the patterns of discourse used in academic settings. Much of this research has been informed by sociolinguistic theories that illuminate the social construction of language and power. The ways in which children learn to access information at home and the values of discourse styles in the home environment have a significant impact on their school experiences. Students whose home talk corresponds highly with school talk will have an easier transition into the school learning environment.

In order to be academically successful, students have to know not only the meaning of words, but also accepted forms and patterns of dialogue in school contexts, and discourse cues that dictate when it is appropriate to speak up and participate or when to remain quiet (Cazden, 1988; Mehan, 1979). School success relies on knowledge of and competence observing unique norms of communication specific to schools, including turn-taking rules, teacher-centered discourse patterns and structures, and communication structures that convey to teachers what students know or have learned.

Teachers use dialogue and inquiry in order to capitalize on students' current understandings and resources. Expanding upon Bourdieu's theory of cultural capital (1977), Stanton-Salazar and Dornbusch (1995) caution against the reproduction of inequality in schools. They believe that students who use the types of cultural and linguistic capital that are valued by schools will be able to transform those forms of capital into further school success. Heath (1986) found that students who do not have these forms of capital are likely to struggle in school contexts. Citing the social nature of learning (Rogoff, 1998; Vygotsky, 1978), some researchers call into question the extent to which an interpreter-mediated education might promote or hinder the cognitive, linguistic, and/or social development of Deaf and hard of hearing students (Schick, 2004; Winston, 2004).

Because many Deaf and hard of hearing students raised in nonsigning families may have limited access to knowledge from their homes and communities, they are not as likely to have the cultural and linguistic capital that leads to school success. Schick (2004) argues, "Access is not just about what the teacher says. . . . A child who can access conversations with peers only by using an interpreter may have reduced opportunities to engage in authentic, rich discussions and debate with peers. These kinds of experiences are essential for cognitive development for any child or youth" (p. 83). Schools are highly social environments in which students create communities of learners that become a resource for continued learning. The extent to which Deaf and hard of hearing students are truly members of these communities remains uncertain (Power & Hyde, 2002; Ramsey, 1997). In order to facilitate the possibility of inclusion, interpreters must be aware of the extent to which Deaf and hard of hearing students in mainstream settings have had access to the cultural and linguistic capital that leads to academic success, especially in comparison to their hearing peers.

Research conducted with college students has shown that hearing students' comprehension of a lecture is significantly greater than that of Deaf students who rely on interpreters, even when the interpreters are highly qualified (Jacobs, 1977; Marschark, Sapere, Convertino, & Seewagen, 2005a; Marschark, Sapere, Convertino, Seewagen, & Maltzen, 2004). Studies have not yet shown what leads to these lower comprehension rates. In spite of all of the questions raised about whether or not an interpreter-mediated education can work, placement of Deaf and hard of hearing students in classes with interpreters continues to be a prevalent practice. Certainly, there is a critical need to discover how the work and decisions of interpreters might be most likely to promote cognitive, linguistic, and social development and find out the conditions in which an interpreter-mediated education could be effective.

Besides a long history of unqualified interpreters in terms of interpreting competency, educational interpreters have reported being underprepared for the realities of working in mainstream settings and the unanticipated situations in which they find themselves. One area of confusion appears to be the roles and responsibilities of educational interpreters.

Jones (2004) identified four primary roles of educational interpreters. Based on a three-state survey of K–12 interpreters, he reported that essential functions of the job include interpreting and/or transliterating, tutoring, consulting, and serving as an aide in the classroom, which he points out "all school personnel are expected to do" (p. 122). He states that confusion may result from overlapping or apparently conflicting roles. Other studies provide further evidence that interpreter roles are not always clearly defined (Kurz & Langer, 2004; Langer, 2004; Hayes, 1992; Jones, 2004; Taylor & Elliott, 1994; Yarger, 2001; Zawolkow & DeFiore, 1986). Furthermore, educational interpreters are responsible for clarifying teacher instructions, facilitating interaction among peers, tutoring, and keeping administrators and other members of the educational team informed about student progress (Antia & Kreimeyer, 2001). In another study, educational interpreters reported negotiating roles and expectations in advance, for example, by asking permission to interrupt a teacher's lecture to request clarification or rephrasing. Collaboration with teachers in this manner would allow the interpreter to share responsibility with the teacher for explaining a concept in different words to ensure it can be more clearly conveyed to the students (Mertens, 1990). Role confusion can be a particular source of frustration for many interpreters in educational settings, especially when the range of roles causes conflicts with the interpreter's primary obligation of interpreting or preparing to interpret (Hayes, 1992).

INTERPRETERS AND DECISION MAKING

Interpreters in K–12 settings must consider multiple factors simultaneously and almost instantaneously make a decision about what to do. Interpreters make choices that affect linguistic output (Davis, 2005), including deliberately and strategically omitting information from the interpretation (Napier, 2002a, 2002b, 2005; Napier & Barker, 2004). However, interpreters do not merely interpret between two languages; they make moment-to-moment decisions about practice based on a complex array of nonlinguistic variables. (Dean & Pollard, 2001, 2006; Turner, 2005). Interpreters must first understand the intricacies of the situations that require a response before they can make appropriate and ethical decisions about how to proceed (Dean & Pollard, 2005).

For many years, interpreters were thought to be unobtrusive neutral parties; yet in the last decade, studies have found that interpreters have a significant impact on communicative events and are actually participants in the interpreted interaction (Angelelli, 2001, 2004; Metzger, 1999, 2003; Metzger, Fleetwood, & Collins, 2004; Roy 2000; Wadensjö, 1998). Although the field of interpreting has begun to explore the impact of interpreters' decisions on interpreted interactions, very little research has explored the range of tasks performed or investigated the factors influencing educational interpreters' decisions while actually at work in K–12 settings.

In a study of an RID-certified interpreter working in a fourth grade classroom composed entirely of Deaf and hard of hearing students from two classes (one at grade level and one below grade level), the interpreter performed various tasks beyond the scope of simply interpreting from one language to another (M. Smith, 2004). Approximately half of the students had moved with their families from Mexico to the United States no more than 18 months before the study and had limited language proficiency. The teacher had invited a graduate student to introduce the students to the study of archaeology. The interpreter significantly altered the class interaction and the hearing guest speaker's pace and style. The interpreter provided unsolicited consultation to the guest speaker, suggesting vocabulary and discourse structures that might be more accessible, considering the cognitive and linguistic needs of this particular group of Deaf and hard of hearing students. She interrupted the speaker to ask the classroom teachers clarifying questions regarding their desired learning objectives. She offered directives to the speaker, for example, requesting that a visual aid not be circulated until it was explained, and she picked up and held objects in the students' line of vision at the time she determined to be most appropriate. This certified interpreter with more than 20 years of experience working in K–12 schools created conditions that resulted in a consecutive style of interpreting so that the students could access the visual information and the accompanying explanations sequentially. She explained turn-taking and the norms of using an interpreter. She also added several explanations to increase the likelihood that the immigrant Deaf and hard of hearing students would be able to understand more of the message. When many students raised their hands to respond to questions posed by the presenter (their eagerness to participate in itself a measure of success), she encouraged the speaker to call on students who had not been able to participate as much as other students. As a result, the students remained engaged in a long presentation (almost 2 hours on a Friday afternoon), and stated in an interview that the interaction was a success. The findings of this study suggest that interpreters may be called upon to do much more than simply interpret. Yet, very little is known about the scope and depth of what K–12 interpreters actually do.

A review of the literature indicates that not only do interpreters take on multiple roles when working in K–12 schools, they have a profound impact on the interaction itself by virtue of the choices that they make while interpreting. Even certification and qualification standards do not guarantee that interpreters will effectively meet the needs of Deaf and hard of hearing students in K–12 settings. Although it is crucial to ensure that interpreters meet at least a minimum level of qualification in terms of interpreting performance, the importance of the effect of interpreters' decisions on an interpreter-mediated education cannot be overemphasized. The question of what interpreters need to do in the classroom in order to enhance school experiences and learning outcomes for Deaf and hard of hearing students remains. More research is needed on the factors that educational interpreters take into account when making decisions about what to do. It is these decisions that determine the actual classroom practice of working interpreters, yet, to date, interpreters have not been given a chance to reflect on their work and explain the thought processes behind their decisions. Comprehensive training for educational interpreters should not be limited to the interpreting process per se. Instead, it should also address the multiple roles and responsibilities they will be expected to perform, language development, the functions of social and academic discourse, and the processes of principled decision making.

In order to determine the skills and knowledge that interpreters working in educational settings need, it is imperative to look at the current practices of interpreters working in schools. Investigation of what educational interpreters do and why they do what they do will deepen our understanding of how interpreters might facilitate or hinder student participation in mainstream settings, and what factors facilitate or hinder interpreters' ability to do their jobs. The primary goal is to expand existing knowledge about what interpreters do in K–12 settings and explore the factors that influence their decisions on a moment-to-moment basis. With this knowledge, expectations of professional practice for educational interpreters can be clearly defined.

Chapter 3

Examining the Work of Interpreters

Through Multiple Lenses

In order to discover what interpreters do and what factors influence their decisions, I investigated the practices and decisions of interpreters working in K–12 settings, including their roles and responsibilities, the strategies they employed, their rationale for choosing particular courses of action, and the ways in which they responded to the complexities of the teaching and learning environment. In other words, I sought to find out what educational interpreters do and why.

Rather than merely asking interpreters whether or not they were certified and the extent to which they felt prepared for their current responsibilities as educational interpreters, I examined what they did and the factors that informed their decisions from multiple perspectives. Observations in the field and video of educational interpreters at work provided data about what interpreters actually do throughout the day. In addition, because making sense of interpreters' actual practice requires an understanding of their own perceptions of the interpreting task and primary obligations at any given moment across various sets of situated realities, recorded interviews provided a venue for interpreters to explain the approaches and strategies they used to make decisions while working in K–12 contexts. Eliciting interpreters' own narrative voices while they watched video of themselves at work similarly illuminated the rationale behind their choices. Furthermore, video of interpreters at work and recorded interview data allowed for iterative analysis of what interpreters actually do and what factors inform their decisions about what to do. My own expertise as an interpreter, interpreter educator, and educational researcher allowed me to provide insights from additional perspectives. As an interpreter, I thought about what I might do in the moment, if I were interpreting. As a teacher, I wondered how best to equip my students for work in educational contexts. As a researcher, I gained interesting insights by observing intently and thinking critically about the data gathered. To capture the complexities of interpreting in educational contexts, the study design provided multiple lenses through which to investigate the work and practice of K–12 interpreters.

The following questions framed the description and analysis of the data:

1. What do interpreters do in the course of their daily work in K–12 classrooms?
2. What factors influence the moment-to-moment decisions of K–12 interpreters?

The study described in this volume not only highlights what interpreters do in K–12 classrooms, it also gives educational interpreters a voice through which they can teach us how they make decisions in the course of their work.

SELECTION OF GRADE LEVEL, SCHOOL SITES, AND PARTICIPANTS

I designed the study to focus on interpreters working in K–12 classrooms with Deaf or hard of hearing students who had been placed in inclusive settings with hearing classmates and teachers rather than in classes with students who relied primarily on oral communication methods such as lipreading, spoken language skills, and/or residual hearing. I focused on interpreters working in elementary schools for several reasons. First, some interpreters and school administrators assume that it must be easier to interpret in elementary settings than in higher grades, because the content and vocabulary commonly used in classrooms with young students is presumably not as sophisticated as the language used in high school or college. For example, the teacher of Deaf and hard of hearing students who was responsible for placing interpreters in her district at one of the three participating school sites reported that the interpreters who pass the in-house evaluation at the first (beginning) of nine levels are always placed in the primary grades (lower primary grades whenever possible). She explained that as interpreters get more proficient and gain a larger signed vocabulary, they often move up to higher grades along with the students that they were originally placed with. After interpreters have spent some time on the job, she said, they are able to do a better job keeping up with the pace of the information delivered in higher grades.

Since lesser-skilled interpreters are often hired to interpret for primary grades and there is a perception that novice interpreters would be better equipped to handle the demands of interpreting in elementary school than more rigorous upper-level academic content, an investigation of what these interpreters are called upon to do was warranted.[6] Moreover, because there were no in-the-field studies based on actual practice that clearly documented the demands of interpreting in elementary school settings, this investigation would be a vital aspect of truly understanding the body of knowledge and set of skills that are needed by K–12 interpreters.

In addition, I decided to focus on the upper primary grades (fifth and sixth grades), based on discussions with teacher educators who suggested that there would likely be lively interactions between teachers and students in elementary schools. In looking at interpreted discourse in academic settings, it was important to investigate interpreted interactions as well as teacher-delivered lecture content. Upper primary grades seemed likely to provide ample opportunities to observe a variety of discourse styles.

Participation was determined by convenience sampling, largely as a result of the complications and restrictions involved with gaining access to classrooms. I extended initial invitations through professional contacts, one national K–12 interpreter discussion list, and a discussion list sponsored by an affiliate chapter of RID. I also sent email invitations to former graduates of an interpreting program at a local community college and to K–12 interpreters working throughout California who participated in a program for interpreters funded by the California Department of Education between 2004 and 2006. Finding interpreters to participate in this study was not difficult. Several interpreters indicated a willingness to participate because of their convictions there is much to be learned about interpreting in K–12 settings and in hopes of making a difference.

I approached nine school districts or educational institutions (one private school), but only three agreed to participate. In accordance with institutional review board (IRB) regulations, I needed the permission not only of classroom teachers, interpreters, and the students in the classrooms and their parents, but also of school principals or their designees, school districts, and administrations. Interpreters, teachers, and Deaf students and their parents—and in one case, even the school

---

6. It is my bias that the most highly qualified interpreters and best language models should work in elementary settings, particularly with those Deaf and hard of hearing students who are not exposed to sign language at home and are likely to be delayed in language development (in both sign language and English).

principal—had already indicated support of the project and a willingness to participate, but several district administrators advised me that it would be better for me to do my research elsewhere. Five school administrators and one school principal's designee stated that it would not be feasible to get consent forms signed by the parents of elementary school students, although this did not become an issue in the schools that did participate. To protect their privacy, any students whose parents did not grant consent or who were not comfortable being videotaped were simply asked by the classroom teacher to sit away from the video cameras.

Ultimately, I was granted access to schools in three school districts in geographically diverse settings. The three schools I chose represent diverse student populations and geographic regions. Via Portal is a K–6 school in an urban community near the U.S.–Mexico border; Azalea is a K–6 school in a suburban coastal community; and Meadowbrook is a K–8 school in a small mountain town not far (an hour by car) from the border between California and Oregon.[7] The participating interpreters worked with a total of four Deaf and hard of hearing students who had varying degrees of hearing loss as well as different backgrounds and linguistic competencies in sign language and English. The families of two students did not sign at all, the mother and sister of another student had achieved a basic level of conversational signing ability, and a fourth student's parents signed fluently.

I interviewed nine interpreters and observed six interpreters in order to seek insights about patterns and trends regarding the work of interpreters in K–12 settings, relying on interviews to draw my attention to factors that they identified as particularly challenging or salient. I observed interpreters with ranges both of educational and language backgrounds and of interpreting experience. (See Chapter 4 for detail on the chosen school sites and settings, teachers, Deaf and hard of hearing students, interpreters, and interpreter qualifications.) Once I had selected settings and participants, the next step was to collect data.

PRIMARY DATA SOURCES

Primary sources of data collected were video of interpreters at work, field notes, group and individual interviews, and video elicitation

---

7. Pseudonyms are used for all schools and participants.

interviews. Since the goal of this research was to investigate what interpreters do in K–12 classrooms and what factors they take into consideration when determining a course of action, video and audio recordings were essential. Sixty-nine hours of field observations of interpreters working with fifth and sixth grade students at three California schools were videotaped during the course of this study. Footage showed interpreters at work, including interactions among interpreters, Deaf and hard of hearing students, and teachers in seven of twelve observed educational settings (e.g., classrooms, the auditorium/gym, the playground, and the library).

In order to examine the decisions made by K–12 interpreters from at least two perspectives (e.g., researcher observations and interpreter explanations), video data were complemented by individual and group interviews. I interviewed nine interpreters for a total of 19.5 hours of interview data. I recorded field notes based on informal conversations that took place between classes or during breaks with classroom teachers and students, in order to gain insights regarding their perspectives on working with interpreters in the classroom as well as additional potentially relevant variables. Finally, I used video clips of each interpreter at work in the classroom to elicit interpreter meta-commentary during video elicitation interviews. During these interviews, interpreters watched video excerpts of their own work and described what was going on. All interviews were recorded on audiotape and transcribed. Table 1 documents the corpus of data collected during this study.

Field Observations and Videotaping Procedures

After obtaining IRB approval for the research design and consent from participants, I had three cameras set up at two of the three schools to record as many interactions as possible among the interpreters, the Deaf and hard of hearing students and their peers, and the classroom teachers. At the third school, space was limited and students moved multiple times throughout the day, so only one camera was transported to dance class in the auditorium, writing class, social studies, and math. Two cameras were used in the homeroom class during language arts and science, as well as morning and afternoon announcements.

Video allowed for subsequent and multiple review and analysis of interactions, interpretations, and classroom discourse. Using more than one camera provided a back-up in the event of technical malfunctions,

TABLE 1. *Corpus of Data Collected at Each School Site*

School site, region, and grade levels observed	Total no. of interpreters observed	Total no. of hours in the field		
		Classroom video/observation	Interviews	
			No. of interpreters	Hours
Via Portal Urban K–6	4	6.5 school days 38 hours	4	8
Meadowbrook Small town/rural K–8	1	3 school days 18 hours	4	9
Azalea Suburban K–6	1	2 school days 13 hours	1	2.5
Total	6	69 hours	9	19.5

as well as gave views of Deaf and hard of hearing students, which was particularly critical when looking at interactions between these students and interpreters. Due to the amount of space and physical arrangements of Deaf and hard of hearing students, classroom teachers, interpreters, and sight lines, videotaping procedures and camera placement were different for each setting. The following describes the typical procedure and setup for camera placement in each of the homeroom classrooms.

Prior to observation at each school site, I arranged a meeting with each classroom teacher to determine the best placement for each of the three cameras and get the teacher's approval. When recording, we made adjustments to camera placement as needed. To avoid backlighting problems, we directed cameras away from windows, and we closed shades and doors when necessary. One camera recorded the interpreter. A second camera recorded the teacher at the front of the classroom. The third camera was directed toward the Deaf and hard of hearing students.

Because my goal was to examine what interpreters do, the interpreter camera provided the main source of data. Control of this camera was maintained to follow interpreters if they moved or to zoom in or out as needed. The camera angle was kept as narrow as possible within the range of motion to allow for analysis of facial expressions and the salient grammatical features of ASL that are demonstrated through subtle facial movements such as raised or lowered eyebrows. The back of the Deaf or hard of hearing student was visible in this camera whenever possible. In this manner, the interpreter tape could be used to determine who initiated an interaction and which sections of video from the student camera might be important to analyze in greater depth.

The interpreter camera captured students giving back-channeling cues (such as nodding to indicate that they were following the discussion or making head movements to indicate confusion about a particular sign or the interpretation of a concept), initiating interactions, and raising their hands to ask a question or make a comment. Sometimes the angle of the interpreter camera also captured students' signed questions and comments. Because there was only one videographer, occasionally the interpreter camera had to be left in a stationary location in order to put in a new tape or change the position of another camera.

The student camera was placed at the front of the classroom, behind the interpreter and directed toward the Deaf or hard of hearing students. The back of the interpreter was visible in the student camera whenever possible, but the primary focus was the Deaf or hard of hearing students to capture interactions with the interpreter, the teacher, and/or peers. The student camera was focused primarily on the Deaf or hard of hearing student(s) so that signed questions, comments, or interactions with the interpreter would be recorded and available for subsequent analysis.

The student camera remained in a single location for the duration of all observations in the hope of not calling undue attention to its presence. Further attempts to reduce the intrusiveness of the student camera included using a remote control, placing the camera out of the line of vision as much as possible (such as in a bookshelf or even up high on a tripod), and changing videotapes between classes or natural breaks, such as when students were given worksheets to work on independently. At the very end of the second day of taping at Azalea, a Deaf student realized that he was being recorded and began to play to the camera. At Via Portal and at Meadowbrook, several of the hearing students asked whether or not the cameras were on. Students at all three schools appeared to pay more attention to the camera that was behind them, because it was being visibly maneuvered and operated, than to the student camera that was facing (and directed toward) them.

The teacher camera was placed at the back of the room and set at a wide angle. Teachers were not visible on the video when they walked to the back of the room. Like the student camera, the teacher camera remained stationary most of the time, unless there was a need to use the teacher camera to record both the teacher and the interpreter in one frame or to get a better view of the interpreter without readjusting the interpreter camera. The time and date functions were set for all three cameras so time codes could be used to compare different angles of the same interaction during subsequent viewings of the video. The interpreter and the teacher cameras were set up at the back and/or to the side of the room and the student camera to the front and side, allowing for tapes to be changed and the two back camera angles to be adjusted without too much disruption.

Consent for videotaping was obtained for all students in the homeroom class of each of the three schools. At two schools, adjustments to videotaping were necessary in other classes to avoid taping students who had not submitted both child assent and parent/guardian consent forms. At Via Portal, the mainstreamed hard of hearing student was pulled out for speech sessions that were not interpreted. She also attended schoolwide assemblies that were observed but not recorded. At Meadowbrook, the Deaf student attended a math class and a P.E. class with hearing students for whom consent forms were not available, so those classes were observed but not videotaped. At Azalea, the students went to several locations during the course of the day. In Mrs. Kendall's math/social studies classroom at Azalea, four students did not return parental consent forms. To ensure that those students were not visible on camera, whenever students began moving around the room, the camera lens was immediately covered or the camera was turned off.

Interview Procedures

I conducted interviews to determine how educational interpreters view and feel about their work in K–12 settings, what kinds of roles and responsibilities they perform, and what factors they take into consideration when making moment-to-moment decisions. All interviews were recorded onto audiotape and were conducted in one of three formats: (a) group interviews, (b) individual interviews, and (c) individual video elicitation interviews.

At Via Portal, I conducted a series of group interviews with the three staff interpreters. Because these interviews took place whenever possible, throughout the course of the workday (e.g., during lunch, on breaks, or after school), sometimes only one or two of the interpreters was present at a given time. All of these interviews occurred after I had observed at least one of the three interpreters earlier in the day. I also conducted a group interview with four of the interpreters working for the Meadowbrook school district. Due to scheduling constraints, this interview took place prior to any actual classroom observation.

I conducted individual interviews with all six of the observed interpreters, including each of the three staff interpreters and one substitute interpreter who worked at Via Portal, an interpreter who worked at Meadowbrook, and an interpreter who worked at Azalea. Most of the individual interviews occurred during lunch or after school hours at the interpreter's convenience. If a conversation occurred while walking between classes or while on a lunch break, I created field notes as soon as possible. As a result, the length of informal and formal interviews ranged from a few minutes to 2 hours.

I conducted video elicitation interviews with at least one interpreter from each of the three school sites, using video excerpts of the interpreter at work as prompts for discussion and commentary. The first interpreter observed stated that affording interpreter participants the chance to justify their decisions might increase their likelihood of "doing what they usually do" rather than doing "what they think I might want to see." Except for the interview with the interpreter from Azalea, an end time was not predetermined. Video elicitation interviews lasted between 2 and 4 hours, as long as the interpreters were active participants and willing contributors. All three of these interpreters expressed appreciation for the opportunity to view video of their work and to provide reasons for choices that they had made. These interpreters hoped to improve their own practice and make a contribution to the field, thereby clarifying expectations and improving interpreter education as well as the state of interpreting in educational settings.

FRAMEWORK OF THE STUDY

Without a doubt, my own experience interpreting in elementary settings as outlined in the introduction to this volume gave me a firsthand lesson on the importance of considering Deaf and hard of hearing students' language proficiencies, far beyond what I had learned as an interpreting student and during my tenure as an interpreter. Additionally, a pilot study (M. Smith, 2004) provided glaring evidence that the work of

K–12 interpreters is not restricted to simply interpreting and/or transliterating. In fact, the study suggested that when certain factors align, an interpreter might be more likely to intervene in order to meet Deaf and hard of hearing students' needs. When I presented the findings of the study at a national conference, interpreter educators were struck by the uniqueness of one situation I reported on, a 4th grade guest lecture on archaeology in which the class was composed of all Deaf and hard of hearing students instead of one or two Deaf and hard of hearing students with a majority of hearing classmates. The interpreter in the classroom was very actively involved in orchestrating the interactions in that particular setting, and the interpreter educator audience at the conference asserted that such a high degree of decision latitude would be extremely rare in K–12 settings. It was intriguing that the same classroom interpreter made different choices when interpreting for a full class of Deaf and hard of hearing students (many of whom had limited linguistic proficiencies) than when I later videotaped her interpreting for a hypothetical Deaf honors student fluent in ASL: While in the 4th grade classroom the interpreter intervened significantly, in the latter case, she simply interpreted in a more traditional sense. The stark contrast between the same interpreter's approach to two different sets of circumstances served as a call to further investigate the factors likely to affect educational interpreters' decisions about how much to directly influence the interaction, as Roy (2000) suggested all competent interpreters do.

Previous research on interpreting in the classroom (reviewed in Chapter 2) also framed my thinking about what I might see. In particular, Winston (1994, 2004) identified issues influencing access in interpreted classrooms, including the effects of information that is filtered by interpreters, academic language, and teacher discourse style on educational access. In addition, she reported that overlapping input (more than one person speaking at the same time) and visual access were problematic for accessing academic instruction and discourse through interpreters, as was the timing delay inherent to interpretation. Literature regarding participation in class discussions (Kurz & Langer, 2004) called for exploration of how interpreters might hinder class participation. Previous research also foreshadowed a variety of roles and responsibilities that might be observed (Antia & Kreimeyer, 2001; Cawthon, 2001; Hayes, 1992; Jones, 1993).

In light of the available literature, it did not seem prudent for me to attempt to discover what interpreters do without concomitantly investigating the constellation of factors surrounding their decisions. Therefore, it was important for me to identify as many potentially new understandings as possible. Because interpreters are not neutral parties (Angelelli, 2001, 2004; Metzger, 1999; Metzger et al., 2004; Roy, 1989, 2000), Dean and Pollard's (2001, 2006) work on decision making appeared likely to have particular bearing on the work of K–12 interpreters, perhaps even to shed light on some of the controversies and confusion regarding roles and responsibilities. Rather than go into the study with a predetermined theory, I followed the theoretical construct of grounded theory (Glaser & Strauss, 1967), which allowed for the emergence of relevant propositions and variables to account for the data. In particular, this approach allowed for the discovery of why interpreters do what they do in different situations.

Grounded theory involves a comparative method of analysis. Although it includes distinct steps, it is not linear. Instead, the researcher interacts with the data, moving between data collection and data analysis recursively and iteratively as often as necessary to identify themes or generate theory (Strauss & Corbin, 1990). The first phase of the grounded theory process is called *open coding*. During open coding, data are closely examined. A label is assigned to represent a phenomenon as evidenced by an observation, an excerpt from an interview transcript, and/or a videotaped instance. In my study, interviews as well as analysis were guided by the central questions of (a) what is going on in this instance, (b) why is that happening, and (c) what led to that decision. The second phase of analysis is called *axial coding*. During this step, the researcher examines the "parts of the data identified and separated in open coding back together to make connections between categories" (Mertens, 1998, p. 352). Through this process, the researcher can begin to identify themes.

As Robinson (1951) suggested, the process conducted in the course of a study is not always intended to be exhaustive. Instead, it provides only a starting point, a partial explanation that can be augmented by the identification of additional variables to provide a more complete description of how and why particular pieces of the puzzle interact to inform the decisions of K–12 interpreters. Although grounded theory influenced the study design of the study, my goal was not to reach the point of saturation, at which point all of the observed decisions and actions could be explained by interview data. However, examples and counterexamples of particular phenomena helped to shed some light on interpreters' priorities, and repeated analysis of video data revealed some of the overarching rationale that led these K–12 interpreters to make different decisions in seemingly similar situations.

DATA ANALYSIS

I implemented a multiphased approach to data analysis, each phase designed to illuminate additional pieces of the puzzle. The phases of data analysis were not sequential, but iterative.

Phase 1: Analysis of Interview Data

After the initial observations, in order to let the interpreters' own narratives guide the discovery process, group and individual interviews were analyzed first. In service of this goal, interview transcripts were coded using HyperRESEARCH, qualitative analysis software that allows for selected excerpts to be marked and assigned descriptive codes.

I intended for initial coding to bring to light a wide range of what interpreters do, and to uncover the breadth and depth of factors that influence their work. I assigned descriptive codes to factors that were perceived as either in service of or hindering interpreters' ability to accomplish a desired goal or task, for example, the availability (or lack) of team interpreters and other resources, the adequacy of professional preparation, opportunities for professional development, and relationships with school personnel (especially classroom teachers). I added codes to the list during subsequent phases of data analysis. (A complete list of codes is provided in the description of Phase 5.)

SELECTING FOCUS INTERPRETERS

To ensure that the sample of interpreters met some recognized standard of qualification for educational interpreters, I narrowed my focus for in-depth case analysis to the three of the six interpreters I observed who had formal interpreter education, recognizable assessment measures, and college degrees. Of the final three interpreters, two met California proposed state standards at or soon after data collection, and one had exceeded state standards. In the latter case, exceeding state standards meant that she had achieved national certification awarded by RID,[8] held a graduate degree in education, and had more than 10 years of postcertification interpreting experience. This interpreter was a native signer, having two Deaf parents who attended residential schools for the Deaf before attending Gallaudet

---

8. AJ held a Certificate of Interpretation (CI) and a Certificate of Transliteration (CT) from RID.

University. Her mother was a retired teacher who taught at schools for Deaf students in two different states. (See Chapter 4 for extensive discussion of interpreter participants and their qualifications.)

After I narrowed the study to three focal interpreters, the remaining corpus of data available for in-depth analysis included 39 hours of field observations and 12 hours of interviews. The following phases of data analysis were applied to video and interview data pertaining only to these three interpreters.

Phase 2: Editing in Preparation for Video Elicitation Interviews

After I observed each interpreter at work, I edited a sample video for use during video elicitation interviews. In order to gain a better understanding of the breadth and depth of what is involved in interpreters' daily work in K–12 classroom, I edited these videos to include not only interpretation of some lecture format and some interactive class discussions, but also a variety of instances in which the interpreter engaged in activities other than interpreting. I scheduled video elicitation interviews within a week of the observation so that interpreters would be more likely to recall the factors influencing their decisions.

Phase 3: Analysis of Video Elicitation Interviews

The goal of video elicitation interviews was for the interpreters to describe what was going on; therefore, I instructed the interpreters simply to describe what was going on at any given moment. Although interpreters could stop the video when they wanted to explain something, they all spoke over the video, leaving me to stop the video during their explanation. If the video showed the interpreter performing a task other than interpreting and the interpreter did not explain, I stopped the video and gave a general prompt such as "Tell me about what is going on here," to initiate discussion about how interpreters made decisions as they pertained to roles and responsibilities other than interpreting. All video elicitation interviews lasted at least 2 hours; the longest lasted 4 hours.

Video elicitation interviews proved to be extremely fruitful in unearthing the implicit thought processes behind interpreters' chosen responses. Although more traditional interviews with individual and groups of interpreters provided valuable insights, even more information emerged when interpreters watched video of themselves and explained the factors influencing their choices. Furthermore, video elicitation interviews kept the focus on specific and actual occurrences rather than hypothetical constructs or general (and sometimes ambiguous) thoughts and feelings.

In addition, iterative analysis of interview and video data provided the opportunity to compare interpreters' rhetoric with actual practice. As such, circumstances in which interpreters made comments indicating a perceived conflict between what they were supposed do and what they actually did served to call attention to multiple overlapping factors influencing decisions. In addition, these conflicts provided a means to examine the question of what took precedence over something else given a specific set of circumstances. In particular, at times interpreters chose very different approaches to seemingly similar situations. I included examples of these in the edited video whenever possible.

Phase 4: Analysis of Video Data

The next phase of data analysis called for preliminary examination of video data. Based on the existing literature, interpreter interviews, and my observations during a pilot study and this study, as well as on my own life experiences and professional expertise, I created a set of descriptive codes using Studiocode (qualitative video software that allows for the selection and coding of instances of observed phenomena). I developed and defined 12 coding categories to analyze video data in order to describe what interpreters were doing and what was going on in the classroom (see Appendix A for coding categories).

Phase 5: Determining the Whats and Whys of K–12 Interpreting

The first four phases of analysis rendered an expanded list of what interpreters do and the types of factors they consider when making decisions (see Appendix B). I intended this list of "what and why" categories and definitions to cast a wide net in order to provide assurances that meaningful understandings would be captured (i.e., not overlooked). The next phase of analysis was to determine which sources of data would answer each of the research questions. I thus had to determine which of the 38 items on the expanded list addressed what interpreters were doing and which were factors that influenced interpreters' decision-making processes. Attempting to make this distinction moved me into a spiraling level of analysis. Specifically, I found myself struggling to identify when a certain factor was a description of what interpreters do as opposed to a reason for why they do it. For example, I observed interpreters assessing student needs: Assessment is evidently something interpreters do, but assessment also came to light as a why—in other words, this assessment is also a factor that interpreters take into account when making moment-to-moment decisions. In fact, it is *because* of interpreters' assessment of student needs and other contextual and human factors that interpreters make a decision to do something. The need to examine the intertwined and interrelated nature of what interpreters do and the factors that influence their choices to do (or not do) something became increasingly apparent.

After I completed field observations and had extensively and repeatedly examined video data, I was struck by the frequency of instances during which interpreters did something outside the scope of what is traditionally viewed as interpreting.[9] It became clear that there were two primary distinctions to describe what educational interpreters were doing in these fifth and sixth grade classrooms: (a) interpreting and (b) what I initially called "beyond interpreting."

The distinction between what was clearly within the bounds of interpreting and what was outside of the scope of interpreting but still performed on a regular basis by these interpreters was not always easily apparent. A narrow definition of *interpreting* was much more subjective than I had anticipated. The ambiguity of this distinction will be explored in greater detail in the discussion of findings. For the purposes of this study, *interpreting* designated not only when interpreters were actually in the process of interpreting, but also whenever they were in place, actively listening and watching, poised and ready to interpret.

I used *beyond interpreting* to describe instances in which interpreters did something other than what is traditionally and narrowly defined as interpreting, especially when the interpreter was on deck to interpret. I used another global delineation, *other tasks,* to designate instances in which interpreters engaged in activities other than interpreting. However, eventually, the designation of *beyond interpreting* proved too broad to be helpful as a descriptive label for analyzing and making sense of video data. As I began to ferret out what this meant, I refined descriptive categories

---

9. In this volume, the term *interpreting* includes both interpreting and transliterating.

to reflect specific tasks, functions, or goals. Codes that more accurately represented what interpreters did and what factors informed their decisions included *tutoring and helping*, as well as *interacting socially with students, deliberate omission,* and *different track.*

However, some of the revised codes were too specific to be informative. For example, the distinction between when interpreters were chatting socially with students, providing praise and positive reinforcement, or tutoring and helping was not always apparent. *Interacting directly with students* was a more useful designation. In addition, it is important to note that there is overlap among codes. To illustrate, *tutoring and helping* might overlap with *assessment, awareness of pedagogy,* and *interacting directly with students,* and each of these designations could also occur while the interpreter was *interpreting* as defined by being in place, poised and ready to produce an interpretation. Although I was initially ambivalent about which code best represented each piece of data, identifying that something other than interpreting was happening most often served the purpose of discovering the scope and range of what interpreters do. Furthermore, preliminary analysis of video data suggested that the designated global descriptive categories of *beyond interpreting* and *other tasks* represented situations likely to further understanding of the factors informing interpreters' decisions through deeper analysis. Multiple iterations of interview and video data analysis led to a working list of five broad categories describing what interpreters do. These primary tasks will be discussed in Chapter 5.

Furthermore, a thorough understanding of what interpreters do and what factors influence their decisions must of necessity consider the context. Thus, the remaining analysis involved careful examination of "the situation or question that has predicated the opportunity for a response" (Dean & Pollard, 2006, p. 121). To shed light on the depth, range, and complexity of interpreters' responses to a perceived need and uncover the story behind the facts, I examined in great depth what interpreters did as informed by the nuances of not only contextual but also of participant-related factors. As I moved back and forth between video and interview data, examining the final list of descriptive categories and considering the literature, four themes emerged as guideposts for further iterative and in-depth analysis: (a) students' visual access, (b) students' language and learning needs, (c) students' participation and inclusion, and (d) interpreters' internal and external resources (see Appendix C). Three of these themes represented rationale behind interpreters' decisions about what to do and prompted a corresponding set of actions. The fourth pertained to the availability and use of resources. *Resources* included external resources (e.g., collaboration with school personnel) and internal resources (e.g., the interpreter's own knowledge and skills), which either facilitated or restricted an interpreter's choices about what to do. They were not deemed to be the stimulus that called for action. Therefore, categories such as the use of resources and collaboration with classroom teachers are described in the section of findings that highlights the five primary tasks that interpreters perform rather than discussed in terms of how they affect interpreters' decisions.

Iterative review of interview and video data revealed that interpreters participated in a variety of activities and took on multiple roles and responsibilities. In turn, each of their attempts to meet the desired goals brought with it another set of actions as well as a multilayered and highly variable constellation of additional factors to be considered. It was evident to me that an understanding of what K–12 interpreters actually do in the classroom would be enhanced not by examining the full array of what interpreters do in the course of their work, a feat that would take a much larger sample size than the current study provides, but by more thoroughly examining the most ubiquitous features of the work of educational interpreters. Thus, I identified three key areas in which interpreters aim to meet the needs of Deaf and hard of hearing students—(a) visual access, (b) language and learning, and (c) social and academic participation/inclusion—and used these to frame my in-depth analysis. I selected instances to describe in great detail and provide examples of what interpreters did in light of these three overarching motivations.

THE ELEPHANT IN THE CLOSET: COMPETING VISUAL DEMANDS

Interpreters must undoubtedly be proficient in both sign language and English in order to produce an equivalent interpretation. However, if an interpretation is not accessible (visible for signed communication), it is without value. Therefore, it seemed vital that I explore the primacy (first in sequence rather than importance) of the visual nature of people who depend on sign language for communication before even beginning to consider the semantic equivalence necessary for effective interpretation. For this reason, I explore visual access rather than focus on the complexities involved with language and interpretation tasks.

General education classroom teachers depend on a multitude of visual aids (such as whiteboards, overhead transparencies, charts, and textbooks) and are accustomed to working with hearing students who can look at visual input while simultaneously listening to instruction. Therefore, teachers typically keep talking while referring to other sources of important visual information, inadvertently creating difficulties for Deaf and hard of hearing students who need to look at an interpreter to access classroom discourse. *Competing visual demands* exist when a Deaf or hard of hearing student must attend visually to a signed interpretation and simultaneously needs or chooses to look elsewhere.

In order to further substantiate the decision to focus on what interpreters do to optimize visual access, the first step was to illuminate the frequency and duration of competing demands for Deaf and hard of hearing students' visual attention. I examined a sample of 14 hours and 20 minutes of video data for the presence of competing visual demands, including at least 2 hours for each of the three interpreters who participated in the study. Nine hours and 54 minutes of this video data included either active instructional time when the teacher delivered information through spoken language or when students and teacher interacted as a class. Competing demands for Deaf and hard of hearing students' visual attention occurred for 8 hours and 50 minutes during the 9 hours and 54 minutes of discourse, or 89% of the time.

To define the conditions under which competing visual demands for attention would be identified as present, I participated in discussions with two teacher educators who had also taught for many years in K–12 classrooms. Both agreed that teachers make deliberate decisions about when to present and remove all types of visual aids. The basic premise is that if the visual input is visible, students can then look at it as often as they want at any time during the corresponding discussion or instruction. Based on this understanding of the goal and function of using visual aids in K–12 settings, competing visual demands were determined to exist from the moment a visual stimulus was first introduced and/or referred to until it was removed or the lesson was wrapped up and no additional references were made to that visual input. For example, if a worksheet was passed out, competing visual demands were identified as present until the worksheet was collected or put away. If the visual input was always visible, such as a map or number line posted on the wall of a classroom, competing visual demands were to be designated as present from the time the teacher first called students' attention to the number line until no further references to the number line were made.

To determine whether my selections of competing visual demands were reliable, a second coding was conducted by outside reviewers. I recruited a Deaf reviewer who was fluent in ASL and had participated successfully in an interpreted educational context. Having two Deaf parents and being Deaf herself, the reviewer I selected was a native user of ASL. She graduated from a large school for the Deaf before attending a university and using sign language interpreters to obtain a graduate degree in Deaf education. The second reviewer was hearing, had completed an interpreting program, held a bachelor's degree, and was working as an interpreter in an elementary school. The same coding software used to code video data was modified for this purpose. Two more code buttons were added, one for Rater 1 and another for Rater 2. As the raters watched video of interpreters at work, they clicked on a designated "visual input" button to mark the beginning and ending points of competing visual demands on the video. Figure 1 shows the Code Input Window from Studiocode used to identify the presence of competing demands for Deaf and hard of hearing students' visual attention.

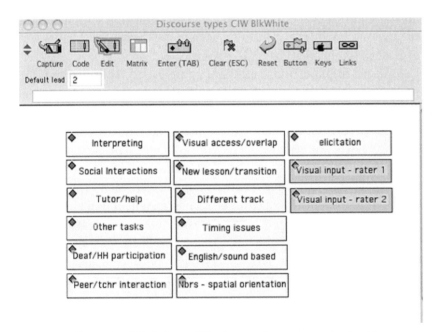

FIGURE I. *Example of Code Input Window used to assign codes to video instances.*

In a sample of just under 6 hours of video, there were 4½ hours of spoken discourse to be interpreted. Competing demands for visual attention as operationalized in this study is defined by the need for Deaf and hard of hearing students to look at an interpretation and another visual referent. Therefore, there must be some discourse to be interpreted in order for there to be competing visual demands. Out of the 5-hour-54-minute video sample, there was spoken discourse to be interpreted for nearly 4.5 hours (4:28:51). I designated 4 hours, 8 minutes (92%) of competing demands for Deaf and hard of hearing students' visual attention in this sample. In contrast, the first outside reviewer indicated 3 hours, 49 minutes of competing visual demands (85%) in the same 4.5-hour video sample (Table 2).

Two main factors account for differences in our selections. First, only the video from the interpreter camera was used to identify competing visual demands. As a result, the Deaf reviewer was dependent on the interpretation and the limited range of the camera angle. At times, the interpreter, in effect, eliminated some of the competing visual demands using one or more of the techniques detailed in Chapter 5. For example, if the interpreter stopped interpreting and waited for the Deaf or hard of hearing student to look at a source of visual input, the Deaf reviewer had no way of knowing that the teacher was still talking unless the teacher happened to be in the same camera frame as the interpreter. Because I could hear the teacher talking whether or not the interpreter was signing, I identified instances of competing visual demands that were not indicated by the Deaf reviewer.

Second, the Deaf reviewer was more likely than I to designate an interaction during which the teacher referred to a group of students at a particular table as a competing visual demand. Although I identified some of these interactions as competing visual demands, I bypassed others that I regarded as somewhat inconsequential or insignificant, as long as the interpreter clearly identified who was speaking. While the Deaf reviewer

TABLE 2. *Comparison of Competing Visual Demands as Determined by Principal Investigator and Rater 1*

Duration of video sample (hr:min:s)	Amount of spoken discourse	Competing visual demands	
		Principal investigator	Rater 1
5:54:20	4:28:51	4:08:24	3:49:44

agreed that a few of the references to classmates were not important enough to be deemed a competing visual demand for attention, for example, "Ten points off of Table 10 for talking," in looking at the data through the eyes of a Deaf reviewer, it became apparent that Deaf and hard of hearing students are likely to turn their visual attention to most, if not all, of a teacher's references to their classmates, whether those references are significant in terms of content or not. This is not surprising in consideration of the highly social nature of educational settings and the highly visual nature of Deaf people.

The second reviewer picked up where the first reviewer left off, coding the remaining 6 hours of sample videos for the presence of competing demands for students' visual attention. Interobserver reliability was even higher between the two hearing raters. During 3 hours and 22 minutes of spoken discourse to be interpreted, I found 2 hours and 53 minutes and the other hearing rater found 2 hours and 49 minutes of competing visual demands (Table 3).

Collectively, the first and second raters reviewed 7 hours and 51 minutes of video data during which there was spoken discourse to be interpreted. A comparative analysis of all three raters revealed that during 85% or more of the video data sampled, there were competing demands for Deaf and hard of hearing students' visual attention (Table 4).

Observations of competing visual demands during the course of this study, coupled with frequent discussions of visual access during interviews,

TABLE 3. *Comparison of Competing Visual Demands as Determined by Principal Investigator and Rater 2*

Duration of video sample (hr:min:s)	Amount of spoken discourse	Competing visual demands	
		Principal investigator	Rater 2
6:06:39	3:22:26	2:53:37	2:49:07

TABLE 4. *Comparison of Competing Visual Demands as Determined by Principal Investigator and External Raters*

Duration of video sample (hr:min:s)	Amount of spoken discourse	Competing visual demands	
		Principal investigator	External reviewers
12:00:59	7:51:17	7:02:01	6:38:51

along with the fact that multiple raters identified frequent and prolonged competing demands for students' visual attention served to pinpoint this as an area of focus for this study. Specifically, I was interested in further exploring how K–12 interpreters make decisions about what to do when Deaf or hard of hearing students need to access information visually.

LEARNING, LANGUAGE, PARTICIPATION, AND INCLUSION AS PRIMARY MOTIVATIONS

All effective translations and interpretations rely on a clear under-standing of the goals of the writer/speaker and the audience for whom the source text or other form of communication is intended. In educational settings, the implicit and explicit goals of the context/teacher and the language and prior knowledge of the students affect all communication. However, in an interpreter-mediated interaction, the communication is processed, and—at least in part—filtered by the interpreter. Preliminary analyses of interview and video data suggest that the filter can be abso-lute, that is, interpreters can and do go so far as to choose to deliberately omit information from the interpretation when they determine that doing so serves a higher and more immediate purpose.

Not surprisingly, I found that many such decisions that K–12 interpret-ers made were prompted by interpreters' assessments of Deaf and hard of hearing students' needs within the school context. Because schools are teaching and learning environments, students' language and learning needs informed interpreters' moment-to-moment decisions about what to do. Several additional factors converged to pinpoint language and learning needs as an important area of focus for this study. First, observa-tions during a pilot study (M. Smith, 2004) highlighted the interpreter's repeated decisions to substantially alter the message so that immigrant students could comprehend as much information as possible. In addition, interpreters' frequent and/or passionate mention during interviews of the importance of students' learning of not only content, but also ASL and English substantiated the need to explore what interpreters do in light of Deaf and hard of hearing students' unique language and learning needs.

Iterative analyses of interview and video data indicated that inter-preters strive to even the playing field so that Deaf and hard of hearing students can succeed academically and socially in mainstreamed school contexts. I observed deviations from the interpretation that could easily be attributed to being responsive to either student language and learning needs or a desire to promote inclusion and participation. Video and interview data illuminated recurring sets of conditions to which interpreters felt obligated to respond in some other manner than remaining in an exclusive and somewhat narrowly defined interpreting role. These primary motivations undeniably influenced interpreters' moment-to-moment decisions about what to do.

Chapter 4

Scenes and Subjects

The three school sites in this study were Via Portal Elementary, Meadowbrook School, and Azalea Elementary. (Pseudonyms are used for all participants and settings.)

VIA PORTAL ELEMENTARY: K–6

Via Portal Elementary is a large urban school near the U.S.–Mexico border in which more than half of students come from primarily Spanish-speaking families and speak Spanish proficiently. At the time of the study, Via Portal served almost 700 students, including 35 Deaf and hard of hearing students. Two of these students were mainstreamed and attended general education classes with hearing peers. The school had three sign language interpreters on staff. Angelina was the only student to be mainstreamed all day.

Angelina's teacher, Mr. Sands, was an Anglo native speaker of English who also spoke Spanish fluently. He intermittently used Spanish throughout the day in the classroom. He was a second-year teacher, but the study year was his first year teaching fifth grade. He had never had an interpreter or any Deaf or hard of hearing students in his room before the beginning of this academic year. He had 2 months of experience with an interpreter in his classroom prior to my first observation, and 6 months' experience by the final observation (four different interpreters were observed). Mr. Sands was responsible for teaching all subjects. There were approximately 40 students enrolled in his class (only 35 attended during language arts). There was also an aide assigned to work with several of the Spanish-speaking students in the class.

At Via Portal, most of the employees spoke a second language — three languages in the case of two of the three staff interpreters. There were three life-sized murals painted on one of the buildings by a former Deaf employee.[10] One showed a student musing that the school is "a cool place" because kids can learn English, Spanish, and American Sign Language (Figure 2).

Another mural depicted a student considering options for postsecondary education, including Gallaudet University (a liberal arts university primarily serving Deaf and hard of hearing students) and the National Technical Institute of the Deaf (NTID), a college housed on the campus of the Rochester Institute of Technology (RIT). The third mural was of three students waiting in line for the water fountain. The students were signing HURRY, WATER, and THIRSTY, respectively (Figure 3).

FIGURE 2. *Mural of student celebrating the school's trilingual learning opportunities.*

---

10. Artist: J. Dorricott. Reprinted with permission. School name has been covered with its pseudonym.

FIGURE 3. *Life-sized mural of students signing at the water fountain.*

For several years, the staff interpreters at Via Portal had followed a rotating schedule.[11] During a group interview, the three interpreters reported that they alternated their duties every 3 weeks in order to ensure that they each had an opportunity to work with and get to know all of the Deaf and hard of hearing students on campus as well as in an attempt to balance the workload. As a result, I observed and videotaped five interpreters at this school, the three staff interpreters and two substitute interpreters (one who subsequently declined to participate in the study), all of whom worked in the same fifth grade classroom. Due to the schedule rotation, I was not able to film any of the three staff members for a full day. As the study progressed, it seemed as if richer data were present when observations and videotaping continued for longer periods of time. This was another reason to narrow the focus of analysis to data collected from AJ, the substitute interpreter at Via Portal, who was observed and videotaped for a day and a half.

---

11. Two months after the data were collected at Via Portal, a teacher of Deaf and hard of hearing students asked interpreters to discontinue the rotating schedules. A compromise was reached that the same interpreter would interpret the same subject area every day, in order to increase the likelihood of consistency when interpreting for each content area.

Meadowbrook School: K–8

Meadowbrook School is located in a rural community near the California–Oregon border. The school had changed its structure from K–5 to K–8 the year prior to this study. There were 18 interpreters employed by the district, with two interpreters working at Meadowbrook for two students, the only Deaf and hard of hearing students attending the school. One of the interpreters worked with a student who was Deaf and also had other disabilities. As was true at Via Portal, only one student was mainstreamed all day.

Mr. Harrison, the teacher of the core class, had been teaching for 19 years. The year of the study was his first experience working with a Deaf or hard of hearing student and an interpreter in the classroom. There were approximately 40 students enrolled in his class. The Deaf student also attended math class with Mr. Lincoln and P.E. with Mrs. Darcy. I observed the interpreter, Camie, in three settings: math; the core class for a tutoring period, language arts, social studies, science, and accelerated reading; and P.E. None of these teachers had ever worked with an interpreter before the beginning of the academic year. At the time of the study, they had had an interpreter and a Deaf student in their classrooms for approximately 7 months.

Azalea Elementary: K–6

Azalea Elementary is located in a suburban coastal community in California. At the time of the study, there were nine interpreters employed by the district. A total of 465 students attended the school, 31 who were Deaf or hard of hearing. Five Deaf and hard of hearing students were mainstreamed at least part of each day, but only two were mainstreamed full time. Mrs. Natale, the teacher of the homeroom class, had been teaching for 22 years. The study year was her third or fourth to have an interpreter in her classroom.

There were approximately 40 students enrolled in each class. I observed one interpreter, Marina, in this school in six different locations: Mrs. Natale's homeroom class for morning announcements, language arts, and science; in the library with Mrs. Natale and the librarian for storytelling and to check out books; in a second classroom with Mrs. Kendall for math and social studies; in the auditorium with Mrs. Jackson for dance lessons; in a third classroom with Mrs. Watson for writing; and on the playground with Mrs. Natale for P.E. activities. Both Mrs. Natale and Mrs. Watson had worked with interpreters in three previous years.

Mrs. Kendall had never worked with an interpreter before the beginning of the academic year.

CLASSES AND TEACHERS AT EACH SCHOOL SITE

At Via Portal, the focal student, Angelina, stayed in the same classroom until the end of the day when she was pulled out for speech. At each of the other two schools, I observed one interpreter working with Deaf and hard of hearing students who moved to different classes for instruction with different teachers throughout the day. As a result, I observed interpreters working with seven different teachers and four Deaf or hard of hearing students across seven different subjects: language arts, math, dance, social studies, P.E., science, and writing (Table 5).

DEAF AND HARD OF HEARING STUDENT PARTICIPANTS

The Deaf and hard of hearing students working with interpreters who participated in this study included four students who had diverse educational and language experiences (Table 6), including state residential schools for the Deaf, self-contained classrooms with only Deaf and hard of hearing students (DHH classrooms), and regular education classes with interpreters (mainstreamed classrooms). None of the students in this study had been fitted with a cochlear implant.[12] All of the students in the study had experienced more than one year in a mainstreamed classroom, and all except for one were being mainstreamed full time. The parents of the Deaf and hard of hearing students in the study had achieved varying levels of sign language proficiency at the time of the study. Angelina's and Miguel's parents were native Spanish speakers and spoke Spanish at home. Their mothers knew a few basic signs but were not conversationally proficient in sign language. Emily's family members

---

12. A *cochlear implant* is a small, complex electronic device that can help to provide a sense of sound to a person who is profoundly Deaf or severely hard of hearing. While hearing aids amplify sounds so they may be detected by damaged ears, cochlear implants bypass damaged portions of the ear, directly stimulating the auditory nerve. Hearing through a cochlear implant is different from normal hearing and takes time to learn or relearn. (Retrieved from http://www.nidcd.nih.gov/health/hearing/coch.htm#a.)

TABLE 5. *Schools, Teachers, and Subjects*

School Site and Grades Served	Grade	Teacher	Class Subject
Via Portal, urban K–6	5th	Mr. Sands	language arts, math, writing, and social studies
Meadowbrook, rural K–8	6th	Mr. Harrison	language arts, social studies, and science
		Mr. Lincoln	math
		Mrs. Darby	P.E.
		Mrs. Natale	language arts, library, science, and P.E.
Azalea, suburban K–6	5th	Mrs. Kendall	math and social studies
		Mrs. Jackson	dance
		Mrs. Watson	writing

TABLE 6. *Demographic Characteristics of Deaf and Hard of Hearing Students*

Student Name and Grade	Student's Primary Mode of Communication	Home Language and Signed Communication	Grades Main-Streamed With Interpreter	Deaf School
Angelina 5th	Spoken English and sign language	Spanish, some English, little to no sign language	4th partial, 5th fully	n/a
Emily 6th	Sign language	English, some sign language	3rd–4th partial, 5th–6th fully	K–2
Kristie 5th	Sign language and spoken English	ASL and English, parents sign fluently	Kindergarten partial, 1st fully	n/a
Miguel 5th	Sign language	Spanish only, little to no sign language	3rd–4th partial	n/a

were native English speakers. Her mother and sister could communicate conversationally using sign language. Only Kristie's parents were both fluent in sign language. Angelina and Kristie used hearing aids at school. They used spoken English to communicate with their hearing classmates. Emily and Miguel did not use any spoken English and communicated with their hearing classmates using basic signs, gestures, and facial expressions. Each of these students, two of whom were in the same classroom at Azalea, had different language and learning needs.

Student Profile: Angelina

Angelina had attended Via Portal since kindergarten. She was in the fifth grade and had been mainstreamed with an interpreter for the first time in fourth grade. According to the school's staff interpreters, Angelina was hard of hearing. Her family spoke Spanish in the home. Angelina learned to sign while participating in the DHH classroom at the school. I observed that Angelina was comfortable expressing herself through sign language and used sign language to communicate with anyone who knew sign. She occasionally used spoken English to ask the teacher questions and to talk to her classmates, and used spoken English in most one-on-one interactions with classmates and teachers. I observed five different interpreters working with Angelina; when Angelina initiated conversations with any of them, she generally used sign language.

At times Angelina appeared to respond to the teacher without the benefit of the interpretation, while at other times she appeared to depend more on the interpretation. The staff interpreters indicated that since Angelina used an auditory trainer, she was able to use some of her residual hearing to hear the teacher's voice. The teacher wore a microphone that sent audio input directly to her hearing aid. The staff interpreters reported that on days that Angelina forgot to charge the battery, forgot to bring the microphone to the teacher, or had an ear infection, she was much more dependent on the interpretation. They also reported that she depended on both her hearing with amplification and the interpreters for support. During my observations, Angelina consistently watched the interpreters. She stayed in the same room except when she and half of her classmates left their homeroom for science on alternating days, for outside or schoolwide activities, and for speech therapy sessions the last 30 minutes of each day.

Student Profile: Emily

Emily was in the sixth grade and had attended Meadowbrook School since the middle of the fourth grade. Emily did not use hearing aids. She depended completely on sign language and visual cues for access to information, and she did not lipread well. Emily did not use spoken English to communicate with anyone during the 3 days I observed her. Her mother and her older sister had been learning sign language since Emily was born and had basic conversational signing skills.

Emily had attended a large school for the Deaf from kindergarten until the middle of the second grade. At that time, her family moved within the boundaries of the Meadowbrook School District, where Emily was enrolled in a program with all Deaf and hard of hearing classmates and a Deaf teacher who signed. When Emily was in fourth grade, the program closed and Emily transferred to Meadowbrook School to continue her education in mainstream classes with hearing peers and hearing teachers. The interpreter assigned to work with her, Camie, had worked in the Deaf and hard of hearing program with Emily before its closing. When I asked Emily which of the school environments she liked best, she responded that because she had a lot of friends at Meadowbrook, she liked it there the best. She added that her interpreter, Camie, was nice.

Camie told me that according to Emily's mother, Emily was previously classified as developmentally delayed based on an assessment conducted for a DHH preschool class. The designation followed her to and through her kindergarten year at the school for the Deaf. Emily's mother was told that Emily scored in the "intellectually challenged" range on the Wechsler IQ test. According to Mr. Harrison, Emily's sixth grade teacher, by March of her sixth-grade year, Emily was performing at grade level in science and social studies. She was significantly behind in math but was assessed at a third- or fourth-grade reading level. She made the honor roll during her sixth-grade year (1 month after data collection) and qualified to join other honor roll students for a special end-of-year field trip.

Student Profile: Kristie

Kristie was in the fifth grade at Azalea Elementary. She had been partially mainstreamed during kindergarten and fully mainstreamed since first grade. The interpreter, Marina, reported that although Kristie was hard of hearing and used hearing aids, Kristie depended on an interpreter for access to spoken language except in one-on-one conversations. According to Marina, Kristie's father was Deaf, and her mother was hard of hearing and used a cochlear implant.[13] Both of Kristie's parents were proficient signers, and her mother used spoken English to communicate as well. During 2 days of observation, Kristie used spoken English to communicate one-on-one with her hearing friends on the playground and between classes, but she signed her questions and comments to them during class and had Marina interpret into spoken English, such as when asking to borrow a pencil. When she communicated with the classroom teacher or with her interpreter, Kristie only used sign language. During lunch, she sat with all of the Deaf and hard of hearing students who attend Azalea and also communicated only in sign language.

Student Profile: Miguel

Miguel was in the fifth grade and had been mainstreamed at Azalea Elementary since the third grade. His parents spoke Spanish at home and did not use sign language. Miguel did not use hearing aids. He depended completely on sign language and visual cues for access to information, and he did not lipread well. Miguel was mainstreamed for all subjects except language arts, writing, and dance. During those periods he attended a class with Deaf and hard of hearing classmates and a hearing teacher who signed. He communicated with hearing friends between classes and on the playground through gestures and facial expressions.

INTERPRETER PARTICIPANTS

At about the time that I was collecting data for this study, the California Department of Education (CDE) developed a three-step process to raise qualifications of the state's underqualified workforce. California proposed that all K–12 interpreters should hold certification from RID or NAD-RID, or score at least a 3.0 on the Educational Interpreter Performance Assessment (EIPA), the Educational Sign Skills Evaluation (ESSE), or a cued-speech testing instrument by July of 2007. By the following year,

---

13. Kristie's mother may very well identify herself as Deaf, even though she uses a cochlear implant.

K–12 interpreters were to have obtained a 3.5 or above if using the EIPA or ESSE to meet minimum qualification standards. Not until July 2009 were K–12 interpreters in California required to demonstrate interpreting proficiency at a 4.0 or higher on these assessments.[14]

I videotaped six interpreters, but only AJ, Camie, and Marina matched two important criteria for inclusion in the analysis of video data: I had observed and recorded each interpreter for at least one full day, and each had passed an interpreting assessment that met California's proposed qualification standards for K–12 interpreters at the time.

AJ was hired as a substitute interpreter when Via Portal Elementary School subcontracted interpreting services from an outside agency. At the time of the study, she held a Certificate of Interpretation (CI) and a Certificate of Transliteration (CT) issued by RID, and had been work-ing as an interpreter for 26 years, 11 years postcertification. Camie, at Meadowbrook School, scored a 3.7 on a 5.0 scale on the EIPA taken 3 years before the study and a 4.2 three months after data collection, at the completion of a distance interpreter education program for K–12 interpreters. Marina took the ESSE 2 months after participating in the study and received a 3.0 on the expressive and a 3.7 on the receptive portions of the evaluation. One year later, she took the EIPA and scored a 4.2. The length of the interpreters' experience ranged from 8 months to 26 years (Table 7).

Each of these focal interpreters had passed a national written exam indicating that they had the prerequisite knowledge necessary to inter-pret as a generalist.[15] In addition, all three had achieved at least an associate's degree and been involved in some formal interpreter educa-tion. All except AJ had completed 2 or more years of formal interpret-ing coursework. All had participated in some formal evaluation or assessment of their interpreting skills prior to being employed in these K–8 schools.

---

14. In 2010, only Nevada, Alaska, Alabama, and California required K–12 interpreters to achieve a 4.0 or higher on the EIPA or hold RID or NAD-RID certification or equivalent. By 2012, the number had grown to 10 states requiring an EIPA score of 4.0 or better. Thirteen more states recognized a score of 3.5.

15. AJ had passed the RID knowledge test required for CI/CT certification. Camie and Marina had passed the National Interpreter Certification (NIC) knowledge test jointly developed by NAD and RID.

TABLE 7. *Characteristics of Focal Interpreters*

Interpreter Characteristic	AJ	Camie	Marina
Type of national or state certification	RID: CI and CT	EIPA 3.7 in 6/03; 4.2 in 6/06	ESSE: Expressive 3.0 Receptive 3.7 EIPA: 4.2 one year after study
Met CA standards	Yes	Yes	2 months after study
Degree	MA/EdS	AA	BA
Field	Psych/Ed	General Studies	Interpreting
# of years signing	40	8	4
# of years interpreting	26	7	8 months
Formal interpreter education	Workshops & national conferences	Certificate from a 2-year program: K–12 specialization	4-year BA program in interpreting
Evaluated at hiring	Sub	In-house evaluation	In-house evaluation: entry-level
Native language	English and ASL	English	English
Interview type	Video elicitation	Individual, group, and video elicitation	Video elicitation

Interpreter Profile: AJ

AJ held a CI and CT from RID. She was also certified at the "qualified" level for teaching sign language by the American Sign Language Teachers Association (ASLTA). She had earned two graduate degrees, including an Educational Specialist degree, and had completed some doctoral coursework in educational technology. Her parents were both Deaf and had attended residential schools for the Deaf before attending Gallaudet University. They relied on sign language as their primary means of communication. Although AJ considered her dominant language to be English, she was a native signer. She had interpreted for more than 20 years and had achieved RID certification 11 years prior to this study; she had also taught ASL and interpreting classes for three colleges in two states. She had taken one beginning Spanish class more than 5 years before the study. I observed and videotaped AJ for a day and a half while she was subbing at Via Portal.

Interpreter Profile: Camie

Camie achieved a 3.7 on the EIPA 2 years and 9 months prior to observation during the course of this study and a 4.2 three months after my observations. She had an associate's degree in General Studies, and she received a certificate of completion three months after data collection from a 2-year community college distance education program for working K–12 interpreters. Camie was a native English speaker who began learning sign language 8 years prior to observations, and she began interpreting in educational settings a year later. Camie had been interpreting with Emily in mainstream classrooms for 2 years and had worked with her in the Deaf and hard of hearing program for the 2 preceding years. Camie took an in-house evaluation conducted by the Meadowbrook School District to evaluate her interpreting proficiency prior to being hired to work at Meadowbrook.

Interpreter Profile: Marina

Marina held a BA in interpreting. Her native language was English. She began learning ASL for university credit 4 years before the study. For 8 months prior to field observations, the Azalea School District had been trying to fill two staff interpreting positions. During that time, they were subcontracting interpreting services through an outside interpreting agency. Although Marina was employed as an instructional signing aide working in the Deaf and hard of hearing classroom and had not yet passed the district's in-house evaluation, she began interpreting on a substitute basis when the agency was unable to send an interpreter. Two months prior to the study, Marina retook the in-house evaluation, passed at the first of nine levels (entry level), and was promoted to the position of interpreter. At the time of the study, Marina had been working with Kristie and Miguel on a part-time basis for 8 months. She had been interpreting in their classes full-time for only 2 months. Marina's scores on the ESSE taken 2 months after data collection were 3.0 on the expressive portion and 3.7 on the receptive portion. Marina attained a 4.2 on the EIPA taken 1 year after data collection.

Contributing Informants

The three Via Portal staff interpreters I observed and videotaped had taken local interpreting evaluations, but they had not yet taken any widely recognized assessments. Therefore, it would have been difficult to provide evidence documenting clearly whether or not they would meet any widely recognized standards in terms of knowledge and skill (Table 8). In addition, these three interpreters rotated in and out of the classroom. I observed the interpreters at Via Portal for a total of 7 days,

TABLE 8. *Characteristics of Informant Interpreters From Via Portal*

Informant Interpreter Characteristic	Francisco	Gracie	Sara
Certification held	None	None	None
Assessment used by school to determine employment readiness	Local in-house evaluations from a public school and a community college—Intermediate level (2 of 3)	Local college in-house evaluation—Beginner level (1 of 3)	Signing skills assessed by the Calif. Dept. of Rehabilitation—Level 1 (Beginner)
Met CA standards	No	No	No
Educational degree	AA	AA	BA
Educational field	General education	Interpreting	Interpreting
Years signing	29	19	7
Years interpreting	19	18	3
Formal interpreting coursework	2 years	AA in Interpreting	AA in Interpreting
Native language	Spanish	Spanish	Spanish
Interview type	Individual and group	Individual and group	Individual, group, video elicitation

TABLE 9. *Characteristics of Informant Interpreters From Meadowbrook*

Informant Interpreter Characteristic	Kris	Kelly	Sabrina
Type of certification	EIPA 2.6 as of 6/03; 3.5 in 6/06	ACCI 3 as of 6/03; 4.3 in 6/06	EIPA 3.8 as of 6/03; 4.0 in 3/07
Meets CA standards	Yes	Yes	Yes
Ed. degree	BA	BA	BA
Ed. field	Recreation Education	Early Childhood Education	Literature and Writing
Years signing	10	9	7
Years interpreting	8	7	6
Formal interpreter education	2-year distance program for K–12 interpreters	2-year distance program for K–12 interpreters	2-year distance program for K–12 interpreters
Evaluated at hiring	No	No	First interpreting job: no; For current job:yes
Native language	English	English	English

but I did not have a full day's worth of observation and video for any of them; for these reasons, I excluded these interpreters from later phases of analysis, such as video and video elicitation interviews.

In addition to interviewing and observing the three Via Portal staff interpreters and viewing their videotaped work, I held a group interview with Camie and three additional staff interpreters working for the Meadowbrook district (Table 9). Through interviews and observations with all nine interpreters, I was able to identify patterns and trends that informed my analysis.

Chapter 5

Opening Our Eyes:

Discovering What Interpreters Do and Why

My investigation revealed that the range and scope of what K–12 interpreters do are multifaceted and variable. I present the results in five main sections. In Section 1, I provide a broad overview of the scope of what interpreters do and the factors that influence their decisions. In Section 2, I describe in detail what interpreters do in light of a particular phenomenon, that is, competing demands for Deaf and hard of hearing students' visual attention. In Section 3, I focus on what interpreters do from moment to moment based on their assessments of Deaf and hard of hearing students' language and learning needs, and in Section 4, I highlight what interpreters do in order to cultivate opportunities for participation and promote inclusion. Whereas in the first four sections I highlight effective strategies interpreters developed for responding to students' needs, in Section 5, I relate situations in which interpreters were unable to effectively optimize students' visual access, facilitate content and language learning, or foster participation and inclusion.

I. WHAT INTERPRETERS DO, AND FACTORS INFORMING THEIR DECISIONS ABOUT WHAT TO DO

The data I collected during this study led me to identify five primary categories of what educational interpreters do during the course of their daily work:

1. Assess and respond to a constellation of contextual, situational, and human factors.
2. Interpret and/or transliterate.
3. Seek, obtain, and capitalize on available resources.

4. Interact with others.
5. Perform aide duties and other tasks; be useful or helpful as needed.

Although these broad-strokes descriptions of what interpreters do may appear to be superficial and obvious, the true story is exceptionally complex. Through analyses of interview and video data, it became exceedingly clear that interpreters' decisions and resulting actions are greatly influenced by unique constellations of multiple factors. A narrative discussion of each of the five primary categories paints a more complete picture of what interpreters do, as informed by an array of factors. Each of these discussions sheds light on the answer to my second research question: What factors influence the decisions K–12 interpreters make from moment to moment while on the job?

Assess and Respond to a Constellation of Contextual, Situational, and Human Factors

I discovered that assessment is foundational to the work of K–12 interpreters. It is impossible to clearly understand what interpreters do without examining their decisions in light of particular sets of circumstances. Interpreters assess and prioritize students' and other participants' needs (visual, academic, cognitive, linguistic, social, emotional, physical, cultural, etc.) in accordance with the school context (e.g., discourse norms, learning objectives, accountability, etc.). Based on these assessments, educational interpreters predict and determine whether they can best meet identified needs within an interpretation or if they need to take another course of action. Although I describe assessment here as one of the primary categories of what interpreters do, the results of the assessment process then inform interpreters' decisions about what to do. In other words, assessment is both a *what* and a *why*, and thereby provides an answer to both research questions. The key to understanding what K–12 interpreters do during the course of their work lies in understanding the contextual, situational, and human factors surrounding their decisions.

Interpret and/or Transliterate

Interpreting and/or transliterating responsibilities are central to the work of interpreters in K–12 mainstream classrooms. The traditional view is that interpreters should or will do one or the other. However, the K–12 interpreters I observed neither interpreted nor transliterated consistently. Instead, they alternated between providing an interpretation that was more consistent with the syntax and lexicon of ASL and providing a transliteration that more closely represented English. All three of the interpreters in this study described the importance of making connections between signed concepts and English vocabulary. One interpreter, Marina, reported that this was one of the most challenging aspects of the job for her to learn. She reported that she tried to sign following English word order whenever the class was reading aloud from a book because she felt it was important for Kristie, a Deaf student, to have access to the English vocabulary.

A lesson at Via Portal on the meaning of suffixes in English provided another example of interpreters alternating in their signing to make connections between ASL and English. AJ, the interpreter, initially transliterated each of the words and phrases in English through a combination of fingerspelling and English-based signs. After doing so, she interpreted the sentences or phrases a second time, using semantically appropriate signs to convey the meaning of the targeted words and phrases. I observed this process of linking conceptually accurate signs to an English representation repeatedly throughout this and other lessons. Although this involved more time and arguably more information than those of the teacher's original utterances, the approach demonstrates AJ's endeavors to construct a bridge between ASL and English and to convey the English terminology and discourse structures for which and by which Angelina would be held accountable.

Seek, Obtain, and Capitalize on Available Resources

Interpreters took time to seek, request, create, and obtain various resources to assist them in carrying out their job obligations. I observed all of the interpreters using the handouts, textbooks, and visual displays available in the classroom, and they often made use of several available resources during a single lesson.

In one situation, Mr. Sands at Via Portal asked his fifth grade students to get out their practice books to get ready for language arts. While students chattered and got their books ready, AJ, the interpreter, looked around the classroom. She saw a chair that was not being used, walked over and picked it up, then brought it back to where she was sitting and placed it next to her own chair. She then began looking around again, signing as she did that she needed a book. Angelina, the mainstreamed student in the class, told AJ to ask Mr. Sands. AJ walked over and asked if he had an extra copy of the practice book that she could use. When he gave her the book, she returned to her seat, placed the book in the adjacent empty chair, and sat down ready to interpret. Mr. Sands wrote two sentences on the board, then the asked students if they knew what the lesson would be about. When nobody could guess, he wrote the word *homophone* above the two sentences and began speaking. AJ turned around to look at what he had written on the board before she began to interpret. As the lesson progressed, Mr. Sands asked the class to open their practice books to page 107. After interpreting his instructions, AJ opened the book next to her and spent 24 seconds reading the specified page.

In this example, AJ made use of a variety of resources. Upon hearing that the class would be using practice books, she immediately found a chair that she could put a book on and look at as needed, leaving her hands free to interpret. Next, she signed that she needed a book. This brief interaction served two purposes. First, it kept Angelina in the loop about what AJ was doing (consistent with Deaf cultural values to keep one another informed). The second benefit, though perhaps unforeseen, was that Angelina became a resource for AJ. Because AJ was a substitute interpreter, she did not know where to locate an extra copy of the workbook. Angelina knew that Mr. Sands had an extra copy, so when AJ signed what was needed, Angelina readily shared that information. The third resource evidenced in this example was the teacher. AJ approached him and requested a book, which he provided. As Mr. Sands began the lesson, AJ looked at the board, capitalizing on a fourth resource to assist her in carrying out her interpreting obligations. As soon as Mr. Sands indicated the page that students would be working on, AJ found the correct page in her own workbook. She did not stop with merely locating the right page, she quickly read as much as she could to determine what information would be covered. In this manner, the fifth resource allowed her not only to see what the students would be working on, it provided a means through which AJ could begin to determine the lesson objectives and prepare mentally to interpret the specific academic content she had read about.

As the lesson progressed, AJ continued to take advantage of these five resources. She referred back to the board repeatedly, looking immediately when Mr. Sands gave instructions such as, "Write just this one word [pointing to the word *threw*] . . . because you have this one [pointing to the word *through*] written already."[16] By that point, Angelina was working ahead of the rest of the class and did not pay attention to these instructions. Instead, she asked AJ if *appear* was the next correct answer. AJ scooted her chair up next to Angelina's desk so they could both look at a sixth resource, Angelina's practice book. Nearly a minute later, Angelina began writing her answers in the workbook. AJ saw that she was writing the wrong word in the designated space because she had missed her teacher's instructions. AJ then used Angelina's book as a resource in a different way. Because she had scooted her chair close enough to see Angelina's book, she could actually reach over and touch it. At that point, the clarification about where to write which of the homophones was directly relevant to what Angelina was writing. AJ repeated the teacher's instructions, touching Angelina's book twice to indicate which of the homophones was already printed and to clarify that the second of the two homophones needed to be written in the provided space. As Angelina erased what she had written and wrote the correct word in the workbook, AJ scooted her chair back to her original position. When Angelina was done writing, she looked back up at AJ, who first pointed at Mr. Sands to indicate that he was talking before she again began to interpret. Almost immediately, the classroom aide walked over and picked up the book that AJ had received from the teacher. AJ turned around and listened to the aide's request, then told the aide to go ahead and take the book. At that point, AJ again scooted her chair up next to Angelina's desk and the two shared Angelina's practice book for the rest of the lesson.

In addition to the six resources AJ used in this situation, interpreters requested a variety of physical and informational resources from teachers and other school personnel: IEP goals, state standards, lesson plans and tutorials, captioned videos, manipulatives for teaching mathematical concepts, dictionaries, and vocabulary and spelling lists. Interpreters also sought information from and discussed strategies with classroom teachers and specialists in order to more effectively meet the needs of Deaf and hard of hearing students. Moreover, interpreters developed and brought

---

16. Text in brackets signifies that I have replaced a pronoun with a specific noun or have in some way clarified the speaker's intent. For example, if the speaker used a gesture rather than an English word, the transcript reflects my chosen word in brackets.

in their own resources, such as materials needed to create sign-related displays for classroom bulletin boards, as well as flash cards and electronic or ASL dictionaries for use during designated tutoring time.

Furthermore, interpreters in K–12 settings made use of internal resources in the course of their work: interpreters' own formal and informal education, reflections on previous interpreting experience, awareness of state standards and academic norms, and life experiences (such as interactions with the Deaf community). In addition, interpreters capitalized on knowledge they had gained on the job, such as previous class content, the needs of Deaf and hard of hearing students, teacher goals and styles, learning objectives, accountability measures, and class progress.

Interact with Others

On a daily basis, interpreters interacted with classroom teachers, instructional aides, specialists (e.g., resource, DHH, or itinerant teachers; audiologists; librarians; etc.), administrators, office staff, and/or other district interpreters. All three of the K–12 interpreters in this study participated in interactions that were both social and professional in nature.

CLASSROOM TEACHERS

Besides Deaf and hard of hearing students, interpreters most commonly interacted with classroom teachers, both socially and professionally. They engaged in polite conversation, shared adult camaraderie, and exchanged light-hearted banter. Interpreters collaborated, negotiated, and brainstormed with classroom teachers about how to make classroom discourse and activities more accessible. In addition, interpreters provided student-related information that they felt teachers should know. Furthermore, they offered assistance (such as reminders about where a teacher had left off) and requested a variety of resources (such as textbooks and handouts).

For example, AJ requested guidance from the classroom teacher after interacting with a student about a class activity. Mr. Sands had directed his fifth grade students to write a paragraph about pizza. Angelina, the Deaf student, asked AJ for help with a "mind map" to organize the writing. Across the table, an instructional aide assisted two dominant Spanish-speaking students with their maps as well. A line of students seeking additional assistance quickly formed in front of Mr. Sands. As students began to write, AJ noticed that Angelina was spelling the word *dough* as *dow*. AJ stated that she did not say anything because she felt it was important for Angelina to get her thoughts down without interruption. After Angelina was done writing the paragraph, AJ prompted her to double-check for spelling. Laughing, AJ explained, "Of course she thought everything was spelled right because she thought it was right. So then I pointed out the word to her, and said that [it] wasn't spelled right and [asked], "How do you spell it? And, of course, she doesn't *know*, so she asked *me*. And I said, "Well, why don't you look it up in the dictionary?"

During the interview, AJ said that she prompted Angelina to look for the word in the dictionary based on her previous experience working with a variety of teachers, but because she was a substitute interpreter for the week, she was not sure what Mr. Sands preferred. When Angelina began to look up the word she had spelled incorrectly, AJ realized:

> D-O-W is a looonng way from D-O-U, and she's never gonna find it. So, that's when I went and asked the teacher, "Do you have them look up words in the dictionary?" to see if I'd even done the right thing. And he was like, "Yeah." So then I told him where she was at, and he was like, "Ohhh, that's gonna be kind of hard, huh?" and I go, "Yeah." So then he just said, "I'll just announce it to the whole class. I'll just tell the whole class."

As soon as AJ recognized that the strategy she had suggested to Angelina was unlikely to be successful, she approached Mr. Sands for three reasons: (a) to find out if prompting Angelina was in line with his typical teaching style, (b) to inform him of Angelina's situation, and (c) to get guidance about what he would like to do or how he would like AJ to respond. After AJ was assured that Mr. Sands would take matters into his own hands, she returned to her seat. As she sat down, Mr. Sands asked the class, "How do you spell *dough*?" AJ did not immediately interrupt Angelina to interpret, but let her continue working on her paragraph. However, when Mr. Sands got the correct answer and wrote *dough* on the board, she waved to get Angelina's attention. With a smile on her face, AJ reported, "I said, 'Look! They're talking about your word!' So then she got to see how to spell it right."

AJ emphasized that ongoing communication with classroom teachers is critical. She provided some examples of relevant information she might provide to a teacher about a Deaf student. "'She gets the right answer a lot, but she won't raise her hand. You might want to consider calling on her even if she doesn't have her hand raised,' or, 'She always *thinks* she has the right answer, and they're always *wrong*. She needs extra help in this area.'" If the interpreter is to help, AJ said, the type of help to be provided should be clearly defined.

In the pizza dough situation, AJ initiated an interaction with Mr. Sands. However, teachers also asked interpreters for their input on how to make activities accessible. For example, Mr. Harrison randomly selected words from the science textbook for his sixth grade students to spell. Camie, the interpreter working in his class, had already taught him that not all English words have a signed equivalent. As a result, Mr. Harrison frequently asked Camie to advise him about selecting words that might be more clearly interpreted so that Emily, the Deaf student in the class, would be able to participate fairly. Interpreters interacted with teachers in order to identify strategies for improving access in an environment designed for hearing students. They participated in discussions intended

1. To collaborate or request guidance and input;
2. To negotiate strategies for accommodation, especially when a technique proved to be unsuccessful;
3. To provide information regarding student progress;
4. To make requests or offer suggestions regarding access;
5. To provide support and reinforcement; and
6. To ask for information or resources.

Besides collaboration, negotiation, consultation, and communication regarding student needs and class activities (including content or access), teacher-interpreter interactions were also social. Camie and AJ both emphasized the importance of maintaining a good rapport and professional working relationship with classroom teachers through both social and professional dialogue.

DEAF AND HARD OF HEARING STUDENTS

The nuances and intricacies of interactions between interpreters and students are intensely complex (I examine their discussions regarding language and/or learning needs in Section 3), but I identified seven common functions of interactions, illustrated in the following vignettes.

To Participate in Social and Personal Conversations

Interpreters did not limit social conversations to teachers and other school personnel; they also chatted amicably with Deaf and hard of hearing students. As Mr. Sands got ready to resume class after lunch, the chatter of hearing students speaking to each other in both English and Spanish filled the room. Angelina, the only hard of hearing student, sat quietly. Soon, Angelina got AJ's attention and signed to her that she had an IEP meeting to go to later in the day. They discussed the meeting for a short time. As the conversation continued, Angelina sat up and began signing animatedly, excitedly explaining that she had begun taking gymnastics. AJ discussed the importance of this type of dialogue between the interpreter and Deaf or hard of hearing students. She explained, "It's rapport building, especially since I let her tell *me* stuff. It's enjoyable to sit and chat with her, and she had stuff she wanted to tell me about. [The other students were] all chatting with each other. And that's the thing too, she doesn't have anyone she can sit and chat with really, so . . . I think it makes the environment somewhat more . . . equal, because she has someone she can talk to if I engage with her."

Not all interactions between interpreters and students were so informal. For example, during free reading time, Kristie, a Deaf student, was reading a book about mummies that she had checked out from the library. She asked Marina, the interpreter, to explain about Egyptian artifacts and references such as King Tut, and for the meaning of English words such as *tomb* and *sacrificed*. This printed English terminology was completely unrelated to class content, but Marina willingly answered to the best of her ability. Kristie also showed Marina some of the pictures in the book, to which Marina responded, "Interesting!" or "That's cool!"

Interpreters discussed physical concerns with Deaf and hard of hearing students, such as a student being hungry, tired, or having a stomachache. Interpreters also talked with students about technical needs, such as Angelina's hearing aid needing new batteries or to troubleshoot problems with the amplification/microphone system worn by her teacher. They discussed and negotiated language and access issues, jointly making decisions about interpreting or the use of certain signs. They collaborated about logistics, such as where the interpreter should sit. In addition, interpreters asked questions about students' visual access, such as "Can you see?"

As AJ suggested, the educational interpreters were often the only people with whom Deaf and hard of hearing students could interact most freely. In fact, interpreters reported that they had been the first adults that Deaf and hard of hearing students approached with questions or concerns about deeply personal matters. Because Deaf and hard of hearing students and interpreters work closely together every single day, sometimes for a number of years, it is not surprising that an interpreter might sometimes find herself fulfilling the role of personal coach or trusted confidante. For example, Camie, an interpreter, had worked with Emily for 4 years, and when Emily started her first menstruation at school, she confided in Camie. Camie reassured Emily and advised her about how to take care of her personal needs. She walked with her to the school nurse and, upon learning that Emily was still confused after leaving the office, Camie explained how to use the provided sanitary products. Later, Emily's mother contacted Camie to thank her for being there when her daughter needed help and emotional support.

To Promote Independence or Encourage Interactions with Teacher and/or Peers

Although interpreters frequently interacted with Deaf and hard of hearing students, these K–12 interpreters emphasized the importance of encouraging students to interact directly with teachers and hearing peers whenever possible. However, they recognized that not all students are ready for the same level of independence as their peers, regardless of age. In one situation, Kristie told Marina that she needed to use the restroom. Marina told her to go ask the teacher. Kristie walked up to the teacher and signed, BATHROOM? Mrs. Natale signed, YES, and wrote her a pass. Marina talked about making different decisions when Kristie and Miguel (two Deaf students in the same class) asked her for permission to get a drink of water or use the restroom rather than ask the teacher directly.

Marina explained, "A lot times she'll ask me, 'Can I go to the bathroom?' [I'll say,] 'I don't know, go ask the teacher.' I mean, I could ask the teacher, '[Can] Kristie go to the bathroom?' But Kristie is independent, and I want her to get used to addressing somebody without using the interpreter." In contrast, she reported that when she prompted Miguel to ask the teacher, he often expressed a reluctance to go ask on his own. Therefore, she reported that she would tell him, "Come on. Let's go ask. I'll interpret."

Interpreters in this study looked for student cues to determine readiness to perform a task or engage in interactions with others independently, encouraging students who appeared cognitively and socially ready but lacked the self-esteem to try. The words and actions of these K–12 interpreters revealed their attempts to strike an appropriate balance between providing adequate support and promoting student independence. This scenario demonstrates how Marina's assessment of student readiness for independence led her to make a different decision with each student. First, she prompted both students to ask the teacher directly. Their responses to her suggestion then determined Marina's subsequent course of action. In Kristie's case, the interaction eventually took place without an interpreter. Marina approached the same situation with Miguel differently: In response to his hesitation, she offered to walk with him and interpret his question to the teacher. In both cases, she did more than simply interpret; she also interacted directly with the students to provide guidance. Her ultimate goal, however, was to facilitate interactions between these two students and their classroom teacher. These K–12 interpreters promoted independence and encouraged Deaf and hard of hearing students to interact as much as possible with teachers and hearing peers. Nevertheless, the fact that interpreters were the only ones in the classroom who shared a common language with Deaf and hard of hearing students was the basis for many interpreter–student interactions.

To Serve as a Discourse Partner, as Well as to Maintain Flow and Promote Efficiency

Interpreters reported a variety of reasons for responding directly to students rather than referring them to teachers or interpreting their signed questions into spoken English. Marina detailed some of the factors she considered when deciding whether to respond to Kristie's signed questions directly, to interpret them into spoken English, or to prompt Kristie to ask the teacher. Marina said that some questions, "like, 'What page number?' if I know, I'll tell her. I'm not going to have her interrupt the whole classroom. If I heard it and she obviously didn't hear it and I have that information, I'll give it to her. If it's something I think she can be independent about, I'll get her to try and do it." Marina described a situation in which Kristie asked what the teacher had just said. She explained that Kristie "was distracted, and she missed it. So sometimes those things I just have to repeat, and she'll ask me again because she was off in 'la la' land. If the teacher is giving information and she's not looking."

Marina elaborated further that hearing students are likely to have multiple avenues to request clarification, but Deaf and hard of hearing students who do not share a common language with their hearing peers are at a disadvantage for seeking repetition and clarification. She explained, "If the teacher is giving information, and [Kristie's] not looking. . . .You know, hearing kids are going to pick it up. Maybe they won't, but they'll hear it, and they'll ask their friends too. Kristie is not going to ask her neighbor, 'What did she say?' She might ask a couple of her friends who sign, but [they don't sign] clearly, so I figure I have that role." Marina made the point that Deaf and hard of hearing students not only more easily miss a piece of information if they do not maintain complete focus, they also have fewer available resources to seek additional clarification. Marina illuminated the difficulty Deaf and hard of hearing students may have when trying to retrieve missed information through a more private channel than asking in front of the whole class, since a hearing peer is highly unlikely to sign well enough to fill them in on missed information. As a result of these factors, Marina felt justified in choosing to answer some of Kristie's questions directly, especially when the information had already been discussed.

AJ concurred that efficiency is another important factor to consider when determining whether to prompt a Deaf or hard of hearing student to direct questions to the teacher. AJ explained that she would be most likely to direct Deaf and hard of hearing students' questions to the teacher if she herself did not know the answer, especially if the teacher had not covered it in class already. She said, "If he has gone over it in class, I sort of look at it as consecutive interpreting. *And* I also look at it as practicality. Why would we go over, stand in line and wait among the five other kids that need that teacher when I know the answer? It just saves everybody time. And he has already talked about it. It's not like I *think* I know the answer. He already *talked* about it, and I'm . . . re-interpreting it, so to speak." All of the interpreters in this study were influenced by the fact that each class had approximately 40 students. Because they recognized that classes were overcrowded and teachers overextended, educational interpreters often chose to repeat information that was previously interpreted. These two situations demonstrate that interpreters repeat information while interpreting as well as during noninterpreting time.

To Redirect Off-Task Students

Interpreters also participated in conversations to redirect students who were not paying attention. Classroom teachers corroborated the importance of attention-getting among elementary school students. The math and social studies teacher at Azalea, Mrs. Kendall, expressed concern about her experiences working with what she called "agency" interpreters as opposed to staff interpreters. For the 8 months prior to my observation, Azalea had been unable to fill two staff interpreting positions. As a result, they had been subcontracting interpreting services through two different outside agencies. Mrs. Kendall reported that some of the interpreters sent by the agencies refused to interpret when Deaf and hard of hearing students were not looking. Mrs. Kendall approached an interpreter to voice her concern and was dismayed by the interpreter's response. The interpreter replied that if the students were not watching, she did not have to sign and it wasn't a part of her job description to get the students' attention. Mrs. Kendall exclaimed, "But they're in fifth grade and they're only 10!" She lamented the fact that one interpreter even "pulled out a book and started reading" during the class session. Mrs. Kendall expressed her appreciation that Marina would tap on the students' desks or wave to get their attention. She explained that she could simply call hearing students by name to get their attention. However, when interpreters refused to get the Deaf or hard of hearing students' attention, she felt it put her in the undesirable position of having to take time away from her focus on the lesson to walk across the classroom and get their attention or to move on without them. Although, in reality, perhaps Mrs. Kendall could have called Deaf students by name, she felt as if she could not. After numerous attempts to address the issue, she was never offered a workable solution or even provided an opportunity to brainstorm with the agency interpreters.

Marina brought up another set of factors to consider when deciding whether or not to get students to pay attention to the lesson at hand. She explained, "I'm sure if [Mrs. Kendall] looked up and saw that they were drawing [she would take care of it]." Like all the interpreters in this study, Marina felt that Deaf and hard of hearing students should be held to the same behavioral expectations as their peers. Interestingly, two interpreters said that they believed classroom teachers were more likely to address the off-task behaviors of hearing students. They explained that because the Deaf and hard of hearing students' off-task behavior was often quiet, it was not as disruptive. Marina said, "They're so quiet that the teacher doesn't always notice them. They're not talkative kids. She notices the kids that are talking in the back and tells them, 'Be quiet, pay attention.' But she doesn't notice that [Miguel and Kristie] are chatting. They're just signing. It doesn't bother the teacher as much, but to me, it bothers me a lot." Because Mrs. Kendall and other teachers were less aware of and therefore less likely to address off-task behaviors, Marina explained that part of her role was to keep Kristie and Miguel on task as much as possible through attention-getting techniques and explicit directive statements. Yet, the decision about how much effort to expend in order to get and maintain student attention is tempered by still other factors.

Camie, the interpreter at Meadowbrook, shed light on even more factors to consider when deciding whether or not to redirect off-task students. In one situation, Mr. Harrison asked students to write down the definitions of a list of targeted English vocabulary words as he dictated them. Emily continued to work on her spelling homework rather than focus on Mr. Harrison's definitions. Camie made several attempts to get Emily back on track, justifying her decision to do so by saying, "It was more important for her to get these vocabulary words to help her with the state testing," but Emily ignored her and kept working on spelling. Camie laughed, "She'll humor me. She's great at patronizing me. She'll look at me like, 'Uh-huh, ok,' and then she's slipping her spelling paper out, so . . . oh well."

Camie tried several tactics to get and maintain Emily's attention: She adjusted the pacing of the interpretation and held the correct responses until Emily decided to look up from her spelling homework. She leaned forward and waved her hand in Emily's line of sight. She asked Emily to put away her spelling and write down the definitions that Mr. Harrison was providing. At some point, she chose to let Emily work on her spelling even though she felt that the stakes were high (state testing). Eventually, Camie chose to let Emily live with the consequences of her own decision. However, in another situation, when students were supposed to be correcting a classmate's paper and Emily was distracted by another activity, Camie moved her chair forward to make sure Emily marked her classmate's paper correctly, providing as rationale that another student's grade was dependent on Emily's corrections. While at times interpreters chose to try to direct students' attention to the task at hand, sometimes they let students make their own decisions about attending to class activities. As they did when deciding whether to respond directly to student questions, when deciding whether to redirect off-task students, interpreters endeavored to discern when to promote independence and when to provide additional intervention or support. Moreover, they considered factors such as accountability measures or the potential impact a Deaf or hard of hearing student's decision might have on a peer.

To Respect Student Momentum and Flow and to Allow for
Independent Choice
At times, although Deaf or hard of hearing students were not staying with the class, they were engaged in activities directly related to the task or lesson at hand. For example, while Mr. Sands was going through

a worksheet with the class, Angelina chose to work ahead. AJ spoke about feeling pulled in two directions—wanting to both meet Angelina's needs and respect the teaching preferences that she determined Mr. Sands valued. She explained that Angelina:

> had whipped through the work and was asking questions about Problems 6, 7, and 8, and the teacher was still talking about Number 2. It was weird because I wanted to be with *her*, and answer *her* questions posed—"in the moment teaching," or whatever. I felt like I had to . . . slow her down because she was way ahead and it seemed to me that the teacher had the priority of everyone should be together at the same place raising their hand answering [his] question, not moving on.
>
> I guess I went back and forth between, like, where she was working and I'd answer *her* questions and look at where *she* was at and help her when she asked me to, but then I would go back to interpreting what the teacher was saying. And she wasn't really looking, because she was doing her work. But I just interpreted it anyway.

When Deaf and hard of hearing students are able to complete a task independently before the teacher has given them free rein to work independently, they may choose to work ahead. In this case, AJ considered conflicting factors to decide whether or not and to what extent she should interpret, whether to respond directly to the questions Angelina posed in the moment or defer to the teacher's pacing. She had to decide whether to get Angelina's attention to interpret the interactions between the teacher and Angelina's hearing classmates or to allow Angelina to work ahead uninterrupted. In this example, AJ intentionally stopped interpreting to some degree for two reasons: (a) to allow Angelina to work ahead uninterrupted and (b) to answer questions as Angelina worked ahead and be responsive to her immediate needs. Although AJ felt obligated to interpret and tried to get Angelina's attention now and then, sometimes she simply continued interpreting without expecting Angelina to watch.

Because the need to complete an assigned task was seen as taking precedence over other classroom discourse, these interpreters often made decisions to deliberately omit information from the interpretation. In other words, sometimes they intentionally chose *not* to interpret. Types of discourse typically omitted were chatter, banter, comments about what teachers saw other students doing, and communication regarded as less relevant to the task at hand. If the communication was not seen as contributing to a more immediate need at the moment, interpreters often chose not to interpret.

For example, when Angelina was already done with one worksheet and had moved on to the next, another student asked Mr. Sands to clarify the instructions for a problem on the previous worksheet. Angelina had already completed the problem successfully, so AJ did not interrupt Angelina to interpret the question and response. In some cases, interpreters in this study summarized information and interactions after the student's work was completed. In other cases, instruction moved forward and the interaction was omitted from the interpretation in the interest of other communication needs. For example, teacher comments directed to an individual who was off-task were often either omitted or held until the Deaf or hard of hearing student completed the task, unless that student also showed evidence of the behavior that the teacher had addressed. In that case, interpreters said that they would be more likely to interrupt the work to interpret the teacher's warnings. These educational interpreters conveyed a tremendous amount of respect for students' desire to work independently when they appeared to be ready to complete a task. There were times, however, that they extended greater efforts to get the students' attention because they predicted that the additional information being presented by the teacher would enhance the student's understanding of the task or concepts being practiced.

To Alert Students to Salient Information

In terms of student attention and missed information, several factors came into play when K–12 interpreters made decisions about whether or not to repeat information, redirect off-task students, or allow students to work uninterrupted (and even respond to their questions in the moment). Camie indicated that sometimes she let Emily make the decision about whether or not to pay attention. At other times, Camie determined that Emily's learning needs and the potential benefit of the information being provided should supersede Emily's desire to keep working. She reported that Emily "knows when she can look up and kind of ignore me and when she needs to pay attention. . . . I just do what I think is best. . . . She'll look at me like, 'Yeah, okay, I don't need to listen to that.' Then I'll [emphasize], 'Yeah, you *do* need to listen to this part, he's telling you something different.' Or, 'He's talking to the whole class now.'" AJ expressed a similar philosophy with regard to deciding to get Angelina's attention when she was working ahead. "At that point I, like, tried to pull her back because the teacher was talking about it. . . . I got her attention to watch what he was saying so that she wasn't just going through it and doing the pattern." In this case, AJ's decision to interrupt was prompted by the fact that Mr. Sands began to discuss a concept that AJ was not sure Angelina fully understood.

Camie and AJ both conveyed that they would deliberately omit information when they determined that Emily and Angelina did not need further elaboration to complete a task, even when teachers were still providing instruction and explanation. They made decisions about whether or not information was pertinent enough to interrupt students and resume interpreting, prioritizing according to which activity should take precedence over another. They valued student momentum and flow, as well as students' right to work ahead. However, interpreters continued to monitor the incoming information, making decisions based on stakes and accountability, student choice, and assessments of what students already knew and could do independently. Sometimes, they interrupted Deaf and hard of hearing students who were hard at work just to let them know about an occurrence that had captured all of the hearing students' attention—for example, at Meadowbrook, a fight between two students outside of the classroom, a boisterous P.E. teacher who poked her head in to give Mr. Harrison a hard time, and a sudden and fierce hailstorm. In all three cases, Camie interrupted Emily's work to make sure she was included in the excitement.

To Provide Immediate Reinforcement and Praise

At least in part because of the timing delay inherent to interpretation, Deaf and hard of hearing students frequently signed their answers after the answer had already been given by another student. Interpreters' shouting out those signed answers after the fact would be inappropriate; instead, interpreters sometimes chose to respond directly to the students. AJ explained the rationale behind her decision:

> I can right there say, "Right! That's a good answer! Right!" And they'll get that out of me, and really, *that's* what education is all about. You know, it's that I-R-E response thing—initiation by the teacher asking for responses, and then the response, and then the evaluation of the response. It's such a *common* interaction in classroom discourse. And with the *interpreter* there, it takes away a lot of it! So, I guess that's my own way of sticking it back in there.

Interviewer: Tell me about "It takes away a lot of it." You think having an interpreter there . . .

AJ: Removes a lot of it for the Deaf student . . . that whole discourse chain, that I-R-E chain. Of course, they get the "I," the teacher asking the questions through me as the interpreter, but they don't . . . they rarely respond, for a million reasons probably. And then when they *do* respond . . . I don't know. It just seems more natural to give them that evaluation. You know, "Right! That's right! That's the right answer!" right there. It's more real that way.

Not only did the interpreters interpret the praise and encouragement that teachers offered to students, they also praised Deaf students directly. Both Kristie and Angelina were highly participatory in class, regularly raising their hands to respond whenever their teachers posed a question. AJ, in particular, was quick to encourage Angelina's participation. She smiled and nodded often, was generous with praise, and responded directly to many of Angelina's signed comments. Perhaps the frequency of praise and reinforcement in this case was attributable to additional factors such as the sharper tone used by this teacher or Angelina's attentiveness and eagerness to participate. However, all three interpreters provided direct praise and reinforcement to Deaf and hard of hearing students.

PARENTS, RELATIVES, AND GUARDIANS OF DEAF OR HARD OF HEARING STUDENTS

By far, most of the interactions I observed or heard about took place between interpreters and classroom teachers or other school personnel, and between interpreters and Deaf and hard of hearing students. However, interpreters also communicated with students' family members. Most conversations with parents took place at school, when students were dropped off or picked up. Some occurred at Deaf community events. Camie said that she and Emily's mother occasionally communicated via telephone or email. One interpreter reported that a teacher she used to work with forbid her from talking to parents; however, Mr. Harrison communicated regularly with Emily's mother through a school-to-home journal. The journal was Emily's mother's idea, and Mr. Harrison quickly realized its benefits. He asked Camie to write in it as well, as a daily practice. He also made sure Emily wrote comments and questions in it, explaining that he felt she should be included in and aware of discussions and decisions surrounding her own education. They used the journal to communicate regarding

1. Academic content
2. Goals and priorities
3. Class activities
4. Communication preferences and needs
5. Signs and vocabulary
6. Personal issues
7. Schedules and availability
8. Absences and health issues
9. Deaf community events and resources

Camie and Mr. Harrison both found the journal to be a beneficial avenue for clear communication; they said that it increased their confidence that expectations between school and home were well aligned.

HEARING STUDENTS

Interpreters also talked to hearing students, often in social interactions. At Azalea, when students lined up to walk from class to class, or when they were at lunch, there was quite a bit of interaction among students. Sometimes Marina interpreted conversations between Kristie and Miguel and their classmates. At other times, she spoke and signed simultaneously as she actively participated in conversations with hearing students. Camie took a similar approach at Meadowbrook. One hearing student was observed hugging a staff interpreter at Via Portal, showing that students develop relationships with interpreters who are in their classrooms day after day.

Other interactions were more instructional. Staff interpreters at Via Portal said that they liked to offer help to hearing students whenever Angelina did not need any help. In their opinion, helping hearing students would reduce the perceived separation between Angelina and her classmates. Camie also provided assistance to hearing students in a group of students with Emily who were asked to complete a class activity. Similarly, Marina helped students in Miguel and Kristie's group by clarifying instructions regarding a class activity (Figure 4).

In one instance, several girls (including Emily) approached Camie after lunch to complain about something another student had done on the playground. Camie listened and, while speaking and signing at the same time, asked if they had been able to speak to the offending party directly.

FIGURE 4. *Marina clarifying instructions for Miguel, Kristie, and a hearing classmate.*

When the girls told her "no" and continued their tirade, Camie nodded empathetically and continued to listen until the bell rang signaling it was time to return to class.

Hearing students often asked interpreters how to sign something. This was especially prevalent at Meadowbrook. Camie would teach the hearing students the signs that they wanted to learn, and then she would sit back and watch, stepping in if needed to clarify for either Emily or her friends. In Emily's case, three or four of her classmates had learned enough signed vocabulary to carry on basic conversations about cute boys, mean girls, and other topics engaging to sixth grade girls. I found it interesting that Mr. Harrison kept this in mind when reconfiguring his seating charts. Although these girls were not always table mates, he said that he tried to keep at least one of them at Emily's assigned table and another close by. The interpreters' willingness to teach signs and problem-solve peer relations led to increased opportunities for Deaf and hard of hearing students to interact with their peers. However, because of language and communication barriers, participation in social relationships with peers was limited.

Interpreters interacted with hearing students on a regular basis. Some of the functions of interpreters' interactions with hearing students were

1. To engage in social conversation.
2. To tutor, help, explain, or repeat.
3. To listen to, support, and problem-solve.

4. To facilitate and promote interactions with Deaf and hard of hearing students.
5. To ask questions regarding sight lines (e.g., "Can you see the board?" when the interpreter was standing in a location that might have blocked a student's view).
6. To facilitate class activities (e.g., "Would you two like to exchange papers?).

Perform Aide Duties and Other Tasks; Be Useful or Helpful as Needed

When there was no immediate need to interpret, interpreters performed a variety of other tasks. At both Via Portal and Azalea, for example, staff interpreters were expected to serve as monitors during lunch and/or recess. These additional obligations decreased the already limited amount of break time for interpreters to eat, use the restroom, or relax. It also precluded the opportunity for interpreters to prepare for upcoming interpretations or quickly collaborate with classroom teachers. These assigned duties did not appear to interfere with interpreters' ability to fulfill their interpreting obligations, however, and in fact, their presence provided some opportunities for interactions between Deaf and hearing students or school staff.

During the course of this study, K–12 interpreters reported or were observed being generally helpful and productive employees in several ways. For example, they passed along items that were in reach; they gave a book to a teacher or picked up and returned a pencil to the student who had dropped it. They turned on lights and closed or opened doors and windows. They erased whiteboards. They watched the class while a teacher quickly ran to use the restroom. They reminded students to adhere to school safety policies (e.g., no running). At Meadowbrook, Mr. Harrison asked Camie to create an ASL-related bulletin board. Camie agreed, explaining during her interview that she had hoped it would increase hearing students' interest in learning more signs and communicating with Emily. Camie stayed after school hours to post pictures of signs on the bulletin board. A resulting benefit was the opportunity it provided for the interpreter and teacher to talk about promoting access and inclusion for Emily while neither was pressured for time. Along with carrying out their primary obligations of facilitating access for Deaf and hard of hearing students, interpreters found ways to be helpful and responsive human beings.

Classroom teachers depend on a multitude of visual aids (such as whiteboards, overhead transparencies, charts, and textbooks) and are accustomed to working with hearing students who can look at visual input while simultaneously listening to instruction. Therefore, teachers typically keep talking while referring to other sources of important visual information, inadvertently creating difficulties for Deaf and hard of hearing students who need to look at an interpreter to access classroom discourse. Competing demands for visual attention exist when a student needs to attend visually to a signed interpretation while also locating and/or viewing another source of visual input. Table 10 lists types of activities during which Deaf or hard of hearing students were expected to watch the interpreter for the signed interpretation of spoken discourse while other visual information was simultaneously being presented.

To begin documenting what K–12 interpreters are doing and considering in the course of their work, I found it necessary to describe in great detail the specific strategies and multiple additional factors that influence educational interpreters' decisions in response to the presence of competing visual demands. The difficulty of the writing task reflects the complexity of interpreters' moment-to-moment decision-making processes. In this analysis, I describe each response separately, although responses in fact shift frequently because of the overlapping nature of the factors affecting interpreters' decisions and because each decision results in a new set of factors to be considered and addressed.

All of the interpreters discussed the challenge of responding effectively to competing demands for Deaf and hard of hearing students' visual

TABLE 10. *Common Sources of Competing Visual Input*

A. Locating materials, such as a particular page of text, paper, pencil, or handouts

B. Looking at visual aids, such as maps, charts, number lines, bulletin boards, props, computer-based graphics or presentations, video (without caption), overhead transparencies, facial expressions, and/or gestures

C. Reading written or printed information, such as on whiteboards or in handouts, textbooks, captioned video, computer-based text, and PowerPoint presentations

D. Generating written information, such as completing a worksheet, correcting written responses, and/or taking notes

E. Participating in a hands-on activity either individually or in groups

---

attention. For example, during Mr. Harrison's sixth grade language arts lesson, he told students to write down a series of dictated sentences that included their spelling words. Students were to spell the words correctly and define each one based on the context of the sentence. While hearing students can listen and sound out the words as they are spoken aloud in English, Deaf and hard of hearing students are engaged in a much different task. Although the language and translation aspect of the activity is in itself worthy of further discussion, the issue here is that Deaf and hard of hearing students need to look at their papers to write the words, then back up to the interpreter to get the rest of the sentence.

While interpreting the lesson, Camie, the interpreter, was frustrated for Emily, the Deaf student. "I hate when [Mr. Harrison] does that because Emily can't do that! That's like telling her brain to go in three different places—look at me, focus on the spelling, focus on trying to figure out what this word is [while writing the sentences]. That's *impossible* to do!" Expressing similar frustrations, interpreters said they had to ask teachers to refrain from talking while presenting visual stimuli; although classroom teachers were receptive to the idea of adapting their teaching style to better meet Deaf and hard of hearing students' visual needs, they still, unintentionally but habitually, created problematic situations.

Competing demands for visual attention result in an intense responsibility for interpreters. Interpreters must respond to students' need to access visual information and attend to the accompanying signed interpretation of spoken discourse, knowing that students cannot look at both sources of information at the same time. Considering the fact that Deaf and hard of hearing students may be put at an extreme disadvantage in such situations, the prevalence of instances of competing visual demands (more than 84% of class time) in the fifth and sixth grade classrooms I observed is disquieting. Interpreters employed multiple strategies in their efforts to optimize Deaf and hard of hearing students' access to various sources of visual input; however, they recognized that, in spite of their best efforts, equivalent access was not always provided, and they struggled to make the most of a less-than-ideal situation.

Common Techniques for Responding to the Presence of Competing Visual Demands

To address competing visual demands, interpreters used four main strategies: (a) adjusting physical position, (b) directing students' attention,

(c) adjusting the timing of the interpretation, and (d) modifying the interpretation itself. While each action is in itself important, responses were highly interdependent and overlapping. Inevitably, the success of one course of action was either facilitated or impeded by the implementation (or lack thereof) of another, and additional responses were often necessary because of the strategies chosen. It is because of the variability of conditions and interrelatedness of factors that the roles, responsibilities, and task of interpreting have heretofore been difficult to pin down.

Interpreters in a variety of settings use these four strategies, but the strategies require particular consideration in the educational context. Interpreters typically position themselves close to the primary speaker and adjust their position as needed to create optimal sight lines. In educational settings, the interpreter usually sits between the teacher and the Deaf or hard of hearing student. Ideally, interpreters are in the same line of sight as both the teacher and other visual input (such as a whiteboard). Deaf and hard of hearing students can then access the other visual input by looking either over the interpreter's head or just to the interpreter's side. The assumption, although arguable and not yet proven, is that while students are looking at the interpreter when the teacher is talking, they can also see the teacher's facial expressions, gestures, and body language either with their peripheral vision or an occasional glance.

Interpreters also frequently point to things and people that a Deaf or hard of hearing participant needs to see. Similarly, educational interpreters typically point to a student or teacher so that Deaf and hard of hearing students can identify who is speaking. However, when interpreters point out salient visual input, they must wait for Deaf and hard of hearing participants to reestablish eye contact before resuming their interpretation. Because of the time it takes for educational interpreters to direct students' attention to visual input, as well as for both the student and the interpreter to visually process the information, interpreters must frequently wait to interpret classroom discourse. If the reference is relatively brief and simple, such as signifying that a different person is now speaking, the corresponding timing delay will be brief and interpreters will simply pause momentarily so that students can see who is talking. If, however, the visual input is more complex or prolonged, the timing delay will increase. In K–12 classrooms, interpreters frequently confront salient visual input requiring students' sustained attention.

A fourth strategy interpreters use to provide access to visual input is modifying the interpretation in some way. Modifying the interpretation often involves adding information to clarify (Metzger, 1999; Metzger & Fleetwood, 2004). For example, if a teacher calls on a student by pointing at him rather than calling on him by name and the interpreter knows the name of the student, a statement may be added to the interpretation of the student response, such as "Patrick says . . ." When interpreters do not know the name of the speaker, they may add a physical description to their interpretation, such as "the boy in the pink T-shirt," so that the Deaf student can more easily locate and identify who is speaking. Interpreters may also reduce or compress the information in some way, such as by delivering a summarized version or even deliberately omitting information as a conscious strategy (Napier, 2002a, 2002b, 2005).

Scenario: Science Lesson on Volcanoes

A science lesson on volcanoes in Mr. Harrison's sixth grade classroom took 1 hour over 2 days (approximately 30 minutes each day). On the first day, students took turns reading aloud from the textbook (there was one textbook for every two students) while each student completed a "directed reading worksheet" to answer questions based on what was read; the next day, Mr. Harrison went over the worksheets with the class. Mr. Harrison's engaging use of visual aids throughout the lesson created competing visual demands for Emily, a Deaf student mainstreamed in his classroom. Camie, the interpreter, responded to Emily's need to access multiple sources of visual input in a variety of ways, often using the four main strategies discussed above. (Not all of her choices were successful. I discuss what went wrong and why in Section 5 of this chapter.)

In the beginning of the lesson, on the first day, Mr. Harrison called on Brenda to read at "When tectonic plates collide." Camie signed to Emily to begin reading at the top of page 203, turning her own book toward Emily to show her exactly where to begin reading. While Brenda read, Camie did not interpret. A few moments later, Mr. Harrison sat down at a vacant student desk in front of the classroom, between Emily and Camie and unintentionally blocking their view of each other. He began conducting an experiment described in the book, pushing two pieces of paper together to see what would happen. As he did so, Camie got up from her seat and walked a few feet to her left, standing while interpreting Mr. Harrison's commentary during the demonstration. As students subsequently took turns standing to read aloud, Camie made sure Emily knew where to read, giving descriptive instructions like, "Second paragraph under 'Predicting Eruptions'"; however, she did not interpret the text as it was read. Whenever Mr. Harrison elaborated on a section of text, Camie waved to get Emily's attention and interpreted what was discussed.

As the lesson progressed, Mr. Harrison used a laser pointer to indicate geological formations at specific locations on a world map displayed on the back wall of the classroom, describing how the movement of oceanic plates will eventually result in the creation of new volcanoes. The students, including Emily, had to turn around to see where he was pointing. The hearing students could hear Mr. Harrison's explanation while they turned away from him to look at the map behind them, but Emily could not see the map and watch the interpreter at the same time. Camie pointed to the map at the back of the room and waited to interpret until Emily looked back at her again. By the time Emily turned back around to see the interpreter, Mr. Harrison was pointing out another location on the map behind her. At one point, Camie pointed to the back of the room for Emily to look, but by the time Emily did so, Mr. Harrison had turned off the laser pointer. Sometimes, instead of pointing and waiting, Camie incorporated the name of the specific location and signed it in a space consistent with an imaginary map in front of her. For example, as Mr. Harrison pointed out the Ring of Fire, North America and South America, or the northern part of Africa and the Cape, Camie signed them in a space corresponding to their actual relative positions.

Further into the lesson, Mr. Harrison said, "Hawaii just looks like a little island like this," and asked students to look at his hands. Camie pointed to him, but because he was keeping his hands in one position while talking about what was happening under the surface of the water, she incorporated his gesture into her own interpretation. Immediately after using his hands to describe a shield volcano in Hawaii, Mr. Harrison said, "Now, here's the weird thing. And I think I'd rather you look there instead of the book." As he spoke, he again shone his laser pointer at the map. At that point, Camie walked to the back of the room. She did not sign while she walked but continued to listen to Mr. Harrison. Once Camie was standing next to the map in a position where she was not blocking any of the students' view, she began interpreting and delivered a condensed version of most of Mr. Harrison's comments about the map thus far, occasionally looking behind her at the map to see what he was pointing out. Because she could not easily see where Mr. Harrison was pointing (Figure 5), she tried to find a better position and moved to her right, closer to the center of the map.

In this position, Camie was blocking some students' view of the map, and she was in the path of Mr. Harrison's laser beam (Figure 6). Camie quickly moved to her left (back to her previous position) to get out of the way. After interpreting a sentence or two, Camie walked all the way over to the left side of the map, hugging the bookcase next to the map so she would not block any students' view (Figure 7).

Mr. Harrison then wrapped up his discussion in reference to the map, and Camie returned to her seat in time to cue Emily where to resume

FIGURE 5. *Camie looking back over her shoulder to view the map.*

FIGURE 6. *Laser beam on back of Camie's wrist.*

FIGURE 7. *Final position next to tall bookshelf (left) with laser beam on map (near Camie's elbow).*

reading. In a few minutes, Mr. Harrison again used his hands to indicate how tilt meters measure the steepness of slopes to predict volcanic eruptions. Camie waved to get Emily's attention before she began to interpret his comments, then alternated between pointing and waiting to interpret, looking herself at Mr. Harrison's gestures and incorporating them into the interpretation, or using a combination of both strategies.

On the following day, Mr. Harrison decided to go through the directed reading worksheets with the class. Camie spent 44 seconds getting a copy of the worksheet packet for her own reference as Mr. Harrison tried to solicit and clarify a student's answer to Question 1. Camie returned to her seat just in time to interpret his comments about the first question and response (omitting the clarification discussion). Mr. Harrison used all of the sources of visual input from the previous day (students' textbooks and worksheet packets) except for the laser pointer, but there were additional sources of visual information for Camie to address. For this lesson, he used a busy whiteboard to draw pictures, used his hands (even in interaction with his drawing) to demonstrate geological formations and characteristics, and used a paper and pen as a three-dimensional model of specific geological phenomena. Emily (as always) had to watch the interpreter almost constantly to access the stream of spoken discourse generated by her teacher and peers as well as other visual input.

Mr. Harrison was asked why lava, if it hardens when it reaches water, doesn't clog up the volcano in Hawaii. He decided to draw a picture to illustrate his response. Camie followed him to the whiteboard, but walked past him so that Mr. Harrison stood to the left and Camie stood to the right. Camie could then see what Mr. Harrison was drawing and which part of the drawing he was pointing to. When it was most relevant to the interpretation, Camie now and then pointed directly at the drawing. Camie also asked Emily whether she could see. When Emily nodded, Camie continued interpreting. As Mr. Harrison drew a second picture close to the left side of the whiteboard, Camie looked to her left (away from the drawing) and determined that moving closer to Mr. Harrison would put her in a position that would block several students' view of the drawing, so she stayed where she was, incorporating features of the drawing and Mr. Harrison's gestures (when she saw them) into her interpretation.

Once Mr. Harrison and Camie had returned to their seats, Mr. Harrison picked up a piece of paper and a pen to create a three-dimensional representation of the geological phenomenon he was discussing. Camie responded by standing up and moving closer to Mr. Harrison so that Emily could see both the interpretation and the demonstration. As he manipulated the paper and pen to demonstrate how oceanic plates move over a magma plume, he rotated his shoulders slightly away from Camie. In order to see his demonstration herself, she stepped and leaned forward, using what she saw to aid in her own comprehension and corresponding interpretation.

On one section of their worksheet packets, students were to match definitions with vocabulary words. Mr. Harrison went fairly quickly, reading each definition aloud, asking students for the corresponding letter, then reading or repeating the word. Throughout this section, Camie interpreted all additional comments, as well as the numbers and their correct answers. The definitions and the words themselves sometimes were interpreted and sometimes weren't. For example, when Mr. Harrison said, "Sixteen. What's the main product of a nonexplosive eruption?" Camie signed only, "SIXTEEN. WHAT'S 16?"

Camie prompted Emily to raise her hand if she had the answer to the question. By the time Emily raised her hand, Mr. Harrison had already called on Hunter, who provided the correct answer. Camie looked at Emily and Mr. Harrison, snapping her fingers as if to say, "Shoot!" Camie then looked back at Emily, signed that Hunter had already said the answer, and cued Emily to look at the next question. In this instance and in several subsequent examples, Camie was actually instructing Emily to jump the gun and look ahead at her answer to the next question. Mr. Harrison read the next definition and called on a student, who gave an incorrect answer. Camie did not interpret what Mr. Harrison said, nor what the student said. Instead, she signed, "Do you know? Do you know? Raise your hand." Emily did, just as the other student gave the wrong answer. Camie told Emily to wait, then at the right time, cued Emily to raise her hand. He repeated the question, "What's magma after it's been exploded out?" He then called on Emily, who gave the correct answer, "pyroclastic material."

Sometimes Emily signed her answers as she raised her hand, and Camie included in her interpretation whether Emily's answers were correct or not and even praised her for correct answers. For example, as Mr. Harrison said that the answer to Question 17 was false, Emily also signed that the answer was false. Camie signed, "False. You're right!" then gave a thumbs up to Emily.

ADJUSTING PHYSICAL POSITION

When Mr. Harrison sat at a vacant desk and obstructed the sight line between Camie and Emily, Camie immediately stood up and moved to Mr. Harrison's left, so that Emily could see what her teacher was demonstrating and could also see Camie (over Mr. Harrison's shoulder) as she interpreted. A few minutes later, Mr. Harrison's use of a laser pointer required Camie to make a more complicated decision about how to optimize Emily's visual access. Camie could have simply followed Mr. Harrison, but it wasn't clear how sustained or repeated the reference to the map would be—if it was a fleeting reference, then choosing to stay where she was made sense. Another factor that came into play was the fact that there was limited space at the back of the room. In this case, she initially chose to stay. She stayed in this position for several minutes, pointing to the map and incorporating Mr. Harrison's geographical references into the interpretation.

In contrast, when Mr. Harrison specified that he wanted students to look at the map on the back wall rather than at their books, Camie waited and listened, then chose to move closer to the map and leave Mr. Harrison behind. In so doing, the potentially important extralinguistic information in Mr. Harrison's facial expressions and gestures would no longer be visually accessible to Emily. However, Camie decided that the map was more important for Emily to see, perhaps at least in part because of Mr. Harrison's explicit directive for students to look at the map on the back wall.

When Camie walked to the back of the room (which took 7 more seconds), she stopped in front of the right side of the map and turned back toward Emily to interpret. In this position, Emily could see both the interpretation and where Mr. Harrison was pointing (around the Hawaiian Islands) with his laser beam without having to turn around. Now, however, Camie had to turn around to see what Mr. Harrison was pointing out behind her, and Emily still had to look back and forth between the left side of the map and Camie on the right. To find a better location from which to interpret, Camie moved further to her right (closer to the center of the map), but in so doing, she blocked some students' view of the map. Moreover, she obstructed Mr. Harrison's laser beam. She danced a little bit to the right and left, trying to quickly get out of the way and find a place where she was not blocking any of the students' view or Mr. Harrison's laser, and where Emily could see the interpretation and the map at the same time without having to look back and forth. After interpreting a sentence or two in this position (still unable to easily see the map herself), Camie walked to the far left side of the map. Because there were built-in bookcases on the left side of the map and shelves in front of and below the map, finding a place to stand that would not block anyone's view required Camie to stand very close to the bookcase to the left of the map. However, standing in this position on the far left side afforded Camie, Mr. Harrison, Emily, and all of the other students an unobstructed view of the map. Less than 2 minutes later, Mr. Harrison wrapped up his discussion of the map and Camie returned to her seat in time to interpret as Mr. Harrison called on Emily's classmate Richard to read aloud and reminded the rest of the students to read along, starting at "Predicting Volcanic Eruptions."

As Mr. Harrison began going through the worksheets with his students during science the second day, Camie did not have to adjust her physical position for almost 15 minutes. She moved for the first time during this lesson when Mr. Harrison decided to respond to a student question by drawing a picture on the whiteboard. After following him to the board, Camie stood on the opposite side of the drawing as Mr. Harrison, where she could see and point directly to specific parts of the drawing or the drawing as a whole. Camie even asked Emily directly whether she could see, making sure Emily's visual needs were met. Camie's physical position allowed Emily to see the drawing, the interpretation, and Mr. Harrison all at once. It also allowed Camie to see and point to specific features of the drawing.

However, when Mr. Harrison decided to draw a second picture, additional factors came into play. Because there was already a chart on the board just to the left of where he had drawn the first picture (near the center of the board), Mr. Harrison drew the second picture to the left of the chart (on the far left side of the board). Rather than immediately moving to a more optimal position closer to the second drawing, Camie looked to her left and determined that if she moved, she would obstruct some students' views, so she chose to remain in place. In Figure 8, Camie is looking to her left (Emily is straight ahead, slightly to Camie's right), checking to make sure that she is not blocking any hearing students' views of Mr. Harrison's second drawing.

After Mr. Harrison returned to a seat at his podium and Camie to her seat, Brett asked a question that prompted Mr. Harrison to return to the board. Seeing him approach, Camie leaned back to let him pass, then followed him to the board, passing him as he stopped to reflect on his first drawing. She returned to a standing position on the right side of the picture and interpreted from there until he returned to his podium.

Camie had to move again when Mr. Harrison began using a piece of paper and a pen to create a three-dimensional model to demonstrate how oceanic plates move slowly over magma plumes. Emily needed to see his demonstration, so Camie stood up and moved closer to Mr. Harrison. As he manipulated the paper and pen to demonstrate the movement of the plates, he rotated his shoulders slightly away from Camie. As a result, Camie needed to step and lean forward to see the model herself, aiding in her own comprehension and corresponding interpretation (Figure 9).

In my observations and interviews, part of what governed interpreters' decisions about where to stand or sit was the degree to which they saw themselves imposing upon the personal space of the speaker and/or disrupting the rest of the students in the class. All of the interpreters expressed concern

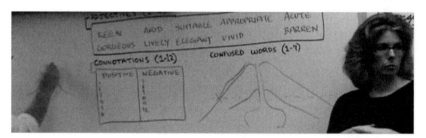

FIGURE 8. *Camie making sure she is not blocking hearing students' view of the board.*

FIGURE 9. *Camie leaning forward to see demonstration of a magma plume under oceanic plates.*

about unnecessarily interrupting the typical flow of classroom discourse. They held a comparable high regard for allowing Deaf and hard of hearing students to maintain momentum rather than interrupting them and getting their attention to interpret every single sound or spoken word. Moreover, physical space can present numerous variables affecting interpreters' decisions about whether, when, and where to move. The physical construction of the classroom, location of shelving, and number and arrangement of desks necessary to accommodate the class size made it more difficult for Camie to secure an optimal position from which to interpret. Securing a position that maintained clear sight lines for everyone (Emily, Camie, Mr. Harrison, and all of the hearing students) proved to be problematic. Furthermore, often complicating the issue of the interpreters' physical position in classrooms is the fact that interpreters are sharing what has been traditionally regarded as the teachers' space. Therefore, a comfortable rapport and solid professional relationship between teachers and interpreters is critical.

The importance of this professional relationship and shared space between teacher and interpreter was evident in comments made by another interpreter, AJ, when she explained what conditions would have to be in place in order for her to approach the teacher and point directly to the board. She said that she would have to be a regular classroom interpreter (at the time, she was working as a substitute interpreter) and would need to have a history and a good working relationship with the teacher. She elaborated, "I would have to feel like this teacher *really is* invested in the Deaf student's education, because if they are not, [having someone up there pointing at their stuff] could really be annoying." AJ went on to emphasize the point that some teachers are less than comfortable with the thought of having an interpreter, another adult, on their turf.

Mr. Harrison and Camie both told me that they had a good professional relationship with each other. Each felt that the other was supportive and helpful, and that they worked as a team to figure out how to best meet Emily's needs. Camie said she felt comfortable sharing the space with Mr. Harrison. By asking Camie questions about what she needed in order to do her job well and by responding to those needs, Mr. Harrison created an environment in which Camie felt free to make decisions that she determined appropriate. He also provided a desk for Camie to store her own copy of class resources and materials as well as a few personal items. Mr. Harrison said he was comfortable working with Camie as well, and stressed that he valued her professionalism and her input about how to work more effectively with Emily. As a result of the excellent working relationship and mutual respect, Camie was able to do as she saw fit in order to meet Emily's needs, even to stand right next to Mr. Harrison at his podium and share the paper he was using to dictate sentences during language arts. Camie felt at ease moving wherever she needed to be in order to optimize Emily's visual access because Mr. Harrison respected Camie's knowledge and expertise regarding how to best meet Emily's learning needs. Rather than be concerned about bothering Mr. Harrison or interfering with the class, Camie was able to move to the right place at the right time, maximizing her physical position in order to afford Emily the greatest opportunity for academic success.

DIRECTING STUDENT ATTENTION

Camie's decisions about optimizing Emily's visual access and alleviating the competing visual demands for her attention depended on, but required more than, her moving closer. Instead of operating under the assumption that Emily could see what she needed to see on the map (or at the board) as long as Camie was close enough to the primary source of visual input, she also showed Emily exactly where to look. The two techniques she used to direct Emily's attention were pointing at the visual stimulus and taking a moment to look at it herself, the latter while keeping her hands down and in a neutral position.

As the lesson began, Mr. Harrison asked Brenda to read at "When tectonic plates collide." Camie signed to begin reading at the top of page 203, then turned her own book around and pointed exactly where on the page to begin, holding the book facing Emily until Emily nodded. Having directed Emily's attention to the right place in the book, Camie kept her hands down and read along in her own book. By choosing not to interpret, Camie eliminated one potential source of visual input (the interpretation) while allowing and prompting Emily to read from the book as her classmates were reading.

Similarly, Camie chose not to try to interpret as she walked to the back of the room, which would have perpetuated the competing visual demand; this choice essentially directed Emily's focus to the remaining source of visual input, the map. Upon taking a position at the back of the room, however, although she stood next to the map, Camie could not easily see where Mr. Harrison was pointing, and thus could not herself point to specific locations on the map when it was relevant. Her final position on the left side of the map, despite being a bit awkward, proved to be the most effective not only because everyone could see the map, but also because Emily could then see both the map and the interpretation. Camie's height also provided an advantage in that she was tall enough so that Emily could see her over other students' heads, as long as they remained seated. In addition, having moved closer to the map, Camie could then point directly at it. She could also touch it to direct Emily's attention to very specific locations at the precise time it was pertinent to the interpretation, even if Mr. Harrison had moved on (Figure 10).

FIGURE 10. *Camie points to a location on the left as the teacher moves on and points the laser at a location on the right.*

Camie used another technique besides pointing. When Mr. Harrison used his hands to represent Hawaii and when he picked up a pen and paper to create a three-dimensional model to illustrate the movement of oceanic plates, Camie stopped signing and looked herself at Mr. Harrison's demonstration, thereby alleviating the competing visual demand and directing Emily's attention to the right place. At the whiteboard, Camie's physical proximity and position were instrumental in enabling her to direct Emily's visual attention to Mr. Harrison's drawing. By standing on the opposite side of the drawing as Mr. Harrison, she had an unobstructed view of the board, and she was again able to look at and/or point directly at the relevant part of the picture in order to direct Emily's attention to the right place (Figure 11).

Had Camie been standing behind Mr. Harrison, her position would have been problematic. Mr. Harrison would have become a barrier between Camie and the drawing, preventing Camie from seeing it clearly herself and using it as a resource (both to aid in comprehension and as a physical prop) for her interpretation. By making a deliberate decision to stand to the right side of the drawing, Camie was optimally positioned for directing Emily's attention to whatever Camie felt Emily needed to see.

Looking at what interpreters do through the lens of competing visual demands for Deaf and hard of hearing students' attention sheds light on one critical aspect of why educational interpreters do what they do in the classroom. It is, in fact, *because* of their efforts to alleviate competing visual demands that interpreters decide when, where, and how to move around the classroom, stand and/or sit, and explicitly direct Deaf and hard of hearing students' attention to essential visual input. To complicate

FIGURE 11. *Camie looking at and touching the drawing of the magma chamber.*

matters further, K–12 interpreters consider the needs and goals of not only Deaf and hard of hearing students, but also other students in the classroom, as well as teachers and other support staff.

Adjusting Timing of Interpretation

Further evidence of the complexity of interpreters' decision-making processes and the intertwined nature of the factors they consider is evident in the frequent timing delays involved during the lesson. Delays are inherent to all interpretations, simply because of the time it takes the interpreter to take in the information, decide how to convey the meaning in the target language, and then deliver the interpretation. Additional delays happen in active and crowded classrooms, where interpretations are often interrupted; for example, a Deaf or hard of hearing student may look away to find and pick up a dropped pencil, to turn to a specified page of text, or to glance (or stare) at a classmate, and cannot follow the interpreter at the same time. Interpreters can choose to simply wait to interpret until they have the student's attention again. However, the choice requires weighing several factors, such as how much time is available for students to look at something in comparison to its relative importance to the task at hand and to gain the knowledge they will need to participate successfully in visually rich and highly interactive school classrooms. As they consider how to ensure that Deaf and hard of hearing students can see salient visual information, interpreters must first evaluate how long a particular source of visual input will be available. For visual references that are temporal, rather than permanent, educational interpreters rely on an additional constellation of factors to make decisions about optimizing students' visual access.

During the full two-part science lesson on volcanoes, Mr. Harrison used various visual aids, some of which were permanent (such as the map itself, printed worksheets, and textbooks) and others that were temporal. When Mr. Harrison told students to begin reading at "When tectonic plates collide . . . ," there was no doubt that the printed words on the specified page would still be there a few seconds later. Camie was able to point out the particular page of text, holding her own book up until Emily indicated that she had found the right place in the text and was ready to read.

By contrast, Mr. Harrison's swift use of his hands as a physical representation of Hawaii (above and below the surface of the water) and to describe how tilt meters work were temporal sources of visual input.

Similarly, his paper-and-pen demonstration of how oceanic plates move over magma plumes was temporal, rather than permanent. In other words, Mr. Harrison could have put the paper and pen down or moved on to something else at any time. Since Camie could not predict how long the model would be visible, she immediately directed Emily's attention to the demonstration as it was taking place, allowing Emily to take in the visual demonstration before attending to the corresponding interpretation. In adjusting the timing of the interpretation by changing the sequence of presentation, Camie optimized Emily's access to the visual input over which Camie had less control (Mr. Harrison's demonstration) while it was visible.

Having decided the information was important enough for Emily to see, and having directed her attention to the demonstration, Camie then had to delay the interpretation long enough for Emily to watch the demonstration. While it may seem like a simple enough judgment, a number of different considerations were at play. Camie had to predict how long Emily would need to look at the model and decide when to interpret the explanation that was meant to accompany that part of the demonstration. She also had to take in the visual information herself and be prepared to quickly redirect Emily's visual attention if necessary.

Once Camie decided to resume the interpretation pertinent to the demonstration, she raised her hands to a clasped position and looked back towards Emily; however, she then had to wait for Emily to reestablish eye contact before again beginning to interpret. Camie lifting her hands signaled that she herself had looked at the visual demonstration long enough and was again ready to interpret. This seemed to serve as enough of a cue for Emily to reestablish eye contact with Camie and indicate readiness for more information. However, sometimes Emily continued watching a demonstration or looking at something other than the interpreter. When she did so, Camie either chose to wait until Emily reestablished eye contact or to wave to get Emily's attention, thereby directing Emily's visual attention back to the interpretation itself. If Mr. Harrison had made a clarification of an earlier point, or elaborated on some piece of pertinent information (e.g., "an understanding of this will help you on the test tomorrow"), Camie would most likely have interrupted Emily's visual observation by waving to get her attention, interpreted the pertinent information, then allowed Emily the opportunity to look again with this newly acquired piece of information. If Mr. Harrison was moving on, once Camie felt there was enough relevant information and Camie would not be able to retain it unless she began interpreting, she would also have waved to redirect Emily's visual attention back to the interpretation of Mr. Harrison's discourse. Interpreters in this study all reported a reluctance to interfere with Deaf and hard of hearing students' right to look at something (e.g., a graphic) or work on something (e.g., a worksheet) that required their visual attention. They frequently made decisions about when precedence should be given to other sources of visual input over the interpretation of spoken discourse and vice versa.

The timing of the interpretation was less of an issue when Mr. Harrison decided to draw on the whiteboard. Since Mr. Harrison's explanations were not as rapid or detailed as some of his other instruction (perhaps because he was also focused on drawing and/or thinking), Camie had ample time to interpret. Also, in her position to the right of the drawing and opposite Mr. Harrison, as when standing to the left of the map, she could point to the picture at the time when it was most relevant to the interpretation. Both of these strategies used in conjunction afforded Emily the opportunity to look at the drawing and take in the accompanying interpretation.

Although the map was a permanent fixture, it became problematic in terms of timing because of the temporal nature of laser pointers (or any other technique used by instructors to point out particular objects, words, locations, etc.). Several factors complicated Camie's decision of whether to adjust her physical position, and/or to direct Emily's visual attention by pointing, and/or to adjust the timing of the interpretation. There was the difficulty of predicting how long Mr. Harrison would leave the pointer in place and the difficulty of directing Emily's visual attention (showing Emily where to look and when) because of Camie's physical position in relation to Emily and the map. A third challenge was the lack of available space. The relative physical positions of Camie, Emily and her classmates, Mr. Harrison, and the map further complicated the decision-making process.

Although Camie could easily point to a student and wait long enough for Emily to see who was speaking before interpreting, she could not rely on the point-and-wait technique for Mr. Harrison's discussion with regard to the map. Camie could not predict how long Mr. Harrison would point at a particular geographic location, but he was not likely to keep the laser beam in place long enough for Camie to interpret before directing Emily's attention to the map. Therefore, Camie initially tried to point so Emily could first look to see where Mr. Harrison was pointing, and then interpret what he said about that location, adjusting the timing of the interpretation by changing the sequence of presentation. This technique worked to some degree, but it soon proved to be inadequate. In one instance, Camie pointed to the back of the room, but by the time Emily turned around to look, Mr. Harrison had turned off the laser. When Emily looked back at the interpreter, Camie signed a brief explanation with an apologetic expression that he had turned it off before she again began to interpret. Here the technique of pointing (directing student attention) and waiting (adjusting the timing of the interpretation) did not work, at least in part because Camie could not predict how long Mr. Harrison would leave the laser in place.

Moreover, because of where Emily and Camie were in relation to the map, it was difficult for Camie to direct Emily's attention to the right place at the right time. Emily could not see the map and Camie without looking back and forth (in front of and behind her). As a result, Emily was often not looking in the direction that would have been most helpful. Camie could not effectively direct Emily's visual attention until she walked to the back of the room and took up a position where both she and Emily could easily see where Mr. Harrison was pointing on the map. Each of these factors and Camie's chosen actions resulted in concomitant timing delays. Whereas some timing delays were deliberate, such as changing the sequence of presentation and waiting for Emily to look at something, others resulted from the particular combination of variables affecting that interaction. Several delays were due to the time it took for Camie to decide on a particular strategy. Even more delays resulted because of where Emily herself chose to look at any given moment. Each of these delays was in addition to the time delay that is already inherent to the process of interpretation.

In addition to making decisions about physical placement and directing students' attention, the need for timing adjustments adds yet a third layer of complexity to interpreters' nearly constant challenge of alleviating the competing visual demands for Deaf and hard of hearing students' attention. Since teachers are accustomed to a style of classroom discourse in which it is acceptable and even desirable for them to speak while referring to visual input, these findings suggest that K–12 interpreters must often intentionally delay the interpretation. Because simply being close to a source of visual input and showing Deaf and hard of hearing students exactly where to look would not sufficiently alleviate competing visual demands, interpreters must also afford students the time to look by deliberately adjusting the timing of interpretations. Timing adjustments then require another series of subsequent decisions and actions. Interpreters need to predict how long a student will need to look at sources of visual input, wait for the student to look back, identify and remember significant instructional points, and construct and deliver a modified interpretation. Accurate predictions about how to optimize visual access for Deaf and hard of hearing students are likely to further complicate interpreters' decisions. In addition, interpreters must prioritize needs, not only in terms of what information is most important, but in which order information must be accessed. Furthermore, interpreters must decide when respecting Deaf and hard of hearing students' need to look at salient visual input is trumped by a greater and more immediate need for some even more important information that also requires their visual attention. Moreover, it is important to understand that the length of time needed for Deaf and hard of hearing students to take in information visually varies across individuals.

Interpreters must be prepared either to meet students' individual needs by waiting as long as necessary for students to attend visually, or they must be prepared to select a different course of action. It is also likely that interpreters may need some time to assess the situation and make a decision. All of these delays are in addition to the delay already inherent to the process of message analysis essential for effective and accurate interpretation. Furthermore, as both references to visual information and corresponding timing delays accumulate, educational interpreters' decisions become more complex and require additional skills in order to alleviate competing visual demands for Deaf and hard of hearing students' attention.

Modifying the Interpretation

Although it is critical for educational interpreters to adjust their physical positions, direct students' attention, and adjust the timing of the interpretations, none of these strategies in and of itself provides adequate means of ensuring that Deaf and hard of hearing students have sufficient opportunity to attend to all salient visual input. In fact, all of these strategies used in conjunction still fail to provide a fully accessible environment when considering a single reality, competing demands for Deaf and hard of hearing students' visual attention. Although these three techniques were valuable and necessary, Camie recognized (whether consciously or not), that further action was imperative. The fourth strategy that Camie used to optimize Emily's visual access was to modify the content of the interpretation.

Modifying the interpretation refers to either adding to or reducing the content of the interpretation in some way. Relatively simple, yet crucial, modifications of the interpretation occurred in this study when a teacher used referents such as *this, that, here, there, these,* and *those* and expected students to look at a visual aid. Modifying the interpretation can involve providing clarifying information. It can also include strategies such as being more specific or more general than the source information, or reducing the original message by paraphrasing, summarizing, or even consciously omitting information.

As previously described, by the time a teacher's instructions to "Take a look at this" have been interpreted, the teacher has often stopped pointing at whatever "this" is, and the visual information is no longer available. Conversely, the discussion of the visual aid the teacher is referring to may be extended, and the teacher expects the students to look at the visual aid while simultaneously listening to his instructions or description. In order to include the visual aid as well as the information accompanying it, interpreters often modify the interpretation by including it explicitly.

In the volcanoes lesson, as Mr. Harrison mentioned and pointed out North America, South America, the Ring of Fire, and Africa, Camie chose to include the names of the specific geographic locations into her interpretation. When she did so, Camie made a deliberate decision *not* to prompt Emily to look at the locations that Mr. Harrison was pointing to (even though he was pointing to them and using referents such as "right here" as he named them). Camie did not direct Emily's attention to the other visual input. In so doing, Camie eliminated the competing demand for Emily's visual attention by giving precedence to interpreting rather than directing Emily's attention to the map. In order for this decision to be a viable choice, Camie had to be cognizant of what Emily already knew. Camie had to know that Emily could identify North and South America, as well as the Ring of Fire, on the map. Camie did use the signing space in front of her and features of ASL to reference the locations Mr. Harrison was pointing out within her interpretation. She simply interpreted the names of these familiar geographic locations without prompting Emily to turn around. When Mr. Harrison talked about how two different plates under Africa were moving in different directions, however, Camie had time to point so that Emily could look to see, waited for Emily to look back at the map and reestablish eye contact, then Camie integrated the specific information directly into her interpretation (such as using classifiers to show how the plate under the northern part of Africa was moving in one direction while the plate under the Cape was moving in another direction).

Camie modified her interpretation again when Mr. Harrison used his hands to talk about the island of Hawaii. As he held his hands in one position, he began to elaborate on the fact that although we can only see a tiny part of Hawaii, the volcano continues under the surface of the water all the way to the ocean floor. Although Camie did direct Emily's visual attention to Mr. Harrison's representation of Hawaii by pointing at it, she then incorporated his hand formations into her interpretation as he continued to speak. Mr. Harrison used his hands as a model to demonstrate how tilt meters predict volcanic eruptions by measuring changes in the steepness of a volcano's slopes. He did this again when discussing the limitations of tilt meters, saying, "So, instead of this, you might get that." In these instances, Camie often glanced at his gestures but did not drop her hands, or point to prompt Emily to look. Instead, she incorporated his gestures into her own interpretation so that Emily would see them at the right time, along with the interpretation of the corresponding description. For example, Camie signed that the slopes change, then incorporated Mr. Harrison's gestures into her own interpretation to show that slopes get steeper as the pressure of magma increases inside the volcano (Figure 12).

There are several advantages to the decision to modify an interpretation by re-creating visual resources (e.g., gestures) within it. When interpreters used this strategy, they often, but not always, also looked at and pointed to the visual aid before incorporating it into the interpretation. This not only allowed both the student and the interpreter to benefit from looking at the visual resource, it also eliminated the competing demands of the interpretation and the visual aid. The interpreter assumed the cognitive

FIGURE 12. *Camie incorporating teacher's gestures to show change in slope.*

burden of looking at and comprehending the visual aid while holding the information still forthcoming in the teacher's discourse, rather than passing on the burden of two visual demands to the student. A third benefit was that once the visual stimulus was re-created within the interpretation, Camie could then choose to refer to the actual visual aid itself, or return to the gesture or other visual information she had incorporated explicitly within the interpretation, or both. In other words, it opened the door to an additional resource for Camie's later use. Once an interpreter has created a representation of the visual information in her own signing space, she creates an option for referring to that visual stimulus even when it is no longer present (e.g., the drawing has been erased from the board, the teacher's hands are no longer in that position, etc.).

The cumulative nature of timing delays further complicates decisions about how and when to modify the content of interpretations. The time delay inherent to interpretation, exacerbated in K–12 classrooms, requires interpreters to compensate for lost time. Even more timing delays arise when interpreters move to a desired location, direct students' attention to the right place, and students take in information visually once they begin looking at the salient visual input.

In this scenario, the delay in the interpretation was particularly prolonged. While Mr. Harrison continued talking, Camie had to listen to him, look at the map, and analyze the incoming message as she walked. Once she resumed interpreting, she had to rely on her memory of what had been said so she could analyze the message and intentionally let go of less academically relevant discourse. Of the range of possible options available to her at that point, Camie chose to deliver a very condensed version of what Mr. Harrison had said, likely influenced by what Emily already knew and Camie's predictions of accountability. Under a different set of circumstances, Camie may have had to seek other options. With introductory material or if students were to be tested on the information, for example, she might have chosen to interrupt Mr. Harrison and ask him to wait, repeat, rephrase, and/or clarify (actions she took on numerous other occasions).

Camie also modified her interpretation when Mr. Harrison prompted students to begin reading at "When tectonic plates collide . . ." and Camie signed to begin reading at the top of page 203. This description got Emily to the same place, but rather than giving her an entire fingerspelled English phrase to look for, Camie chose a description that would likely be faster, thereby allowing more time for Emily to locate the specified excerpt.

As Brenda began to read aloud, Camie modified the interpretation by choosing not interpret. Such read-alouds, which are common in K–12 class-rooms, require interpreters to decide whether or not and to what extent to interpret the text being read aloud. An interpreter can choose not to sign, eliminating the competing demand by omitting information from the inter-pretation, or to interpret, knowing that the students will not be able to see the printed text—in other words, the interpreter must choose whether the interpretation or the text should be given precedence. Educational inter-preters experience a great deal of conflict (expressed uncertainty) about the decision. If interpreters are making these decisions without teacher input, they may not be aligned with the most appropriate learning objec-tives. Camie, like many educational interpreters, also reported that con-cerns about physical injury (e.g., repetitive motion injuries) contributed to her decision not to interpret extended and designated read-aloud sessions, which were prevalent during my observations. (She did, however, interpret printed instructions and handouts that were read aloud.)

Information read aloud included printed instructions and questions (e.g., handouts), passages from textbooks, information written or posted on the board, audiotaped recordings of scripted information, and cap-tioned videos. On a weekly basis, Mr. Harrison's class was asked to recite a poem they had memorized. Emily was excused from this activity. As a matter of fact, there was only one instance of a Deaf or hard of hearing student actively participating in any read-aloud activity during the course of the study. According to the interpreter (Marina), this was likely a result of the researcher's presence in the room rather than standard practice. Alleviating demands for Deaf and hard of hearing students' visual atten-tion is highly problematic during read-aloud activities.

Decisions for optimizing visual access make the already complex and cognitively challenging task of interpreting even more difficult. The choices involved are not necessarily intuitive, and most of them need to be made while interpreters also continue to process teacher-delivered instruction for meaning, determine an equivalent interpretation, and deliver a signed interpretation clearly. Furthermore, the process of con-densing and summarizing instructional content involves academic exper-tise which interpreters may or may not have. Generating a consolidated version of salient academic points is a process which, in and of itself, depends on fairly advanced linguistic skills in *any* language, especially in a second language. It becomes even more challenging because interpreters are processing two different languages at the same time. Add to that the fact that these decisions are taking place in an environment known for being inundated with visual and communicative activity. So while interpretation in K–12 classrooms may seem no more complex than interpreting in any other context, close observation of Mr. Harrison's science lesson shows that even something as simple as walking across the classroom is neither simple nor merely about walking.[17]

3. WHAT INTERPRETERS DO TO FACILITATE LEARNING OF CONTENT AND LANGUAGE

K–12 interpreters' decisions about what to do, including when, whether or not, and to what extent they should interpret or transliterate or do something else are often in response to the presence of competing visual demands for Deaf and hard of hearing students' attention require a great amount of finesse and choreography. However, these moment-to-moment decisions become even more complicated because of interpreters' own assessments and perceptions of the students' language and learning needs. In order for an interpreted interaction to be effective, Deaf and hard of hearing students (as well as interpreters themselves) must be linguistically and cognitively equipped to participate in this highly interactive, visually rich educational context. If they are not, further support is critical.

A lesson on the Dewey Decimal System that involved watching a captioned video, as well as other examples, demonstrate how interpreters' consideration of individual students' educational placements and reading proficiencies, academic stakes and accountability measures, and students' personal preferences and socioemotional well-being all impact interpreters' moment-to-moment decisions about what to do. Their assessments compel interpreters to provide additional support of learning as needed, including tutoring, helping, explaining, making connections to prior knowledge, supporting language development in both ASL and English, and making explicit connections between ASL and English.

---

17. Much of the previous section of this chapter has been published as "Opening Our Eyes: The Complexity of Competing Visual Demands in Interpreted Classrooms" in K. M. Christensen (Ed.), (2010). *Ethical Considerations in Education Children Who are Deaf or Hard of Hearing.* Washington, DC: Gallaudet University Press.

Scenario: Library Lesson on the Dewey Decimal System

There were two Deaf students in Mrs. Natale's fifth grade class at Azalea Elementary. Kristie was mainstreamed all day. Because Miguel was not mainstreamed for language arts, writing, and dance, he started his school day in the Deaf and hard of hearing class and joined Mrs. Natale's class for second period. Once a week after morning announcements, the class went to the library to check out books. One morning, the teacher announced that they would be going to the library early. Miguel had not arrived by the time they left the homeroom class. When they got to the library, Mrs. Natale said they would be viewing a DVD to learn about the Dewey Decimal System. As students found seats on the floor and Mrs. Natale answered questions for a few individuals surrounding her, Marina (the interpreter), asked the librarian if she could use the phone. She then called the Deaf and hard of hearing classroom and asked the staff member who answered to deliver a message to Miguel informing him that the class was in the library. After she hung up, she asked Kristie whether she would prefer to read the captions independently or if she preferred to have them interpreted. Kristie told Marina she wanted to read the captions. Marina pulled a chair to the front of the group of students but off to the side where she could see both Kristie and the video. Although Marina was not interpreting as the video began, she remained attentive. She alternated her gaze between watching Kristie and the video. Occasionally, Kristie looked at Marina quizzically. Marina either provided a brief explanation or interpreted what had just been said.

As soon as Miguel arrived, Marina walked directly under the TV monitor and, still standing, began to interpret information on the video. When the video was over, Mrs. Natale asked students to find a book using the information they had just learned. After interpreting these instructions, Marina had a short conversation with Kristie and Miguel. As Kristie went to find a book independently, Marina helped Miguel to find a book, pointing out the numbers and letters on the spines of books as they looked. In this example, Marina clearly did more than simply interpret and/or transliterate; multiple actions and decision points are evident in this scenario.

1. Marina asked the librarian to use the phone.
2. She called the Deaf and hard of hearing classroom and asked the staff member who answered to give a message to Miguel so he would know where to find the class.

3. She made a decision that because Kristie was reading at grade level, it would be appropriate to let Kristie choose to read captions or to watch Marina interpret.
4. Marina asked Kristie which she preferred.
5. In response to Kristie's stated preference to read the captions, Marina pulled a chair to the front of the room where she could see both Kristie and the video.
6. Although she did not interpret, she remained watchful and attentive, alternating her gaze between Kristie and the video.
7. Marina assessed Miguel's ability to access the captions independently.
8. Considering the content and Miguel's reading ability, she decided to interpret.
9. When Miguel arrived, Marina stood up and walked directly underneath the TV, as close as possible, so that Miguel (and Kristie if she chose) would be better able to see both the video and the interpretation.
10. Marina began to interpret.
11. After interpreting the information on the video as well as Mrs. Natale's instructions, Marina had a brief conversation with Kristie and Miguel.
12. She stayed with Miguel and helped him to find a library book, referring back to information presented in the video as she did.

This example documents 12 distinct decisions and actions other than interpreting, illustrating clearly that interpreters do more than interpret and transliterate. However, the complexity of the situation is illuminated not by what Marina did, but by her consideration of shifting priorities that influenced her to make particular choices. Initially, Marina made sure Miguel knew where to find the class. Since they did not adhere to their daily routine, Miguel would have gone to his homeroom class only to find that they were gone. Although he may have then proceeded to the library, at the very least, he would have wasted time. As it was, he had already missed the beginning of the video, putting him at a disadvantage in comparison to the rest of his classmates.

Making the phone call to the Deaf and hard of hearing classroom is arguably beyond what has been traditionally viewed as the interpreter's role. However, because Marina knew how to reach the Deaf and hard of hearing classroom and readily get a message to Miguel, this decision made sense. Even if Mrs. Natale had left a note on the door, Miguel would have had to waste more time getting to the library. While the teacher took a few minutes to respond to several students grouped around her to ask questions, there was not a need for Marina to interpret. Instead of conversing, reading a book, checking for texts, or relaxing for a few minutes, she determined that a more productive and important use of her time was to make sure Miguel was able to join them as quickly as possible.

Considering Educational Placement and Student Reading Proficiencies

As soon as Marina had ensured that Miguel knew where to find the class, she turned her attention to determining how to best meet Kristie's needs. Marina explained to me how Kristie's educational placement affected the decision about whether or not to interpret. Because Kristie was mainstreamed all day as well as reading at grade level and therefore able to understand the captions, Marina felt that it would be equally appropriate for her to interpret or for Kristie to read the captions herself; she tried to respect Kristie's preference and let Kristie choose whenever possible. She elaborated, "Kristie might look at me to see what I am saying, but she won't look at me for the information. She can get it from the TV just fine."

Although she was not interpreting the video, the fact that it was captioned did not provide Marina with the opportunity for a break. Taking a position that would allow her to watch both the video and Kristie, she could check the captions for accuracy (as there are occasionally too many errors to make reading captions a viable option). In this case, the captions were accurate, but she remained watchful and attended to both the video and Kristie. When there was any indication that Kristie needed additional information or clarification, Marina responded by interpreting or offering a brief signed explanation. My observations confirmed Marina's claim that she was always ready to provide whatever information Kristie might have missed.

In contrast, because Marina's priorities shifted when Miguel arrived, she chose to interpret at that point. She explained her decision: "[Miguel] is not a fast enough reader or is not skilled enough in English to follow along with the sentences that are across the bottom of the TV, so he needs a lot more support. [The video in the library] was about the Dewey Decimal System. He would have never followed along with it."

Considering Academic Stakes and Accountability, Student Preferences, and Socioemotional Well-Being

Marina's decisions about interpreting the captioned video may appear to be as simple as interpreting audible printed or scripted text when students are not reading at grade level and letting those who are reading at grade level read independently. But her decision making was far more complex, also including consideration of academic content, stakes, and accountability. In contrast to her approach to the Dewey Decimal DVD, Marina did not interpret during the animated movie *An American Tail* that was shown in Miguel and Kristie's history class the previous week. Marina said she felt that because the content of the movie was not technical in nature, because it was not important for Miguel's school success, and because he would not be held accountable to understand or use the information for academic success, she could honor his preference to watch or have her interpret. Given the option, Miguel said that he preferred to watch on his own.

Yet, there is still more to understanding Marina's considerations and the factors informing her decisions. She mused, "I don't know if it is an embarrassing thing or he doesn't want to bother to look from the TV to me, and he's fine just watching the animated movie. But if I ask, 'Do you want it interpreted?' a lot of times he'll say 'No,' but then I pay attention, and he'll look at me and say, 'What's that word?' or, 'Why is that happening?'" Marina described the importance not only of considering a student's reading ability, the content presented in a video, and the student's personal preference, but also of remaining focused and attentive, even when the student says he does not want the video interpreted. It is important to recognize that Marina still had no way to know if Miguel would have understood more of the movie had it been interpreted or if it would have increased his appreciation of the story. However, not interpreting eliminated the need for Miguel to split his attention and to watch the visually engaging animation. In this case, and with occasional support to explain the meaning of the English captions or elaborate on what was going on in the movie, Miguel was free to enjoy watching the movie without having to look away from the screen to see the interpreter. In addition, he retained the privilege of deciding when to request additional explanation and support.

In addition to making decisions about how accessible printed English was likely to be to each student, the content and difficulty of the video being presented, academic stakes and accountability, as well as student preference, Marina also considered students' social and emotional needs. Although I chose not to focus on the socioemotional effects of relying on interpreters for educational access, all of the interpreters I spoke to raised concerns about the possibility of Deaf and hard of hearing students feeling embarrassed or singled out in mainstream classrooms. In the case of *An American Tail*, it was unclear whether Miguel did not want the movie interpreted because he truly felt embarrassed to be perceived as needing the interpreter by either his hearing peers or Kristie, or if he simply wanted to watch because it would be entertaining.

Considering Readiness for Independence

After students watched the video on the Dewey Decimal System and were instructed to use what they had learned to find and select a library book, Marina checked in with Kristie and Miguel. Kristie went to find a book on her own while Marina stayed with Miguel to help him. As they searched, Marina took advantage of the opportunity to elaborate on some of the information from the video. She explained to me that she helped him simply because she determined he needed the support. Kristie had headed off to find her book, and there was a line of students waiting for Mrs. Natale. Marina had time available, understood the information that had just been presented in the video, knew how to use the library, and decided to be useful. Furthermore, Miguel had missed the beginning of the video, and he appeared happy to have the help. The two chatted amicably and Miguel asked questions (which Marina answered) as together they searched for a book. With this approach, Marina's decisions were well aligned with and in service of the goals and learning objectives of the lesson on the Dewey Decimal System.

Educational interpreters consider students' readiness for independence when deciding whether they will encourage Deaf and hard of hearing students to get their personal needs met by interacting with others. Another example of this emerged when Kristie indicated she needed to use the restroom, Marina instructed her to go ask Mrs. Natale. Yet with Miguel, Marina offered to go with him to interpret the same request to the same teacher. In a different situation, when Emily got her first period and Camie realized that she was still confused about what to do with the sanitary napkin she received from the school nurse, rather than encourage Emily to go back into the office she had just left (where she chose not to express her confusion with the nurse she did not know very well), Camie just explained what to do. Camie determined that Emily was not ready (e.g., felt too uncomfortable) to have that conversation with the nurse and explained herself how to use a sanitary napkin, probably to Emily's relief.

Yet another layer of factors that interpreters take into account when considering Deaf and hard of hearing students' readiness for independence is the degree to which each student is able to participate in academic activities and how well equipped each student is to interact freely and participate equally with their peers, especially during collaborative group work. Kristie and Miguel's English language proficiencies came into play—not only with reading, writing, and language arts—but in all subject areas and for an array of academic tasks. During social studies class, Mrs. Kendall created work stations around the classroom designed for students to learn about a particular era in U.S. history. Students were randomly assigned to small groups of five or six students to complete specific tasks, following printed instructions on cards posted at each work station. On the first day of this activity, Kristie and Miguel were assigned to separate groups. Marina stayed with Miguel's group and Kristie participated in her group without an interpreter. Marina looked over intermittently to monitor how things were going in Kristie's group. Kristie read the instructions on the cards and used spoken English when communicating with her classmates.

The fact that there was only one interpreter and two Deaf students in separate groups required Marina to make a decision about what to do. Marina explained her rationale for choosing to interpret in Miguel's group. She said, "I'm going to make sure he's caught up because he just needs a little bit more explanation. He's not going to be able to read the directions card. He is slightly more motivated, but he doesn't have as much language . . . access to written language that she does, so that's why I choose to focus on him more and make sure he's getting it." Marina chose to stay with Miguel because he needed more support than Kristie in terms of his ability to access written English. Because the instructions were written on cards for students to read at each workstation, Marina believed Kristie would be able to read the instructions and participate in the group activity. In addition, although speaking was not her preferred means of communication, Kristie was able to communicate with her peers through spoken English and lipreading. Marina was also able to look over at Kristie's group occasionally to ensure that she was participating. Furthermore,

Kristie would have been able (and assertive enough) to get Marina's attention and ask her to interpret if something was not clear. If the activities had not been in writing, or if Kristie was not reading at grade level and was unable to communicate with her peers, Marina would have selected another course of action; she might have approached Mrs. Kendall and asked her to assign Kristie and Miguel to the same group. The following day, Mrs. Kendall did assign them to the same group. If she had not, Marina would have had to decide whether a repeat of the previous day's approach was indeed an acceptable option or to request that both students be assigned to the same group.

Assessing Student Learning Needs

Further evidence of the complexity of the unique constellations of factors considered at any given moment can be seen in the frequency of educational interpreters' efforts to assess student learning needs. Besides relying on information based on a student's educational placement (e.g., a student who was not mainstreamed for Language Arts and Writing was probably not reading and writing at grade level), K–12 interpreters determined student learning needs through various other means. I observed educational interpreters often deviating from the interpretation to initiate dialogue with Deaf and hard of hearing students in order to assess comprehension of academic content, and they habitually checked in with students to determine whether they were on the right track. For example, when Mrs. Kendall was using overhead transparencies to help students correct their math homework, Marina asked Kristie and Miguel what their answers were. When they indicated correct responses she explained that she would tell them, "'Okay. Good. That's right.'. . . I just want to see if they're really getting it right or just going, 'Uh-huh, uh-huh.' I get feedback to make sure they're following."

Camie said that when she asked if Emily understood a concept, Emily would often indicate that she did. Camie explained that although she initially took Emily at her word, "after a while, I started catching on, so I would say, 'Well, then, explain it to me.' Or I would ask her a question about what I just said. I would say, 'Why do think that is?' or whatever. Then she would look at me like, 'Oh, crap.' Then finally she'll say, 'I don't know.'" Because these K–12 interpreters recognized that student self-reports are not always accurate, they favored open-ended questions to assess Deaf and hard of hearing students' learning needs. They also watched as students worked to determine what students could do independently. However, AJ explained that assessing student learning could still be difficult to ascertain. Moreover, students may not be open to additional explanation at any given time. In one case, even though Angelina had moved ahead of the rest of the class, AJ could not clearly determine whether Angelina truly understood a concept. "She was doing the kind of worksheet where once you figured out the pattern, you could just do it based on the pattern and not really know why you were doing what you were doing. At some point I'm like, 'Hmm. . . . She might just be doing the pattern thing, and does she really know what she's doing?'" AJ asked questions to see if Angelina understood, but Angelina was too focused on her work to accept AJ's invitation to discuss content. AJ said that when she decided to inform Angelina that two of the answers were wrong, Angelina just changed her answers. AJ explained the ineffectiveness of that particular approach in this case: "She knows that if one's wrong the other one's wrong because it's A, B, C, and you only use each one once. So she just switches it; she didn't learn anything from it. I tried to explain the answer, which the teacher did later in the lesson too, but you know, it's like [Angelina is thinking], 'Blah, blah, blah. OK, I got the right answer. Now let's move on.'" In that case, AJ chose to let it go, at least for the moment.

Interpreters desire to even the playing field for Deaf and hard of hearing students in comparison to their hearing peers emerged as a theme during my observations and interviews. Interpreters used hearing peers' skills and knowledge to gauge when additional support or explanation might be appropriate. This required them to consider and assess the learning needs of not only the Deaf and hard of hearing students, but all the students in the class.

AJ described what she chose to do when she could not clearly discern whether or not Angelina had totally understood a particularly complex concept. "I'm not sure that a lot of people in the class understood it. . . . She was probably no better or worse off than anyone else in the classroom. I guess that's just where I wanted to leave it." She added that she would often "ask kids questions while I'm interpreting that the teacher isn't necessarily asking, but I'll ask them stuff to just to see if they get it and see whether or not to reinforce something, but only to the level that the rest of the class should be at." In this case, she chose to continue interpreting rather than pursue another course of action because Angelina was on the same playing field as her peers. Similarly, Camie explained she would leave further explanation up to Mr. Harrison "if I look around, I don't think the other kids get the full grasp of the meaning or the concept, the theory, or whatever he's trying to get across either." When interpreters perceive that all of the students are in the same boat, they are more likely to allow Deaf and hard of hearing students to flounder, struggle, or deal with the ambiguity. Assessments of what Deaf and hard of hearing students knew and could do in comparison to their hearing peers greatly influenced interpreters' moment-to-moment decisions.

Tutoring, Helping, and Explaining as Needed

Determining that a Deaf or hard of hearing student is not equally equipped to successfully perform a task or participate in a specific activity prompts a new corresponding set of actions. When they were not actively interpreting, all of the interpreters in this study helped students as needed, such as when Marina helped Miguel find a book. In addition, all of the interpreters took on tutoring responsibilities, either formally for an extended and specified time designated for tutoring, or intermittently throughout each day. Tutoring frequently occurred during time allotted for independent seat work. However, deciding how much help to offer was in itself a complex decision. AJ, who was a substitute interpreter who was assigned to work at Via Portal for a week, reported the difficulty of determining an appropriate level of support when working with younger students. She explained, "Especially when you're used to working with adults all the time where you take kind of a hands-off approach, you go into an elementary school and you don't know what these kids need. You don't know how much they need you to be there, or if they're gonna be like, '*Back off*!' or if you *should*. I mean they might *need* your help. They might not, and you don't *know*." AJ explained that when Angelina asked for help, she was willing to help, such as by answering Angelina's in-the-moment questions when she chose to work ahead.

Assessment is one of the tools that K–12 interpreters rely on to determine how much support to offer. In particular, interpreters made decisions based on what Deaf and hard of hearing students knew and could do in light of the knowledge and skills necessary to successfully participate in or to complete an activity. Marina explained the factors she considered when deciding when and how to interpret word problems in math for Miguel. She said, "It depends on if I know he knows it. A lot of times, it will have the information, so I'll sign the whole thing to him. And if he still doesn't [understand], I'll say, 'Okay, what is it asking you? What do you need to know? How many bags?' or whatever. And then I'll sign it again without the useless information, and he usually gets it. I don't usually tell him, 'That's the answer,' but I'll help set it up better. If they don't get it, help." Marina first tried to interpret the questions to see if that was enough support for Miguel to successfully complete word problems in math. If that proved to be inadequate, she would then provide additional help as needed (Figure 13).

Like the other interpreters, Camie tutored Emily when students were engaged in independent seat work, but she also tutored Emily at length in two additional settings. During first period math, Mr. Lincoln gave a short lesson every day and then let students work independently. When students completed a module, they were to approach the teacher so he could check their work. After receiving his approval, students were free to move on to the next module. Students who had questions for the teacher lined up at his desk with those waiting to have their work checked. Camie tutored Emily during this time, answering questions that Emily asked, providing explanations about math concepts and procedures, and asking questions to assess what Emily could do. If Mr. Lincoln interjected instructions or explanations, she did not interpret right away. Instead, she let Emily continue working

FIGURE 13. *Marina interpreting math questions for Miguel.*

and interpreted if and when the information was directly relevant to what Emily was working on at that particular moment. When Emily was done with a module, Camie would wait in line with Emily and interpret the interaction between Mr. Lincoln and Emily as he checked her work. Camie also requested the teacher's guidance about the mathematical concepts that Emily needed to focus on.

Following first period math, Camie was expected to work in the homeroom class with Emily for one hour a day. Camie was responsible for finding appropriate materials and resources to use during this extended designated tutoring session. She worked outside of regular school hours to research, locate, and develop materials. She made flash cards to help Emily learn multiplication tables and key vocabulary. She brought in an electronic dictionary for Emily's use. Camie checked in with classroom teachers, an itinerant teacher, and a resource specialist to get materials and instructional objectives to work on with Emily, but she reported that teachers rarely approached her with suggestions about what to cover during that hour. Although all of the teachers were helpful and supportive when Camie requested specific materials and input, none of the general education teachers, teachers of Deaf and hard of hearing students, administrators, nor Camie's supervisor approached Camie with instructions or materials for Camie and Emily to use during these one-on-one tutoring sessions.

Camie was expected to determine the subjects and lessons with which Emily needed the most help. In order to identify Emily's learning needs, Camie depended on formal and informal assessments of what Emily could do. Camie related how she determined what to work on during designated tutoring time. She reported that during that time, they often worked on math. She said, "I try to support whatever they're doing in class. Originally it started with money and time and stuff like that—that they didn't cover in class that she didn't know."

Camie said that she looked for opportunities to fill in some of the gaps in Emily's skills and knowledge, especially in comparison to her peers. Camie explained her rationale for choosing to work on borrowing in math, "Basically, I was trying to catch her up with the rest of the kids because for some reason the rest of the kids could do that." Camie said that sometimes she decided what to cover during tutoring based on informal assessments throughout the course of the school day, sometimes as a result of conversations between classes. She explained, "I just see what she's having a problem with—even if it's maybe a conversation that we have during the day and I'm trying to explain something to her—something that most people know at the age of 13 and she doesn't know it. Then I'll go into more depth [about] that later."

Camie attributed the gaps in Emily's skills and knowledge to previous educational experiences such as changing schools when her family moved, transitioning to a mainstream program mid-year because the DHH program closed, as well as to a lack of access to the incidental learning most hearing students benefit from. Whether for the purpose of making decisions about interpreting or whether to pursue an alternate course of action, ongoing assessment of the needs of Deaf and hard of hearing students informed K–12 interpreters' moment-to-moment decisions.

Making Connections: Prior Knowledge

Because most parents of Deaf and hard of hearing children are not fluent signers, many of these children miss out on incidental knowledge that hearing children overhear during dinner conversations and on news broadcasts or other television shows about pop culture, even children's shows (e.g., *Sesame Street* or *Jake and the Neverland Pirates*) designed to broaden awareness; expose children to concepts such as numbers, letters, vocabulary, and rhyming; or teach manners and social values. Besides providing tutoring, helping, or explaining, interpreters in this study also capitalized on their own awareness of Deaf and hard of hearing students' personal experiences. They endeavored to make explicit connections between prior knowledge and a concept currently being discussed. Camie explained that she sometimes integrated additional explanatory information into an interpretation. She reported that Emily was not as likely to be as familiar with some information as her hearing peers, such as references to popular culture or current events. For example, Mr. Harrison talked about the South Pacific region of the Indian Ocean as being the area where a tsunami had occurred the previous year, a phenomenon that was covered extensively in the news, on talk shows, and on commercials seeking financial contributions. Camie explained why she asked Emily if she remembered when (a staff interpreter) Kelly's daughter was in Thailand the previous year during the tsunami. "She learns really, really well (I figured this out) by scaffolding—by relating it to one of her experiences or what she already knows. Or if I'm trying to explain something and I give her an example of something that's related to my family or something that happened to me in the past, then she's just, totally focused . . . she gets really interested if you can relate it to something that she can relate to . . . then all of a sudden she's interested." In this case, Camie's approach reflected the common pedagogical practices of educational scaffolding and of helping students make connections between prior knowledge and new learning. Using her own knowledge of what Emily knew, she built a connection between familiar and new information.

Supporting Language Development: English

Educational interpreters not only assess all students' mastery of academic content and Deaf students' ability to successfully participate in class or school activities, they also consider the language proficiencies of Deaf and hard of hearing students. Pursuing a more direct course of action such as tutoring, helping, or explaining becomes complicated even further because K–12 interpreters recognize that most Deaf and hard of hearing students are on a path of language development that does not mirror that of their hearing peers (or even of other Deaf students, since each student's exposure to both signed and spoken languages at home and school has traditionally been highly variable). During a language arts lesson, Mr. Harrison's students were to replace a specified adjective with a synonymous adjective. Camie explained that she fingerspelled the word *sharp* to let Emily know "that's a key word. After that, I tell her, 'Okay, now I want you to replace the word, and then I spell it again, *sharp.*'" However, when Emily still looked confused, Camie provided additional explanation about how the word was being used. She said, "I kinda elaborated a little bit more than what he said actually for the sentence, so she would understand what the word meant. 'Dogs have a sharp sense of smell.'. . . I want her to know that in that sentence, the word *sharp* didn't mean like a knife. It meant they are expert at smelling, they are really good at smelling. It was important for her to understand what the actual word meant, so that's why I expanded."

Interpreters using fingerspelling to convey key English concepts and terminology while taking care not to give away the answers is also evidenced in a lesson on homophones. To begin, Mr. Sands called on Rashid to read two sentences written on the board. Rashid read: "Doug's fear grew during the course of the hike," and "He watched Charlie lick her fur with her coarse tongue." AJ transliterated using fingerspelling and English word order:

D-O-U-G-'S FEAR GROW DURING T-H-E C-O-U-R-S-E O-F T-H-E H-I-K-E.

H-E WATCH C-H-A-R-L-I-E LICK HER F-U-R WITH HER C-O-A-R-S-E

TONGUE.[18]

AJ relied heavily on fingerspelling and adhered to English syntax when signing these sentences rather than using semantically equivalent signs that would give an unfair advantage to Angelina over her classmates. By transliterating, AJ provided the opportunity for Angelina to answer a question that was posed to elicit students' understanding of English vocabulary and spelling. Mr. Sands continued by asking for a volunteer to tell the class what a homophone was. In response, Julio explained, "Homophones are words that mean the same . . . no, that sound the same way but mean something different, and they're spelled different. Like *hare* and *hair*." AJ signed:

<u>rh-</u>   <u>topic</u>
MEAN WHAT H-O-M-O-P-H-O-N-E? MEAN WORD IX + (alt. left and right)
     <u>nod</u>   <u>topic</u>
SOUND SAME-AS, BUT THEIR+ (alt. left and right) MEANING DIFFERENT,
          <u>topic</u>
AND THEIR+ (alt. left hand then right) SPELLING DIFFERENT. LIKE
H-A-R-E (left)
          <u>nod</u>
AND H-A-I-R (right).

This time, AJ chose to interpret. She used a form of signed output that adhered to ASL grammatical rules and was much less consistent with English than when she had transliterated and fingerspelled so many words in the sentences that Rashid had read. She also omitted Julio's self-correction from the interpretation. She chose to fingerspell only the

---

18. In this volume, ASL signs are represented in small capital letters, nonmanual grammatical markers are indicated with a line above the corresponding signs, fingerspelling is indicated by dashes between letters, and spatial structuring is described in parentheses. It should be noted that the ASL transcriptions here are not intended to be complete, but to provide sufficient documentation of the principle being discussed in these results.

three key words in these sentences: *homophone, hare,* and *hair.* In both cases, her fingerspelling was clear, making sure that every letter of each of the key words was easy to see so that Angelina would have access to the fundamental English terminology; however, she did not adhere as closely represent English lexicon and syntax when the point of the discourse was to explain the meaning of a homophone.

While the class was still discussing the first set of homophones, *through* and *threw,* AJ read the next set of sentences along with Angelina, who had chosen to work ahead. AJ then watched Angelina, who cautiously fingerspelled

<u>   y/n   </u>

A-P-P-E-A-R? AJ looked at her own book before looking back at Angelina to nod in confirmation. As Angelina wrote the answer, Mr. Sands read, "As she climbs, objects below seem to get smaller." He continued, "We're on Number 2" and repeated, "'As she climbs, objects below seem to get smaller.' We're looking for the definition of *seem*. So what is the definition of *seem*? What is the definition of *seem*?" AJ interpreted:

<u>   wh   </u>

WORD S-E-E-M MEAN WHAT? Angelina was looking at her book and did not see the question interpreted. When Angelina looked up again, AJ repeated:

<u>   wh   </u>

WORD S-E-E-M MEAN WHAT?

Because the point of the question was to determine if students knew the definition of the word *seem*, AJ did not give away the answer by using the sign for SEEM. Instead, she fingerspelled. In this manner, Angelina was able to access the English terminology that was fundamental to the current task and had the same opportunity as her classmates to respond to the question Mr. Sands had posed, "What does *seem* mean?" As the lesson on homophones continued, AJ was diligent about representing English through transliteration and making connections to interpreted academic concepts without giving away the answer before it had been discussed in the class.

Supporting Language Development: ASL

Deaf and hard of hearing students' language proficiencies not only in English but also in ASL heavily influenced interpreters' decisions about what to do. Camie discussed the responsibility of considering Deaf and hard of hearing students' language development in ASL. She said, "Hearing kids don't just automatically know English. They have to learn. So why would it be any different for a Deaf student? It seems to me along with vocabulary and everything, she [Emily] would have to learn the classifier concepts, and the nonmanual markers, and all of that. . . . They don't just automatically know that." AJ echoed the necessity of modeling grammatically correct use of ASL when interpreting a lesson about the number line. She discussed the importance of maintaining the signer's perspective according to ASL conventions and explained that she turned around to face the board (thereby making sure that left on the number line corresponded with Angelina's view) only when Mr. Sands continued to emphasize the point that numbers to the left of zero are always negative. Although none of the students in this study had the opportunity to study ASL formally, all of the interpreters were at least aware of the need for students to develop ASL skills. In particular, interpreters working with students who rarely had the opportunity to interact with other fluent signers emphasized the importance of modeling ASL to the best of their ability.

During Camie and Emily's tutoring sessions, Camie used literature as a means to foster the development of ASL vocabulary as well. When Emily encountered vocabulary she did not know while signing stories, she would fingerspell the word or use an English-based (conceptually inaccurate) sign. Camie explained, "I started by stopping her all the time and trying to explain it, but then it was too hard for her to keep track of the story [while] stopping 10 times in a one- or two-page story, so I just started underlining them. Then I would have her look them up later and then write the definitions down on a piece of paper, and then we'd go over the signs for them." Camie initially came up with this technique to build English vocabulary, but she soon realized that the activity was teaching Emily ASL vocabulary as well. As Emily's reading comprehension improved, Camie explained that she began to challenge Emily more about the meaning of particular English words and phrases and how to sign them according to meaning in context. For example, Camie discussed the idiomatic phrase *silence fell across the room*. Camie said that at first, Emily would just sign word for word. Camie said, eventually, "I started asking her, 'Does that make sense? Can silence fall?' And then she would look at me like, 'Oh, no. I guess not.' So I said, 'So now that your comprehension is building, and you are understanding the stories, and you have most of the signs down, start thinking about what the story means. What does that mean? Does it mean there was nobody in the room? Does it mean there [were] people in the room but nobody was talking? You know, what does it mean?'"

Supporting Language Development: Connections Between ASL and English

Because English is the language of accountability in schools, these K–12 interpreters endeavored to support student learning of English structures and vocabulary. In addition, they recognized that Deaf and hard of hearing students are also learning ASL, and, therefore, they stressed the importance of supporting student learning of ASL vocabulary, structures, and other linguistic features. Furthermore, they attempted to make explicit connections between ASL and English whenever possible.

In a lesson about volcanoes, Mr. Harrison said, "The explosive ones have the thick, viscous lava that stops up the vent . . . that closes the vent up." While watching her own interpretation of that particular concept, Camie reflected, "Normally when I sign *volcano*, I will just sign *volcano* and then show the lava coming out more [switching to sign language and using classifiers to show a slow lava flow]. Because he said 'explosive,' I was trying to show that with more emphasis like it exploded, but I should have fingerspelled." In this example, Camie noted that the specific English adjective *explosive* might prove to be important in terms of testing and accountability. Camie also said that classifiers (features of ASL that are used for descriptions of formations and movement) must be used in conjunction with the fingerspelling of specific English vocabulary. "With younger kids, you would have to spell *explosive* instead of just [using the classifier]. . . . You would have to explain what that means." She elaborated that although Emily would be more likely to understand the ASL depiction of an explosive volcano, she might not be able to comprehend it if she saw the printed word. Camie recognized that Mr. Harrison wanted students to understand not only the concept of "explosive" but also to recognize the printed English word. Camie wondered about the degree to which language development in ASL could be fostered by modeling appropriate use of ASL and wanted to be sure to make explicit connections between key English terminology and ASL interpretations.

Returning to the homophone lesson illuminates that supporting content learning as well as facilitating the development of language skills in both

ASL and English is likely to require explicit and repeated exposure. As the lesson progressed, students began to respond accurately to the teacher's question, "What does *seem* mean?" Mr. Sands called on Jacob, who said, "Appear?" Mr. Sands thanked Jacob for his answer, and AJ interpreted by fingerspelling, A-P-P-E-A-R. Mr. Sands called on several students, asking each one to provide a definition of the word *seem*. AJ interpreted

‾‾‾‾‾‾‾‾ wh ‾‾‾‾‾‾‾‾

WORD S-E-E-M MEAN WHAT?

Initially, AJ completely avoided signing SEEM, and she always finger-spelled when Mr. Sands asked for the definition of the word. However, when students began to provide the accurate response, *appear*, AJ some-times fingerspelled A-P-P-E-A-R and sometimes signed SEEM then immediately fingerspelled A-P-P-E-A-R. In this way, AJ began to make connections between English vocabulary and semantically equivalent ASL vocabulary. However, even repetition and the fact that Angelina had written down the correct answer and was working ahead proved to be insufficient confirmation of Angelina's understanding of the targeted vocabulary.

Mr. Sands continued, "Okay, I'm going to repeat the question. We're on number two. 'As she climbs, objects below seem to get smaller.' We need to know the definition of the word *seem*. What does *seem* mean? 'As she climbs, objects below seem to get smaller.'" AJ interpreted by signing:

‾‾‾‾‾‾‾‾‾‾ when ‾‾‾‾‾‾‾‾‾‾

I WILL ASK-YOU AGAIN. NUMBER TWO. WHILE S-H-E CLIMB, THING+
UNDER SEEM S-E-E-M BECOME SMALLER. WE WANT KNOW

‾‾‾‾‾ wh ‾‾‾‾‾   ‾‾‾‾‾ when ‾‾‾‾‾

WHAT S-E-E-M, WHAT MEAN? WHILE S-H-E CLIMB.

As Angelina began to fingerspell A-P-P-E-A-R, AJ nodded, but when Angelina used a semantically incorrect sign (APPEAR as in SHOW-UP), AJ emphasized:

‾‾ topic ‾‾   ‾‾ y/n ‾‾

SHOW-UP DIFFERENT MEANING. Angelina then signed, SEEM? AJ replied, (nod)
RIGHT! SEEM. SEEM (nodding while mouthing *appear* both times). To clarify further, she added, SEEM, S-E-E-M, SEEM (mouthed *seem* and signed to left), A-P-P-E-A-R SEEM (mouthed *appear* and signed to right)

SAME-AS SIGN (nods). After Mr. Sands confirmed the correct definition, he asked, "Now, who thinks they can come up with a homophone for that word?" AJ interpreted:

```
                                    wh
───────────────────────────────────────────
WHO CAN FIND H-O-M-O-P-H-O-N-E FOR WORD S-E-E-M?
```

Mr. Sands asked students to write the homophone in the corresponding space in their workbooks and waited quietly for them to write. AJ scooted her chair up next to Angelina's desk and looked at Angelina's practice book. AJ then signed SO, leaned forward and pointed to *seem* in Angelina's book, and then signed,

```
topic
─────
SEEM-left (pointing at the list of words in the book and waiting until

                                    y/n            ─────
Angelina looked back at AJ), HAVE ANOTHER? ITS-left (possessive)

     y/n
─────────────
H-O-M-O-P-H-O-N-E?
```

AJ touched Angelina's book and slid her index finger down a list of provided homophones from which students were to choose, then touched the word *seem* again and tapped it a few times, leaned back in her chair and signed:

```
  t                                 wh
─────────────────────────────────────────────
SEEM WHERE (sliding her finger down list of words in the book) ITS-left

           wh                    y/n
──────────────────────   ─────────────
(possessive) H-O-M-O-P-H-O-N-E? YOU CAN FIND?
```

AJ leaned forward in her chair again, pointed at *seem* in Angelina's book, and waited for Angelina to look at the book to see what AJ was pointing to. When Angelina looked back up, AJ signed SEEM.

```
                                    wh
───────────────────────────────────────────
WHERE (sliding her finger down list of words in the book) ITS (IX-
possessive toward

        wh                yn
─────────────────   ─────────────
book) H-O-M-O-P-H-O-N-E? YOU CAN FIND?
```

AJ put her hands in her lap and waited, still leaning forward and watching as Angelina looked at the list of words. Angelina pointed to a word in her book as Mr. Sands

FIGURE 14. *AJ clapping her hands in a silent cheer for Angelina.*

said, "Okay, raise your hand." AJ looked at the word Angelina had pointed out, looked at Angelina with a smile, clapped her hands silently (Figure 14) and signed RIGHT while nodding. Mr. Sands finished the question, ". . . if you have the homophone." Angelina raised her hand to respond. Throughout the rest of the lesson, AJ alternated between using conceptually accurate ASL vocabulary and fingerspelling to convey key English vocabulary. Moreover, AJ provided guidance and correction regarding Angelina's use of a semantically incorrect ASL sign in order to help Angelina make connections between ASL and English.

4. WHAT INTERPRETERS DO TO CULTIVATE OPPORTUNITIES FOR PARTICIPATION AND PROMOTE INCLUSION

Because of competing visual demands, communication options, the pace of classroom discourse, and the time delay inherent to any interpretation, it can be a challenge for Deaf and hard of hearing students to keep up with the rest of the class and participate fully. Regardless of whether the teacher explicitly asked students to raise their hands or implied that students who knew the answer should do so, interpreters in this study frequently prompted Deaf or hard of hearing students to raise their hands (Figure 15).

AJ said, "Usually the teacher is going at a pace that's much faster than the Deaf student can keep up with—just because of having to look

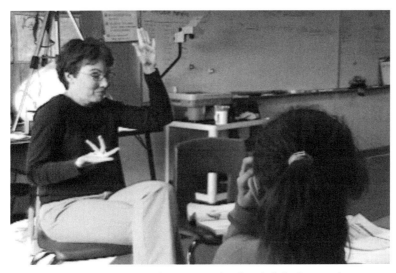

FIGURE 15. *AJ prompting Angelina to raise her hand if she knows the answer.*

at the teacher, look down at the paper and do whatever, and try to get it all at once. So usually the student is behind and I'm trying to help them get caught up." Correcting answers on worksheets or tests was a common class activity that illustrated the orchestration of competing visual demands. One of the simplest techniques interpreters used when students were asked to correct their own or a classmate's paper was to sign the number of the problem with one hand and the answer with the other, holding both until Deaf or hard of hearing students made any written corrections that were necessary (Figure 16).

However, this two-handed technique was not adequate when answers were longer or more complex. Mr. Lincoln and Mrs. Kendall both used overhead transparencies to help students correct math problems. When Mrs. Kendall provided the answers to math homework on an overhead transparency, she asked students to raise their hands to indicate which problems they had answered incorrectly. If several students raised their hands, she wrote out each step on the overhead transparency. Marina explained that by the time Miguel and Kristie saw the interpretation of Mrs. Kendall's prompt, "Raise your hand if you got number five wrong" then looked at their homework to see whether they had the answer right or not, they were too far behind. She said, "By the time they get it, they put their hand up for number *six* when they meant number *five*."

Two of three interpreters in this study used similar strategies to create opportunities for Deaf and hard of hearing students to participate actively

FIGURE 16. *AJ signing* ONE *and* A.

and publicly. During Mr. Harrison's lesson on volcanoes (Section 2 of this chapter), Mr. Harrison's students were to choose the correct answer on their worksheets. Mr. Harrison moved through the multiple choice answers quickly, reading each question before asking students for the corresponding letter. Once he received a correct response, he then provided a comment or added an explanation. Mr. Harrison asked, "What's the main product of a nonexplosive eruption?" Camie signed only, SIXTEEN. SIXTEEN WHAT? Emily indicated that she wanted to respond, and Camie encouraged her to raise her hand, but Mr. Harrison had already called on Hunter, who gave the correct answer. Camie snapped her fingers as if to say, "Shoot!" She then looked back at Emily and explained that Hunter had given the answer, then told Emily to look at the next question. In this instance, and in several others, Camie was actually prompting Emily to look ahead to determine the next answer in advance. Mr. Harrison read the next definition and called on Priscilla, who gave an incorrect answer. Camie did not interpret what Mr. Harrison read to the class. Instead, she signed, "Do you know? Do you know? Raise your hand." Emily nodded that she did just as Priscilla was called on. Emily put her hand down. Priscilla gave an incorrect answer. Camie told Emily to wait. She watched Mr. Harrison as he repeated the question, "What's magma after it's been exploded out?" At the right time, Camie again prompted Emily to raise her hand. Mr. Harrison called on Emily, who fingerspelled the correct answer, "Pyroclastic material."

Camie made deliberate decisions to omit several types of information from the interpretation in order to make up for the time delay inherent to interpreting. For example, she chose not to interpret Mr. Harrison's admonishment of a student for not being on task. Furthermore, as Mr. Harrison read the question for Number 19, Camie signed only the number 19, using ASL grammatical markers to indicate a question, as in, "How about 19?" Sometimes Emily signed her answers as she raised her hand, and Camie informed her whether or not the answers were correct and even praised her for correct answers. For example, when Mr. Harrison said that the answer to Number 17 was false, Camie interpreted that it was false and then gave a thumbs up to Emily.

AJ used a similar strategy so that Angelina could participate actively in class discussions. When Mr. Sands began the lesson on homophones (Section 3 of this chapter), he wrote two sentences on the board. He then asked students if they knew what the lesson would be about. When nobody could guess, he wrote the word *homophone* above the two sentences. After Rashid had read the sentences and Julio had defined *homophone,* AJ waited for Mr. Sands to write the definition on the board. She then interpreted as he told the class they would do another example together but turned around to look as he wrote two more sentences on the board. This time, instead of waiting for Mr. Sands to write, AJ immediately asked Angelina where the homophones were in the first two sentences. She put her hands down and waited for Angelina to respond. When Angelina gave the correct response, AJ signed, RIGHT! GOOD! She then asked Angelina for the homophones in the next two sentences. After doing so, AJ kept her hands down, looking at the sentences on the board and back to Angelina while waiting for a response. By that time, Mr. Sands had pointed out the homophones in the first two sentences and was asking the class who could find the homophones in the second set of sentences. So, as Mr. Sands read from the board, "The sun shone down hotter and hotter as he climbed. To think that a cougar had shown him how to get around the ledge," AJ did not interpret. Instead, she continued waiting for Angelina's response to the question that, by that time, Mr. Sands had asked and AJ had already interpreted. Angelina fingerspelled the first homophone, S-H-O-N-E, as Mr. Sands began, "This time, raise your hand . . ." Angelina fingerspelled S-H-O-W-N. By the time Mr. Sands instructed students to raise their hands if they knew the homophones for the second sentence pair, Angelina had fingerspelled the correct two words to AJ. At that point, AJ prompted Angelina to raise her hand in time for Angelina to do so at the same time as her classmates.

By using visual resources productively and proactively, and by making principled choices about what to omit from the interpretation, these interpreters mitigated the time delay that so often precludes the participation of Deaf and hard of hearing students. Rather than let the students get behind, as is typical of (and inherent to) interpretation, the interpreters pursued a course of action that, in effect, created more time and actually let the students get *ahead*. As the class progressed, both teachers eventually caught up with Camie and AJ, and Emily and Angelina were able to raise their hands along with their classmates. Camie and AJ's strategies cultivated opportunities for participation rather than simply maintaining the status quo of interpretation that relegates Deaf and hard of hearing students to bystander status. However, it took a tremendous amount of effort for them to orchestrate a single opportunity for Emily and Angelina to respond publicly.

Cultivating opportunities for active participation in class activities was complicated not only by competing demands for Deaf and hard of hearing students' visual attention and the timing delays inherent to interpretation. Deaf and hard of hearing students are often isolated as a result of communication barriers, even to the point of systematic exclusion from certain class activities. Perhaps even more pervasive was the fact that Deaf and hard of hearing students have few opportunities to interact with hearing teachers and peers. None of the interpreters in this study chose to limit student responses to only those which were shared with the teacher and class. They also encouraged students to reply privately, in sign language by responding to student questions and providing praise. Interpreters in this study had to decide whether or not to interpret Deaf and hard of hearing students' signed discourse into spoken English. They frequently chose not to interpret signed student comments, questions, and responses to teacher-initiated questions. The following example illustrates AJ's decision-making process about whether, when, and to what extent to interpret the class discourse, to intervene in some other manner, or to interpret Angelina's signed discourse into spoken English.

Scenario: Language Arts Lesson on Suffixes

In language arts class, Mr. Sands asked students if they could remember the two suffixes that they had previously discussed. Josie said, "ing." Mr. Sands said that although *ing* was a suffix, it wasn't one of the two they had talked about. He wrote *ous* on the board and Angelina mouthed "Oh!" and slapped her palm to her forehead. She then looked up toward the ceiling before looking at AJ to fingerspell W-A-R-D, just as Mr. Sands was writing it on the board. AJ turned to look at the board. When she saw that Angelina was correct, she smiled and nodded at Angelina. Angelina covered her eyes with one hand and fingerspelled W-A-R-D, then opened her eyes, looked at AJ and signed that it was hard to remember. Mr. Sands pointed to the board where he had written *ward* and said, "Let's start with this one." While pointing at the board indicating that Angelica should look, AJ turned around herself to see where he was pointing. Mr. Sands asked, "Who can think of a word that uses *ward* as the suffix?" AJ interpreted the question and kept her gaze fixed on Angelina while holding the signs and grammatical facial markers of ASL that indicate a response is desired. Angelina looked at AJ and fingerspelled, B-E-W-A-R-D. AJ fingerspelled, B-E-W-A-R-E, pointing and tapping with her nondominant index finger at the fingerspelled letter E to emphasize the correct spelling (Figure 17). Angelina cupped her hand over her mouth as if to say, "Oops!"

Mr. Sands continued, "Who can think of a word that has this suffix: *ward*? AJ again interpreted the question as "Can you think of a word with *ward* at the end?" This time, AJ looked around at all of the students in the class while interpreting the question. As Mr. Sands waited silently for students to think of words, AJ looked directly at Angelina and asked if she could think of another word. Angelina shook her head. Holly provided the word *reward*. Angelina began to write in her notebook. Brian gave the word *backward*. When Angelina looked up and saw the second

FIGURE 17. *AJ emphasizing that* beware *ends with an* e.

word was *backward,* her eyes widened as she wrote it, showing with her facial expression that she had thought of a word. Dustin offered the word *upward.* When Angelina was done writing, she raised her hand high and waved it to be called on. She then put it down, looked directly at AJ and fingerspelled T-O-W-A-R-D. Although AJ was ready to interpret the third word on the class list, she waited and watched as Angelina fingerspelled. AJ nodded and signed that the word was a good one, then continued to interpret the third word on the class list, *upward.* Angelina again raised her hand, squirming in her seat and waving her hand even more eagerly than before. Soon Mr. Sands called on Nathan, the student seated next to Angelina, who gave the word *forward.* Angelina put her hand down and looked away from the interpretation to watch Nathan's interaction with Mr. Sands. AJ did not interpret. After a few more students added words to the list, Mr. Sands called on Angelina, who had again raised her hand. She spoke for herself rather than signing to give her answer. She very softly said, "Tow-ird?" Mr. Sands did not respond right away. Not recognizing the word, he said, "Pardon me?" AJ signed for Angelina to say it again. When she did, another student said something at the same time and the word was not pronounced as clearly as it had been the first time. Mr. Sands remained quiet. Sensing his reluctance to ask Angelina to repeat her answer a third time, AJ looked at Mr. Sands and repeated, "Toward." As Mr. Sands repeated "toward" for the class and wrote it with the other words listed on the board, AJ looked back at Angelina, smiling and nodding while she signed "Good!" After being called on, Angelina flipped through the pages of the book she had sheltered in her lap behind her desk, glancing back and forth between the interpreter and the book. AJ continued to interpret, although Angelina was watching intermittently and did not appear to be paying much attention. When she found the page in the book that she wanted, she began writing the list of words from the board. AJ continued to interpret as Angelina wrote.

Although AJ interpreted throughout this lesson, it is clear that there was much more going on.

1. AJ interpreted a question the teacher posed to the class.
2. She pointed to Josie to indicate who was called on.
3. She interpreted Josie's response to the question presented.
4. She watched and waited as Angelina covered her eyes while fingerspelling the suffix W-A-R-D as Mr. Sands was writing it on the board.

5. AJ chose not to interpret Angelina's signed comment into spoken English.

6. AJ turned to see that Mr. Sands had written the suffix *ward* on the board.

7. She looked at Angelina, nodded, and smiled to confirm that Angelina got it right.

8. She watched Angelina sign that it was a hard suffix to remember as she practiced spelling W-A-R-D.

9. AJ chose not to interpret Angelina's comments into spoken English.

10. When Mr. Sands said, "Let's start with this one," AJ immediately turned to look at the board.

11. She saw that he was pointing to the suffix *ward*.

12. She interpreted *this one* by fingerspelling W-A-R-D.

13. AJ interpreted as Mr. Sands asked who could think of a word that uses *ward* as the suffix as, "Can you think of a word that ends with W-A-R-D?"

14. She looked directly at Angelina when interpreting the question and paused after the question, thereby cuing Angelina to respond.

15. She watched as Angelina fingerspelled B-E-W-A-R-D.

16. She did not interpret into spoken English.

17. She looked at Angelina and fingerspelled B-E-W-A-R-E. As she got to the final E, she held it for several seconds while pointing at it with the index finger of her nondominant hand, then signed that it was different.

18. She watched Angelina put her hand over her mouth as if to say, "Oops!"

19. She did not interpret Angelina's comment.

20. When Mr. Sands repeated his question about who could think of a word with the suffix *ward*, AJ interpreted the question, this time directing it to the whole class by looking around at all the students and gesturing with both palms outspread as if to say, "Well?"

21. She looked directly at Angelina and asked if she could think of another word.

22. She watched Angelina shake her head, but she did not interpret Angelina's response.

23. She interpreted as Holly offered the first word, *reward*.

24. She interpreted Brian's word *backward* as Angelina got out paper and began to write.
25. Although a third word had been provided, AJ chose not to interpret.
26. She waited for Angelina to write.
27. When Angelina looked up and began to fingerspell T-O-W-A-R-D, AJ watched but did not interpret Dustin's word, *upward*, Angelina's word, *toward*, or Nathan's word, *forward*.
28. AJ nodded and smiled as she told Angelina that her word was a good one.
29. AJ then interpreted that the third and fourth words were *upward* and *forward*.
30. When Mr. Sands called on Angelina, AJ did not interpret as Angelina said, "Tow-ird."
31. AJ waited for Mr. Sands to respond. When he did not reply after a second or two, she looked to see what he was doing. As she did, he said, "Pardon me?"
32. She interpreted the teacher's response, "Pardon me?" as "Say it again."
33. She listened to Angelina's response and realized he still may not have heard it clearly.
34. She looked at the teacher and as she saw his quizzical expression, she repeated, "Toward."
35. As Mr. Sands repeated the word and wrote it on the board with the other words, AJ looked at Angelina, smiling and nodding while signing "Good!"
36. AJ continued interpreting while Angelina got out a book, even though she was only paying partial attention to the class discussion.

In this scenario, AJ made several decisions to do something other than interpret. In fact, interpreting or transliterating accounts for only nine out of 36 separate actions (25%). In addition, AJ optimized visual access by directing Angelina's attention to words written on the board, by adjusting the timing of the interpretation and waiting until Angelina looked up or opened her eyes, and by modifying the content of the interpretation and providing more specific information such as fingerspelling W-A-R-D when Mr. Sands said, "Let's start with this one." While Angelina was writing, Mr. Sands asked who could remember the two suffixes the class had discussed. AJ waited for Angelina to look up before she interpreted the question. In the meantime, by the time Angelina saw the question interpreted, Mr. Sands was already writing the answer on the board. Even though Angelina gave the right answer, AJ chose not to interpret Angelina's signed response into spoken English. Since Mr. Sands was already writing the answer, Angelina's delayed response would have been out of place. Although AJ relied on multiple strategies to alleviate competing demands for Angelina's visual attention, there is much more than meets the eye. In this case, the complexity and depth of AJ's decision making comes to light by looking at what was happening when AJ chose not to interpret and by examining the rationale behind the interactions between AJ and Angelina.

In several instances, Angelina signed comments that AJ chose not to interpret into spoken English. AJ simply watched as Angelina covered her eyes and fingerspelled W-A-R-D, signed that it was a hard suffix to remember and practice fingerspelling, fingerspelled B-E-W-A-R-D, clapped her hand over her mouth, and fingerspelled T-O-W-A-R-D. In each case, AJ praised Angelina by saying, "Good job!" or by nodding and smiling to confirm that Angelina's responses were correct. When Angelina fingerspelled an incorrect answer, AJ gently corrected Angelina, emphasizing that the word she was thinking of was *beware* spelled with an *e* at the end. Angelina's response hints at embarrassment at getting the word wrong, even though only AJ knew what had happened. AJ simply redirected Angelina by explicitly asking if she could think of another word. When Angelina indicated she could not and Mr. Sands repeated the question, AJ interpreted the question again, this time using discourse cues to direct the question to all of the students so Angelina would not feel singled out and on the spot. AJ recognized Angelina was trying to participate in the activity and respond to her teacher's request for words with the suffix *ward*. However, she chose not to interpret Angelina's comments about the suffix or her incorrect responses. In addition, when Angelina did come up with a correct answer, AJ still chose not to interpret. In fact, Angelina did not have an opportunity to participate directly in the discussion until she raised her hand and was called on to respond. AJ honored Angelina's choice to give her answer in spoken English and initially did not interpret the spoken response. When Mr. Sands indicated that he had not heard the response, AJ prompted Angelina to say it again. Rather than ask her to say *toward* a third time, AJ then repeated the word for the benefit of Mr. Sands when he remained silent and leaned forward to indicate he still hadn't caught it. Closer examination of the rationale behind AJ's decisions not to interpret many of Angelina's signed questions or comments illuminates another critical set of overlapping factors that complicate the work and decisions of educational interpreters.

Recognizing Student Discourse Cues and Communicative Intent

AJ explained that discourse cues are crucial when she determines whether or not to interpret students' signed comments and questions into spoken English. She told me that she makes her decisions based on "the rules of the language. So, if she looks at me and kind of [signs] in a low space, like in a one-on-one conversation space, then I feel like it's just to me. But if she's looking *not* at me, if she's looking to the class or looking to the teacher and signing it sort of bigger, like to the bigger space, then that to me would *definitely* be, "Shout this out. I'm shouting this out," as opposed to just telling you. Marina concurred that discourse cues were important to consider when deciding whether or not to interpret what Kristie signed into spoken English. "If it's related to the signs, like it has nothing to do with the rest of the class, you know, it's just between me communicating with her, I don't voice that. If it's something that I can tell—she turns her body pretty clearly and says something—you know, she is looking at [Kate] behind her, and she is trying to get her attention and ask her about something. I'll say, '[Kate], do you have a pencil I can borrow?' or whatever."

In addition to discourse cues, AJ discussed other factors she takes into account when deciding whether and when to interpret signed questions and comments into spoken English. She described the potential harm of choosing not to interpret what a Deaf or hard of hearing student signs. She said, "I've struggled with it for a long time. I always wonder, you know, am I shutting this person down? Am I . . . not shutting them down, but, am I . . . further separating them from the classroom and from the teacher by doing that? I don't know. I struggle with it because I don't know." However, she felt that the benefits of taking a conservative approach far outweighed the potential risks. She explained, "I would rather err on the side of not voicing in case they don't [intend it]. Because I think that's a lesser error than shouting out something that the student doesn't want voiced. I think that's humiliating and embarrassing and punishing and I would not do that. That would be my last choice because of those results." She discussed the importance of trust between interpreters and Deaf students. "I guess I'd rather err on the side of assuming it's for *me* than assuming it's for the class and it ends up being sort of a betrayal. In my experience, when people do want it voiced and I didn't voice it, they'll tell me. They'll just say, 'Tell them' and then I just do. And then you can fix it. But once you've said something that wasn't intended, you can't fix that."

According to AJ, the potential severity of the consequences of the decision to interpret into spoken English so everyone can hear when communication is intended to be private outweighs the potential negative consequences of the decision not to interpret into spoken English. However, the fact that failure to interpret into spoken English could inhibit inclusion and membership is cause for alarm. This realization should serve as a reminder for interpreters to be on the lookout for other opportunities to promote inclusion through participation and social interactions.

Evening the Playing Field: Responding Directly to Students

Only two of the four Deaf and hard of hearing students participating in this study routinely raised their hands to respond when their teachers asked questions. The other two frequently signed their answers to the interpreter and only occasionally volunteered a response publicly unless the teacher called on them specifically or when all of the students were expected to participate in turn. Three of the four students frequently checked their answers with the interpreter while or prior to raising their hands. Sometimes the interpreters would give an indication of whether or not the response was correct. In other instances, the interpreters would shrug or explicitly encourage the student to reply publicly to the teacher. The fourth student in this study responded almost exclusively to the interpreter, and then only when she asked him questions directly.

Interpreters discussed the importance not only of student readiness for independence and participation, but also of building trust and rapport with Deaf and hard of hearing students. AJ explained that decisions about whether to interpret into spoken English or respond directly to students' questions are influenced by additional factors. As AJ watched the video of herself at work, she called attention to what happened when Angelina fingerspelled the word *toward*. She exclaimed that the "first time she just told me, which was why I thought that was for me. And *this* time, she raised her hand. She wanted the *teacher* to respond to her, but she also *checked* with me, and maybe it's because the first time she didn't get it right. And how I could tell she was checking with me—she had her hand raised, but she looked at me, fingerspelled the word she was going to say, and I said, "Yes, that's right," and so she kept her hand raised.

AJ shared additional reasons that she was willing to allow students to check their answers with her before the replied publicly. She said, "I think, especially with these Deaf kids in these hearing classrooms, it's already a tough fit. They already are going to have a harder time fitting in because they're not like everybody else. . . . So if *they* want to check with me first, I think that's part of the support of them being out there. They get a chance to check their answer before they put themselves out there in front of their whole class." These types of judgment calls are made on a daily basis by K–12 interpreters who strive to even the playing field in a context designed for hearing students.

To complicate matters further, Deaf and hard of hearing students are operating within a bilingual context, often acquiring and learning English as well as sign language in addition to academic content. When Angelina fingerspelled B-E-W-A-R-E, rather than interpreting into spoken English, AJ signed that the response was incorrect and provided clarification that they were looking for words with the suffix *ward*. AJ explained that along with recognizing student discourse cues and intent, and understanding that Deaf and hard of hearing students often have a harder time fitting in, her recognition that Deaf and hard of hearing students are often learning English as a second language influenced her decision about whether or not to interpret into spoken English. She explained that Angelina "gave out the answer, *beware*. But really he is looking for words that end in *ward*. So I just corrected her myself instead of spitting her answer out to the class . . . because for me I guess it's sort of an English thing. It's her second language and it just saves her from saying a word that's incorrect in front of the class."

It may appear that AJ's repeated decision not to interpret might preclude Angelina's opportunity to participate in the class discussion. However, Angelina still had the opportunity to call out her response and, in a way, be held accountable by having the interpreter to serve as a witness or audience. In addition, AJ recognized Angelina's unique language needs and lack of opportunity to fully participate in academic and social interactions in K–12 schools, evening the playing field by serving as a sounding board, providing correction and guidance, and being someone for Angelina to talk to. Contrary to shutting Angelina down and thereby relegating Angelina's school identity to one of passive learning, which AJ was afraid of doing, AJ deliberately cultivated opportunities for Angelina to participate actively in class discussions.

Camie and AJ had each devised a sequence of steps to cultivate opportunities for participation. In addition to prompting students to interact directly with teachers and peers, they responded directly to students' questions, participated in social conversations, and repeated or clarified information that had already been interpreted. They also encouraged students directly, providing positive reinforcement for correct answers and gentle guidance for incorrect responses. To facilitate opportunities for Deaf and hard of hearing students to participate publicly in class discussions, they relied on an elaborate sequence of steps to compensate for lost time and ensure students were ready to raise their hand along with their classmates. They relied on visual resources and predictions of where a lesson was headed, assessed and determined student readiness to respond, made principled and strategic decisions about what to omit from the interpretation, and they prompted Deaf and hard of hearing students to raise their hands at exactly the right time. If the Deaf or hard of hearing student was not called on, the interpreters would begin the sequence again.

5. IN SEARCH OF BETTER OPTIONS: WHEN INTERPRETERS DO NOT KNOW WHAT TO DO

All three of the interpreters I observed met some widely recognized level of qualification and had demonstrated interpreting experience and education (see Chapter 4 for interpreter profiles and individual qualifications). Nevertheless, they—as well as the other interpreters who participated in the study—admitted not always being sure about what to do or being equipped to interpret every situation they encountered. One interpreter who initially agreed to participate subsequently withdrew when the first observation included a lesson on homophones, stating that she did not feel comfortable interpreting the subject matter. Five of six educational interpreters who initially agreed to participate expressed uncertainty about whether or not their approach was the "right thing to do" or "what other educational interpreters do." They asked what I would do or what I thought they should do. One (reflecting his recognition of the lack of status awarded to K–12 interpreters in comparison to interpreters certified by RID and/or NAD) asked what "real interpreters do." I myself observed interpreters in various situations that exceeded their level of expertise.

The Struggle to Optimize Visual Access

During the volcano lesson, as Mr. Harrison used a laser pointer to refer to locations on the world map on the back wall of the room, Camie eventually found an appropriate place to stand. It was not until her sixth position that Camie found a place where Emily could see and Camie did not block other students' view or the laser pointer. However, Camie did not make a decision to move until more than 6½ minutes after Mr. Harrison first used the laser pointer. During that time, she struggled to direct Emily's attention to the right place at the right time. Complicating the issue was the fact that even if Camie chose to interpret a particular concept, she had to stop when Emily looked away. Naturally, whenever the students around her looked back toward the map, Emily looked too. In so doing, whatever Camie was signing was lost. Moreover, Mr. Harrison's visual referents were missed several times. For example, he explained, "Magma has risen up through the continental crust, through the lithosphere and is extruding pyroclastic material." After Camie interpreted that magma came through the continental crust, she pointed to the back of the room, directing Emily's visual attention to the map. By the time Emily turned to look, Mr. Harrison had turned off the laser. Emily looked back to Camie, who explained apologetically that he had turned the laser off. Camie tried a variety of strategies, each to no avail. She tried pointing and waiting, summarizing information whenever possible. She tried changing the sequence, but when she was interpreting, Emily looked away to follow the gaze of her classmates. She used specific names of geographic locations and geological features, which worked to some degree, but left Emily without the opportunity to see and be reminded of where each was located.

In spite of Camie's willingness to move in other situations in order to create clear sightlines, several factors converged to contribute to her reluctance to move in this particular instance. First of all, because of the physical layout of the room, the shelving, and the seating arrangement, there simply was not a good place for Camie to stand. Another constraining factor was Camie's lack of ability to predict how long Mr. Harrison would be referring to the map. In the meantime, he also told students to look at his hands to demonstrate another phenomenon. Because he was at the front of the room and the map was at the back of the room, this added yet another visual referent to further complicate the situation. In addition, students were looking at their worksheets as well as their textbooks (and Emily was also supposed to be watching the interpreter), so Camie had to prioritize between several sources of visual input (the interpretation, the map, the book, and the worksheet that Emily had at her desk, and Mr. Harrison). Emily made her own contribution to the choreography when she looked away from the interpretation (often in the middle of a sentence) because her classmates looked to the back of the room en masse.

Camie finally chose to stand 6 minutes and 20 seconds later when Mr. Harrison said, "I think I'd rather you look there [at the map] instead of the book" and pointed with his laser to the map at the back of the room. Although she stood and could visibly be seen considering her options, she did not move yet. After another round of visual ping pong, Camie finally chose to move to the back of the room. However, Camie's conundrum became immediately apparent upon her arrival, as she chose positions that blocked Mr. Harrison's laser pointer, Emily's view, and other students' views. In her haste to get out of everyone's way, Camie even retreated to a previous location that did not allow Camie herself to see the map and the laser pointer. Finally, Camie crossed to the opposite side of the room and stood to the left side of the map. She pressed herself close to a bookshelf and reached to point at the locations on the map when they were most relevant to the interpretation (several seconds after Mr. Harrison had pointed them out with the laser). The position that she finally settled on may not have worked as well if Camie were not tall. A shorter interpreter would have had to stand closer to the map and very likely blocked the view of at least a few students. It took nearly 8½ minutes for Camie to find a location from which she could effectively direct Emily's visual attention. By the time she did so, Mr. Harrison was ready to put away the laser pointer for good (less than 1 minute later).

The Struggle to Facilitate Learning of Content and Language

Besides the difficulty of alleviating competing demands for Deaf and hard of hearing students' visual attention, Camie also described her struggle to interpret subject matter that was more challenging for her to understand. She reported being mentally and physically drained because of the amount of effort expended while interpreting back-to-back social studies and science lectures. Furthermore, she lacked confidence in her ability to interpret them clearly. She reported, "The lectures are frustrating. I think that's when I really just get totally exhausted . . . because I feel like I'm out of my element, so I'm trying to focus that much more, and trying to get the concept down, and it's just taking that much more energy." She described, "When it comes to P.E. time, I'm just like, [slumps over in feigned exhaustion, then laughs], because social studies and science are back-to-back."

In one day, Camie tutored Emily in mathematical concepts, worked with Emily to help her read and understand a story from her literature book, interpreted an audio recording about ancient Chinese civilizations, and interpreted a language arts lesson that focused on adjectives, words with positive versus negative connotations, commonly confused words like *later* and *latter,* and homophones. After lunch, she interpreted Mr. Harrison's review of answers to directed reading worksheets on volcanoes before interpreting a DVD about volcanoes. She then interpreted the rules of flag football for Emily's P.E. class, saying that by that time, interpreting P.E. was "a lot more fun! I mean, there again, she says, 'Nice juke!' I'm like, 'What's that?' I don't know what that means! [Laughs.] I don't know this football lingo!"

Because of Camie's own lack of confidence regarding the quality of her interpretations of science and social studies lectures, she checked in more frequently with Emily. However, Camie lamented that even if Emily indicated that she did not understand, Camie would not necessarily be equipped to explain the concept more clearly. She elaborated, "I would question my abilities as to whether I could explain it to her in a better or more efficient way for her to understand it because I'm not so sure *I* really understand it." She said she frequently asked Mr. Harrison to clarify and was grateful that he was always willing to elaborate. When I asked what she does when she suspects that Emily is not understanding the content, she said that she would have to follow up the next day during their tutoring session. However, she felt that Emily would be disadvantaged because the information would not be as "fresh" or relevant at that time.

Marina also struggled to interpret a science lesson effectively. She floundered while trying to interpret a lecture on wind, air pressure, and temperature. The interpretation was incomplete as well as inaccurate. Marina began to use incorrect signs that she had used correctly during previous observations. Moreover, sentences were grammatically inaccurate and incomplete. In addition, she struggled with decisions about where to direct students' visual attention, giving conflicting messages by pointing to indicate that they should look at the teacher who was showing how to make a barometer, then immediately waving to get their attention in order to interpret. Although the interview ended before she could explain what had happened, it is clear that interpreting the lesson was beyond her current level of expertise.

Before interpreters can even begin to identify an equivalent meaning in ASL, they must be able to understand the content. Interpreters with college degrees may be more likely to successfully negotiate the academic language of school contexts; however, even these interpreters who did hold college degrees had strengths and weaknesses when it came to their own academic competencies. In addition, their linguistic proficiencies and interpreting expertise significantly affected the quality of the interpretation. The task of not only clearly conveying academic content and the meaning of specialized vocabulary but also making explicit connections between a signed interpretation and key English terminology can be daunting. Moreover, the content of instruction, as well as the mode and rate of delivery, were often detrimental to interpreting effectiveness.

All of the interpreters in this study attempted to make connections between signed concepts and English words and phrases throughout many lessons and across subject areas, but sometimes they did not have enough time to make those connections as explicit as they would have liked. I observed AJ's work for a day and a half, less than time than I was able to observe any of the other interpreters. During that time, she was able to maintain control of the interpretation and convey the information accurately. However, in some cases, she was forced to make compromises.

During language arts, Mr. Sands went through a list of suffixes written on the board. AJ first directed Angelina's attention to the board as Mr. Sands pointed to each word and allowed enough time for Angelina to read it. As he used each of the words in a sentence, AJ fingerspelled each word and paired it with a semantically equivalent ASL interpretation of meaning. As Mr. Sands increased his rate of delivery and hurried through a list of suffixes written on the board, AJ adapted her interpreting style by reducing the number of ways that she represented the information. Instead of directing Angelina's attention, fingerspelling the word, and then interpreting the meaning of the word, she changed her approach. In response to the increased pace, she stopped fingerspelling each word. She still directed Angelina's attention to the board and allowed her enough time to read each word as Mr. Sands pointed. This appeared to be a coping strategy rather than what AJ would have ideally continued to do had more time been available. In other words, a more effective interpretation was sacrificed in the interest of keeping up with the teacher's increased rate of delivery.

In this situation, AJ reverted to simply optimizing Angelina's visual access rather than also making explicit connections between ASL and English. Several factors aligned to make this a valid choice. First, Angelina was doing well in the class and was reading as well as her classmates. Second, Mr. Sands wore a wireless microphone that amplified his voice for Angelina, helping her to hear some of what he said. If Angelina had not been reading at grade level or was not doing well, AJ might not have been as willing to compromise or may have determined that another course of action (such as interrupting and asking Mr. Sands to repeat or slow down, or perhaps following up with Mr. Sands at the end of the school day) was necessary. In fact, the resulting interpretation still seemed to work based on Angelina's continued participation in class discussion and activities. In other cases, meeting the language and learning needs of Deaf and hard of hearing students proved to be extremely difficult.

Whether a student's lack of understanding was due to ineffective interpretation or the student's language and learning needs, interpreters made choices to fill in the gaps. Especially when interpreters perceived that the learning situation was unfair, interpreters reported that the equitable choice was to even the playing field. For example, if they attributed a lack of knowledge to the fact that students did not have access to the news, radio, and dinner conversations, or access to peer interactions and incidental learning, or exposure to English vocabulary and phonetic cues and clues, interpreters would fill in the gaps. However, it was sometimes difficult for interpreters to determine an adequate level of support that would not provide an unfair advantage.

In one situation, Mr. Harrison was trying to quickly expose students to vocabulary before the upcoming state test. Camie explained that students had to select which of two words was correct in the context of a given sentence, for example, "Terri will [*accept* or *except*] the award by giving a speech." After interpreting the lesson as students were quietly reading at their desks, Camie returned to the worksheet in order to reflect on and determine the most effective way to interpret the sentences without giving away the answer. She said that because the two words are signed differently in ASL, she was not sure how to avoid giving Emily the answer. Camie reported wondering:

> How should I set it up to give her choices about which one is right? I was thinking about it and that's why I was going through that book to see some other examples. I thought maybe I could do, "Terry will accept the award by giving a speech [simultaneously signs TERRY WILL ACCEPT AWARD after pointing at index finger], or, the second one, "Terry will except the award by giving a speech" [pointing at second finger and signing TERRY WILL EXCEPT/SPECIAL AWARD]. So that's what I was doing, going over in my mind how to give it to her without giving her the answer.

Camie took advantage of time when interpreting was not needed to reflect further on how to improve the quality of future interpretations of a similar nature. In this case, she was concerned with how to avoid giving answers away, which would eliminate an opportunity for Emily to participate equally. However, Camie was even more concerned about clarity of meaning and language development than she was concerned about giving Emily an unfair advantage.

Interpreters gave priority to making sure language input was sound and academic content was conveyed clearly, especially when it came to the development of English language skills. Camie discussed some of her concerns pertaining to decisions about interpreting impromptu spelling. On a weekly basis, Mr. Harrison randomly selected words from the students' science textbook and asked students to spell them. Neither Camie nor the students were given a specific list of words in advance. Students lined up across the back of the classroom. When he gave them a word, such as *subterranean,* students who spelled the word incorrectly were asked to sit down. Camie explained:

> When we first started doing these spelling bees, I struggled with [what to do]. I wanted her to be able to see how the other kids were spelling it and why they were getting it wrong and sitting down. So I would copy what they were spelling. I would spell it how they were spelling it, which would be wrong. Eventually, I started thinking—especially for a word like this that I don't think she has ever seen before, nor does she know what it means. So, I give her all of these wrong spellings from all of the kids. . . .Then finally after a while I [began to] say, "This is how you spell the word." Then I will spell it for her [once] the right

way, and then I'll continue on with all of the wrong ones. So she *does* know, "That's how you spell it, but all of these other kids, this is how they are spelling it." So I'm getting it to her how they are spelling it, but I want her to know how you really do spell it.

Although Camie and other interpreters tried to avoid giving students the answers whenever possible, in this case, she decided that Emily's English language development and need to access the correct English spelling were paramount. Camie chose to fingerspell each word correctly once. The rationale for her decision was that the classmates (a) were more likely to have been exposed to the English word and (b) received the benefit of phonetic cues. Because Camie spelled slowly and clearly, Emily was involved in a different task. While her classmates were eliminated for not knowing how to spell a word, Emily was eliminated only if she could not memorize and recall the correct spelling that Camie had provided. Camie's choice might have worked if she had fingerspelled the word rapidly. In this manner, the shapes and patterns of combinations of fingerspelled letters would have been parallel to, and much like, the phonetic cues that hearing students were provided. However, in Camie's effort to create equity, she tipped the scales in favor of Emily.

THE STRUGGLE TO INTERPRET PRINTED TEXT: READ-ALOUD SESSIONS AND DVDS

Perhaps one of the most basic and yet complex decisions K–12 interpreters grapple with emerges when they are faced with printed text: Should they interpret, stop interpreting, and/or intervene in some other manner? Although students could not watch the interpreter and simultaneously follow along with the printed text, interpreters often chose to interpret when the text was relatively short, perhaps only a few sentences in duration. For example, interpreters most often chose to interpret when teachers read worksheet instructions or lists of words written on the board, or when students took turns reading sentences from the board, handouts, or worksheets. However, when visual input was dense, sustained, and/or complex, as was the case with audio recordings of textbooks, passages of books read aloud by students or teachers, and captioned movies, it was not possible for interpreters to effectively interpret and transliterate, much less make effective connections between ASL and English. Interpreters expressed a great deal of conflict and uncertainty about their decisions regarding the interpretation of printed or scripted text.

Camie said that when she first started working with Emily, she tried to interpret all of the text that was read aloud. She said, "As far as interpreting the text or having her read it herself and then me interjecting his comments or whatever else he adds to it, I know that I definitely need to do that." Camie went on to explain that competing visual demands was one of the reasons why her chosen approach changed over time. "I always struggled. . . . because in the beginning of the year, I would sign everything . . . from the book and everything. But the rest of them are supposed to be following along and reading in the book as well, so it was too many places for her to look. Then he'd say, 'Second paragraph,' or whatever. I found it easier to just let her read when they are reading."

Although on the surface, the practice of reading out loud may simply appear to be another competing demand for Deaf and hard of hearing students' visual attention, in reality, there is more for K–12 interpreters to consider. Camie reported she felt it was more beneficial for Emily to see the printed English words in the text than to watch an interpretation of the text. She also explained that Emily would read independently but look up when Mr. Harrison added commentary relevant to the text. However, Camie's expressed uncertainty conveyed a lack of confidence in either approach. It is apparent that an internal conflict existed because she was unable to think of a more effective option.

Camie's own physical health was another factor influencing her decision to stop interpreting text as it was read aloud. Although repetitive motion injuries are common among interpreters who work hours at a time without a team interpreter, K–12 interpreters are often still expected to work alone. None of the three interpreters in this study was given a break. Between classes or class periods, they often talked with Deaf students or teachers, or prepared to interpret an upcoming lesson. Marina was assigned to take a turn monitoring the Deaf and hard of hearing students for the last half of the lunch break. In terms of Camie's decision not to interpret text, she explained, "Another reason that I stopped doing it is because my hands are starting to hurt at the end of the day, to do all of the stories and everything, and all of the textbook [reading]."

Camie gave several reasons for her eventual decision not to interpret when printed or scripted text was delivered in an audible mode. She said that she felt it was easier and, in some cases, more important for Emily to see the words. She lamented that it was "impossible" for Emily to watch the interpreter, look at the book, and simultaneously think about the meaning of words in sentences. In addition, she expressed concern regarding the quality of the interpretation due to mental and physical fatigue. She was anxious and fearful about the possibility of physical repetitive motion injuries (which had already been a problem). In addition, Camie's assessment of her own skill limitations came into play when making decisions about whether or not to interpret text. She explained, "[In] literature I think I can be fairly clear. I start questioning my abilities when you start talking about interpreting text. I just do. I don't know why . . . but when we get into science, and social studies, and ancient civilizations, and China and the Phoenicians, and the way they traveled and traded, I think it's more beneficial for her to read it herself."

In spite of her robust list of rationales, Camie was clearly not confident with a decision not to interpret text. As a matter of fact, in contrast to her stated preference, she almost always interpreted shorter texts, such as printed instructions or sentences on worksheets and other class activities. She also interpreted a captioned DVD on volcanoes. She did, however, stop interpreting as students read aloud from their literature books. Perhaps one of the factors leading Camie to a different decision in the latter case was the fact that students had access to the textbook, whereby the DVD would only be viewed once during class time. Camie was generally reluctant to interpret printed text because neither choice (interpreting or not) was in itself satisfactory, she lacked confidence in her ability to interpret text clearly because of the content and pacing, and she was concerned about physical injury and mental fatigue. However, in spite of Camie's preferred approach not to interpret printed text, Emily's need to access information took precedence over all of the other factors when it came to Camie's decision about interpreting captioned DVDs.

Marina described the difficulty of representing specific English words and phrases while effectively interpreting the meaning using ASL signs. In particular, she emphasized her inability to make connections between ASL and English within the time constraints imposed by printed text being read aloud. She said, "Sometimes it takes more time for me to explain the concept. I can't just go word for word." For example, Marina struggled to convey the meaning of the English word *sparkling* in terms of the expression "a bright sparkling personality." In trying to convey the meaning of a single English word, Marina said, "I signed, 'It's like a good attitude.' I don't know. 'Like a bright sparkle in a person's personality,' and she was like, 'A diamond sparkle?' And I was like, 'No, like a bright personality, like a shiny personality'. She was like, 'Okay.' I don't know if she really connected the word or not. I tried."

Marina recognized that the interpretation of even a single word did not appear to be effective as she tried to use signs that would accurately convey the meaning of the word. Interestingly, the word was somewhat incidental in this particular situation because it was not one that had been called to students' attention as targeted vocabulary. The conversation occurred because Marina had decided to transliterate and adhere more closely to English vocabulary and syntax rather than interpret in ASL. When she heard the idiomatic phrase, she chose to fingerspell *sparkling*, which then led to Kristie asking what it meant in that context. In the meantime, the rest of the class continued with the narrative, much of which was omitted from the interpretation.

Like Camie, Marina also reported that she did not always interpret audible text. Instead, she stated that she gave Kristie the option of reading the captions when DVDs were presented. However, when students read aloud from their literature books and Mrs. Natale read from the science textbook, Marina interpreted. In one case, she said that she interpreted because Kristie looked bored and was not following along, however, this did not appear to account for the differences observed because she did not always wait to see what Kristie would do. These inconsistencies between what Camie and Marina reported that they did in comparison to what they actually did provide evidence that a decision not to interpret text, although easy to justify, was not always perceived as satisfactory.

Although AJ was highly qualified (and exceeded every state's minimum qualification standards) and clearly interpreted throughout the day and a half of observations, she described a situation for which she was unable to interpret effectively. She reported that she was sent to a high school English class as a substitute interpreter. When she arrived, she found that the class had been working on a poem. On this particular day, teams of students were to come to the front of the class and explain the meaning of each line in their assigned stanza. AJ said:

This is the *very first time* I am hearing this poem, and it's *poetry*. So, the kids are up at the board going [AJ makes inarticulate slurring, mumbling sounds, then laughs]. I don't know what they've said, and I haven't read it. I don't know what they're talking about. It's up on the board, but that's not helpful to me at the moment. Because I can't even... *plus* it takes *so much* interpretation. I've got to *have* a minute to be able to even *interpret* it. I can throw the *words* out, but *even then*, they're going a million miles an hour and I don't even know what the *words* are.

AJ outlined several challenges that she encountered when trying to interpret the poem, even though the words were written on the board. She explained that the rate of delivery, her lack of understanding of what the poem was about, and the fact that she could not hear students clearly contributed to an inability to interpret effectively in this situation. At that point, she looked for other options about what to do. She considered the feasibility of using the board, but discarded it in terms of her own use because of her lack of familiarity with the particular poem. Even if she read the words, she recognized that spontaneously interpreting poetry is incredibly difficult.

In this particular case, she was fortunate enough to have been assigned to work with another interpreter who was a staff member at the school and also happened to have recently graduated from an interpreter training program (ITP). Unfortunately, AJ reported that the team interpreter with whom she was working was "apparently of the mentality that when you're not up in the chair [interpreting], you're back there reading a book, so she wasn't there for me at *all*. So I'm like, crap! [Laughs.] Which I mean, I don't know what she would have done to help me anyway. She just needed to be there *instead of* me. She just really needed to be there."

AJ explained that she finally chose to have the Deaf and hard of hearing students read each stanza on the board (which meant she reconsidered the use of the board as a resource from a different perspective). She said that because the students had been working on the poem for several days, "*They* knew it better than *I* did. So I just had them read it because *luckily* it was up on the board. So I just I had them *read* the words and then I interpreted what the kids *said* about it which wasn't as hard. [When the team of two Deaf or hard of hearing students] went up to the front, they spoke for themselves. Thank goodness, because I was a little worried!"

At that point, AJ made another decision. "So [because of] the fact that I haven't been there every day working up to this assignment, I was like, 'Oh, my God.' The girl that *works* there every day, I asked, 'Can you get up here and do this?' because she *knew*, and she did great job with it because she had *been* there. So as a freelance interpreter walking into a setting like that, I felt like an ITP graduate. I couldn't do it." In contrast, AJ reported that her team interpreter, "who *was* a recent ITP graduate," was better prepared to interpret. She added, "I was *so* impressed with her work."

In this situation, lack of familiarity with the content, lack of time to adequately prepare, and lack of support from the team interpreter led AJ to choose a response that she felt was less than ideal. Several factors aligned to make the choice reasonably effective: The students already knew the poem, the poem was written on the board, and the students spoke for themselves rather than signing when it was their turn to present. At that time, AJ took advantage of another resource and asked the less experienced staff interpreter to take her place. If the lesson had continued for longer than a single class period, it might not have been feasible to ask the team interpreter to interpret the whole time by herself.

Although many school districts do not provide team interpreters, this one apparently recognized the fact that physical injury and mental fatigue should be avoided in order to be assured of healthy employees and more accurate interpretations. Unfortunately, the staff interpreter did not remain attentive, but she was willing to switch upon AJ's request. If there had not been a team interpreter, if the students were not familiar with the poem, or if the students did not speak for themselves, this situation would have called for AJ to identify another course of action. For example, she might have done her best to interpret and/or transliterate, or she could have moved her chair closer to point to the poem in one of the students' textbooks so they could read along (if she determined they were reading at grade level). Additionally, she might have subsequently chosen to follow up with the teacher after the lesson, by which time students would have already missed out on the opportunity to access either a clear interpretation or the printed text.

Marina's frustration at not being able to adequately convey the meaning of particular English words and phrases in ASL was echoed by other interpreters, especially when it came to interpreting printed or scripted text that was presented in an audible mode. AJ described the difficulty of interpreting poetry without an opportunity to prepare in advance, reporting that a novice interpreter who was familiar with the poem being discussed was better equipped to interpret effectively than she was as a substitute interpreter hearing the poem for the first time.

READ-ALOUD SESSIONS AND LACK OF ACCOUNTABILITY

Additional problems related to the difficulty of interpreting read-aloud sessions came to light during this investigation. In particular, the task of reading aloud is different for Deaf and hard of hearing students than it is for their hearing peers. When Mr. Harrison interjected commentary and instruction, Camie, like all interpreters in this study, always got Emily's attention and interpreted. For this part of the activity, at least, the experience of Deaf and hard of hearing students was somewhat equivalent to that of their hearing peers. However, it is unclear whether Emily knew exactly which part of the text the commentary made reference to; indeed, it is likely that she did not.

As hearing students took turns reading out loud, they knew at exactly which point Mr. Harrison interrupted to provide further elaboration. Even if Emily was reading at grade level and could keep up with the rest of the class, it is unlikely that the interpreted explanation took place precisely when it was relevant to the portion of the text she had just read. Camie had no way of knowing whether or not Emily had even read that portion of the text yet. Therefore, Emily may or may not have had the opportunity to see the targeted concept or vocabulary word used in context. If she had not read it yet, it is possible that she would recognize the reference when she subsequently read it, but that assumption cannot be made with certainty.

Because of Deaf and hard of hearing students' unique language learning needs, their experience more nearly parallels that of English language learners who are accessing print in a language other than their dominant language. In order to address Emily's language learning needs in the moment, Camie read along and made decisions about English vocabulary and phrases that Emily was less likely to know. Based on Camie's predictions, she then intervened by getting Emily's attention to engage in a dialogue about the English vocabulary or academic concepts that seemed important, in Camie's view, for Emily to know. In so doing, however, Emily had less time to read the text than her hearing classmates, who were for the most part reading text written in their dominant language.

Clearly, Emily's task during read-aloud sessions was more complex than that of her classmates. Not only was she reading the text in a language that she had never heard, she did not have access to her classmates' or her teacher's pronunciation of vocabulary to help her determine meaning. Furthermore, it is doubtful that Mr. Harrison's instructional comments and Camie's explanation of key vocabulary were offered at the time when the explanations would have been most appropriate and relevant.

The rate of delivery and density of information in scripted material were problematic for all of the interpreters in this study to convey.

In addition, other factors such as competing visual demands, student preferences and language abilities, and interpreters' own physical and skill limitations influenced interpreters' decisions about whether and when to interpret printed text. The length and type of the text influenced interpreters' decisions, as did the possibility of alternative options for subsequent follow up. Furthermore, AJ described that a lack of opportunity to prepare to interpret poetry or other literary works (such as when working as a substitute, or when teachers spontaneously decide to bring in additional material) makes it exceptionally difficult to interpret effectively. Whether choosing to stop interpreting or continue interpreting, interpreters remained on deck, monitored class interactions and student work, offered guidance and support, remained attentive to student needs, and responded to requests for help, clarification, or validation. However, interpreters' uncertainty and lack of consistency in their chosen approach suggest that the prevalence of the practice of read-aloud activities in mainstream classrooms presents a barrier to inclusion that interpreters are ill-equipped to alleviate.

The Struggle to Tutor Effectively: Developing Reading and Language Skills

All of the interpreters in this study reported unsuccessful attempts to clearly interpret printed text, especially for students who were not proficient readers. Because Camie had the option of subsequently working on literature with Emily during one-on-one tutoring sessions, her decision not to interpret literature may have been appropriate. However, she reported that education and training specific to K–12 interpreting had significantly impacted her work and decisions. Camie's approach to working on literature and reading during designated tutoring time changed significantly after working with Emily for a year and a half. Camie described the revised tutoring process she had designed for working with Emily to help her not only with her reading, but also with her English and ASL skills. First, Camie watched as Emily signed a narrative from her literature book. Rather than frequently interrupting when Emily did not use the correct sign for a concept, Camie simply underlined the word in her own copy of the book. Next, Emily would look up each word in the dictionary and write the words and their definitions on a piece of paper. Finally, Camie and Emily would discuss the meaning of particular words and phrases by using sign language.

Camie explained that the convergence of two factors led to the decision to change her approach. First, Camie was at the end of her second year of a specialized interpreting program designed for K–12 interpreters. The second factor influencing Camie's decision to change her approach to working on the development of Emily's reading skills was Camie's recognition of Emily's readiness to do more than simply sign each word in the story. In order to engage in this type of activity, and for Emily to have a meaningful reading experience, Camie needed to be able to recognize not only different levels of expertise in reading, but also language fluency in both English and ASL. It was only through specialized training that Camie came to realize that signing words without regard for meaning is no more than simple decoding and is unrelated to either reading comprehension or appropriate language use. Once Camie had a more accurate understanding of learning objectives that were specifically tailored to Emily's unique language needs, Camie was able to guide Emily to a deeper level of learning.

It is important to note that until Camie had received specialized training regarding tutoring, learning, and language development, she was unaware of the need to make such explicit connections. Even with all her interpreting experience and high assessment scores, she was not well informed about Deaf and hard of hearing students' unique language and learning needs until she received specialized training. Although an interpreter may not be the ideal choice to provide reading support for Deaf and hard of hearing students, clearly someone who is a fluent bilingual and understands the difference between signing words and comprehending them must be available to monitor and work with students on a regular basis.

Difficulties Cultivating Opportunities for Participation and Promoting Inclusion

In accordance with the common initiation–response–evaluation/ feedback (IRE/IRF) pattern of academic discourse identified by Cazden (1998) and earlier work by Mehan (1979), teachers in this study initiated the cycle by asking a question, which was usually interpreted. However, because of timing delays and differences in communication modes, Deaf and hard of hearing students rarely had the opportunity to respond to the teacher. Instead, the sequence continued with students signing their answers to the interpreter. The evaluation portion of the cycle was parallel to the teacher's discourse if it was applicable to the student's signed response. For example, if the student who was called on gave the correct answer and the teacher said, "Right! Good job!" interpreters would do the same (often while looking directly at the Deaf or hard of hearing student rather than the hearing student who had replied to the teacher). If the student who was called on gave an incorrect answer and the teacher provided further clarification, the interpreter would interpret the clarification. However, sometimes when the Deaf or hard of hearing student gave an incorrect reply and the hearing student replied correctly, the interpreters would take ownership of the evaluation phase of the sequence and provide additional correction or guidance themselves.

In spite of AJ and Camie's frequent and diligent efforts to encourage participation, most of Angelina's and Emily's responses were private. They simply did not get called upon as often as their classmates. To compensate for this reality, all three of the interpreters responded to students' privately rendered responses. Whether conscious of the rationale (as in AJ's case), or because all three interpreters were products of the educational system in this country and therefore had internalized the prevalent I-R-E sequence of classroom discourse, all three interpreters felt it was crucial for students to respond in some way rather than not at all. While they recognized its value, it should not be mistaken for the ideal. True inclusion and full participation would mean Deaf and hard of hearing students are able to participate equally. During this study, in accordance with many previous studies, Deaf and hard of hearing students rarely had the opportunity to participate, in spite of interpreters' best efforts.

Besides question-and-answer sessions and other class discussions, participation was restricted in two primary areas: (a) read-aloud sessions and (b) social interactions. For example, on a weekly basis, Mr. Harrison's students recited a poem that they had been asked to memorize the previous week. Emily leafed through her notebook as her classmates stood and recited a poem by Wordsworth. Although their classmates took turns reading aloud from handouts, literary works, and passages from text books, none of the Deaf or hard of hearing students were asked by their teachers to take a turn reading. Furthermore, other than Angelina (who chose to use spoken English during class) none of the Deaf or hard of hearing students even raised their hands to volunteer during the course of these observations, in spite of teachers' diligence in making sure "every" student had the opportunity to participate. In fact, although read-aloud activities were observed several times a day, there was only one isolated instance of any Deaf or hard of hearing student actively participating in a read-aloud activity during the course of my observations.

Students in Mrs. Natale's fifth grade class were reading a historical fiction story called *Elena*. Using a microphone (as was her general practice), Mrs. Natale gave a brief introduction before reading the first paragraph aloud. When Mrs. Natale was done reading, she gave the microphone to Zachary. She instructed him to read a paragraph and then pass the mic to Shelby, who had not read yet. During this "popcorn reading" activity, in which students are asked to call upon each other for a turn to read, Mrs. Natale repeatedly asked students who had not read yet to raise their hands and directed the students who had just read to choose one who had not read yet. Neither of the two Deaf students in this class raised their hands when the teacher asked who had not read yet. Eventually, Devin handed the microphone to Kristie. Without hesitation, Kristie placed it on her desk and looked at the interpreter. Marina picked the book up from her lap, leaned slightly forward towards Kristie, smiled and gave her a slight nod. At that time, Kristie signed as Marina read out loud from the book, following along in her own copy of the book as Kristie signed.

Marina relied on the printed text to produce a spoken English equivalent for the class. Since no two languages are exactly alike, Marina based her spoken English interpretation on the English text so the interpretation would be consistent with the hearing students' and Mrs. Natale's expectations of what they should hear when students read aloud. Matching Kristie's timing required Marina to hold the book and divide her visual attention between Kristie's signing and the printed text. Kristie's accuracy or fluency as a reader was obviously not the point of being able to read aloud, since Mrs. Natale only heard Marina reading from the text and the interpretation could not accurately reflect either student comprehension or reading errors. The learning objectives of this lesson were not clear, and although Kristie was actively involved by taking her first turn to read for the class, her participation was not being monitored in any way. No discussion took place during or after this activity between Mrs. Natale and Marina to identify possible means of accountability and options for correction, such as providing the correct sign when Kristie made semantic errors while reading aloud in sign language.

An additional factor unique to this situation was Mrs. Natale and her students' use of the microphone. Marina did not use the microphone when Kristie was reading aloud, stating as rationale that she felt she could project loudly enough to be heard clearly. In my opinion, she did not project loudly enough to be heard clearly; however, since all of the students and the teacher were following along in the book, they still had access to the text. The choice to pick up the microphone might have been less noticeable in terms of the volume differential between student readers, but it would have given Marina one more item to manage. She would have had to hold the microphone in an appropriate position near her mouth while simultaneously holding the book to follow along with the printed text. Along with being cumbersome to hold the microphone in the correct place near her mouth and hold the book where she could read it and still see Kristie would have been difficult enough. However, Marina also had to divide her visual and cognitive attention between the printed text and Kristie's signs.

Although popcorn reading had been a frequent class practice during the previous seven months, Kristie had never before been given the opportunity to read. According to Marina, the student who gave Kristie the microphone was a class clown, and Marina believed Devin gave Kristie the microphone to see what would happen because video cameras were there to record class interactions for this study. Interestingly, during an interview two days later, Marina reported that in the two school days following the popcorn reading scenario, Kristie had raised her hand and had been called on to read aloud several times. Marina exclaimed, "Before yesterday she wasn't raising her hand, and she never had the floor. I don't know if she never had the confidence to do it, not realizing that I'll just voice whatever she signs."

In addition, Marina said that Kristie had been trying to persuade Miguel to volunteer to read. When Miguel resisted, Marina defended him to Kristie explaining that he did not have to volunteer to read if he was not yet ready. Although Kristie was arguably engaged in a different task than her classmates, this example provides a compelling argument that Deaf and hard of hearing students are not automatically included simply because a sign language interpreter is present. Whether the goal of read-aloud sessions is participation, the development of reading fluency, or comprehension of content, the existence of competing visual demands and the lack of clear learning objectives specific to the needs of Deaf and hard of hearing students are likely to result in exclusion.

The participation of Deaf and hard of hearing students was frequently and severely limited, in spite of interpreters' best efforts. Students were at an extreme disadvantage when it came to participating actively and fully in class and group discussions, they were regularly excused from read-aloud activities, and even when given the opportunity to read, there were no support structures in place to monitor and improve their reading skills at the time of the reading. In addition, social interactions between Deaf and hard of hearing students and their hearing peers were rare. Except for Kristie and Miguel, Deaf and hard of hearing students interacted socially with interpreters more frequently than they did their peers.

Because Kristie and Miguel were mainstreamed together for some classes, they were able to talk to each other frequently during transitions between class activities, during group projects, on the way in and out of class, and even during class. When Miguel was not present, Kristie interacted more frequently with the interpreter than with anyone else. For all four students, most of their in-class interactions with their peers were limited to those explicitly assigned by a teacher, such as working in pairs or groups. However, even when Miguel was assigned to work with a group in social studies, he watched what they had to say, but his comments and questions were directed to the interpreter.

The Struggle to Make Effective Interactional Decisions

Interactions between interpreters and classroom teachers were both frequent and essential. The interpreters said, however, that development of rapport and a good working relationship was not always intuitive. For example, Camie described that she was initially unprepared for how to interact with a boisterous P.E. teacher. She explained that the P.E. teacher

> likes to give me a hard time. It's like, she lives for seventh period P.E. so she can make me suffer. So I just play along with it, and I scream back at her or whatever, which the kids all think it's funny, so it works. It's not like we're really screaming at each other. But in the beginning though, I have to say, I didn't know how to handle it. Because she would do things that I thought were totally unprofessional. And I would look at her like, "Okay, I'm not used to that kind of behavior. I don't know what to do with that."

Although Camie reported having an excellent working relationship with Mr. Harrison, she told stories about some of the things he had done that made her feel as if he did not respect her professionally. Camie's decisions about how to interact with various classroom teachers were not based on skills she had learned during her education; instead, she relied on her instincts to develop rapport and resolve interpersonal conflicts. AJ substantiated the importance of being sensitive to teachers' needs and styles. In addition, even with her extensive background, she was admitted to not always being sure what the teacher wanted. Because she was a substitute, she relied on her knowledge of academic norms not only from her own educational experiences, but also from working with an array of other teachers; she said that teachers' attitudes towards Deaf and hard of hearing students greatly influenced her decisions about how and when to approach teachers regarding access issues.

Even interpreters who had been working with the same teachers for several months had few opportunities to collaborate, and certainly not on a regularly scheduled basis. Instead, quick interactions took place as needed, immediately prior to, during, and/or after class activities and squeezed in between lessons.

Interpreters were not always certain about appropriate roles and boundaries when it came to their interactions with Deaf and hard of hearing students. For example, it was difficult for interpreters to decide the degree to which they should redirect students who were not paying attention. All of the interpreters made different choices regarding when and to what extent they should redirect students' visual attention, especially when the student clearly indicated a desire to focus her attention elsewhere. When Angelina chose to work ahead of her classmates and was completing a worksheet correctly, AJ alternated between waving to get Angelina's attention and interpreting what Mr. Sands said, responding to Angelina's direct questions and providing guidance as well as reinforcement, and continuing to interpret without any expectation that Angelina would watch.

Camie explained the tension between choosing when to let Emily keep reading or work ahead and when to interrupt her in order to interpret what Mr. Harrison was saying. She clarified when she might interrupt by explaining, "Usually if it's something that [Emily] really needs to pay attention to, then I tell her, 'Hey, he really wants you to pay attention,' or, 'He wants everybody to know this.' I just do what I think is best. I don't know if it is, but I think I am." Camie's uncertainty about whether she always made the right choice about getting Emily's attention is clear. She used her judgment to let Emily know if the teacher was working hard to get everyone's attention or if it was information that she would be held accountable for, such as information that would be covered during state testing. However, as previously described, when Emily had made up her mind to not pay attention, Camie respected Emily's choice (albeit reluctantly). In that case, even though stakes were high because Mr. Harrison was providing definitions of words similar to those likely to appear during state testing, Camie tried several times to redirect Emily's attention. When Emily persisted in working on her spelling and Camie was sure Emily knew that she was missing something likely to be on the state tests, she stopped interpreting and allowed Emily to continue to work uninterrupted.

Camie and Marina both talked about feeling frustrated when teachers did not hold Deaf and hard of hearing students to the same behavioral standards as hearing students. They suggested that Deaf and hard of hearing students' off-task behavior was less likely to be noticed by the teacher, often because the behavior did not involve noise (such as the chatter of hearing students). Another reason that teachers overlooked Deaf and hard of hearing students' off-task behaviors is likely attributable to the fact that interpreters and students interacted regularly. Because discussions occurred frequently, even as teachers continued to deliver instruction, it would be difficult for teachers who do not know sign language to recognize which interactions were integral to the process of interpreting (e.g., discussions regarding content or the interpreting process and preferences) and which were not. Therefore, although interpreters wanted teachers to hold Deaf and hard of hearing students accountable to the same behavioral standards as their hearing peers, they did not appear to recognize that teachers were very likely unaware of the situation and would remain so unless the interpreters initiated a dialogue.

In contrast to situations in which interpreters felt the equitable choice was to fill in the gaps and even the playing field, when students' lack of understanding was due to their own choice not to pay attention, interpreters chose not to fill in the gaps in understanding. In contrast to those situations in which interpreters perceived that the learning situation was unfair and reported that the equitable choice was to even the playing field, when students were off-task, all three of the interpreters in this study ultimately let students suffer the consequences of their own decisions. However, the frequency and length of attempts to redirect off-task students depended on another multilayered level of analysis. Interpreters first assessed what Deaf and hard of hearing students knew and were able to do in comparison to their hearing peers. Next, they attempted to direct students' visual attention to the interpretation or other source of salient visual input. Third, they made sure students knew what was being missed. At that point, interpreters' decisions appeared to differ according to personal preference and bias, such as a belief that students could do better if they tried harder.

Interpreters working in K–12 classrooms do far more than we have recognized thus far. As is true of all interpreters, they must think critically as they simultaneously listen to and analyze the source message for meaning and function; consider a host of additional factors regarding context, language, and culture; and engage in the inherently cognitively demanding task of interpreting. In addition, K–12 interpreters must monitor and assess Deaf and hard of hearing students' visual needs along with additional language and learning needs. Moreover, interpreters seek to cultivate opportunities for active participation and true inclusion.

Chapter 6

What Remains to Be Seen

Although many Deaf and hard of hearing children access education through interpreters, research on educational interpreters is scant and has focused on revealing inadequacies of underqualified interpreters rather than examining exactly what it is that qualified interpreters do. This volume provides the most thorough description to date of what K–12 interpreters do and what factors inform their decisions. My examination of interpreters at work and in interviews revealed the complexity of classroom interpreting. While educational interpreters certainly (a) interact with others and (b) interpret or transliterate, they also (c) assess and respond to a complexity of contextual, situational, and human factors. Moreover, interpreters (d) seek and capitalize on resources needed to do their jobs more effectively. Finally, K–12 interpreters (e) take on additional responsibilities as situations arise and needs present themselves. Furthermore, what interpreters do is largely affected by what is going on at any given moment.

Based on my observations, I chose to focus on what interpreters do in response to contextual, situational, and human factors relating to just three desired objectives for the students with whom they worked: optimizing visual access, promoting learning of language and content, and cultivating opportunities for participation and inclusion. I did not include myriad additional factors likely to affect interpreters' decisions, such as working with teachers who are not as open to adjusting their teaching styles or working with Deaf and hard of hearing students who have more serious social, cognitive, linguistic, or behavioral issues. Neither did I address how Deaf and hard of hearing students might participate fully in social interactions with their peers outside of the classroom and in extracurricular activities. Much still remains to be seen about the roles interpreters play. What is clear, however is that educational interpreters need specialized knowledge and skills in order to meet the unique visual as well as language and learning needs of Deaf and hard of hearing students. Additional support structures and systems must be put into place if the promise of inclusion is ever to become more than merely a promise.

Much has been written about the illusion of inclusion, especially in regard to the lack of interpreter qualifications (Jones, 1993; La Bue, 1998; Russell, 2006; Schick et al., 2006), but also in terms of power dynamics (Glickman, 2003), social implications (Power & Hyde, 2002) and accessibility of the school context and academic discourse (Ramsey, 1997; Winston, 1994, 2004). "Philosophically, inclusion implies more than mainstreaming. Inclusion refers to full membership in a regular classroom" (Seal, 2004, p. 1). Many Deaf and hard of hearing students attend regular classrooms with interpreters, yet concerns about the efficacy of an interpreter-mediated education remain.

Certainly the school experiences of Deaf and hard of hearing students working with interpreters are far different than those of their peers. According to Kurz and Langer (2004), "A constellation of factors has to be properly aligned to achieve adequate access to education through an interpreter. Even if that alignment were achieved, these participants are quite aware that they still would not have equal access to education because of inherent alterations associated with the interpreting process" (p. 11).

The popcorn-reading scenario is one of several school situations I observed in which inclusion and equal access were not achieved. Certainly, participation is of the utmost importance. Students who do not have the opportunity to participate regularly are likely to become observers, relegated further and further from the core of the classroom interactions and school culture. Educational interpreters must avoid making decisions that contribute to the creation of discourse patterns and expectations in which the Deaf or hard of hearing student becomes a passive learner, in danger of drifting further away from her classmates both socially and academically.

Creating change in the learning experience of Deaf and hard of hearing students is imperative in light of the dismal statistics regarding their educational outcomes. To date, schools have largely failed to effectively meet the needs of Deaf and hard of hearing students (California Deaf and Hard-of-Hearing Education Advisory Task Force, 1999; Commission on Education of the Deaf [COED], 1988). In a 2007 State of Education address, California's State Superintendent of Public Instruction reported that only 8% of Deaf students and 15% of hard of hearing students scored *proficient* or above on English language arts standards (O'Connell, 2007). Other studies confirm that Deaf and hard of hearing students' reading and writing competencies often plateau at about the fourth-grade level, and these students do not perform as well academically as their hearing peers (Allen, 1986; Holt, 1993; Marschark et al., 2002; Schildroth & Hotto, 1994). One study found that only 3% of Deaf 18-year-olds read as well as their hearing peers (Traxler, 2000). According to Cuculick and Kelly (2003), about 83% of students admitted to the National Technical Institute for the Deaf (NTID) at the Rochester Institute of Technology (RIT) in 2001 and 2002 did not have freshman-level literacy skills.

To work effectively in K–12 settings, which hold students accountable for and through written English, interpreters must have attained mastery in both interpreting and transliterating, especially in light of the highly unique learning needs, cognitive proficiencies, and experiential backgrounds of Deaf and hard of hearing students. Even so, this volume documents the fact that interpreting expertise is just one small part of the whole picture.

Assuring interpreting proficiency is not enough to guarantee interpreters are adequately prepared for the complexities of interpreting in K–12 settings. Focusing attention on linguistic flexibility and interpreting skill provides only a myopic view of the complexities of the participants and interactions in context. Although California and other states are taking steps in the right direction by establishing clear minimum competencies for interpreters working in K–12 schools, certification and licensure for any professional denotes only entry-level readiness. Interpreters who do not have adequate knowledge, skills, and resources at their disposal may not make effective decisions quickly. A lack of professional preparation will result in more delays, at the very least. Therefore, the likelihood that Deaf and hard of hearing students will miss out on salient information could increase proportionally, and leave additional educational gaps.

The interpreters I observed and interviewed reported that, in spite of their best efforts, they were not consistently able to effectively meet the wide array of student needs likely to be encountered in highly interactive, visually rich educational environments. This volume provides compelling evidence that the fundamental knowledge and skills required to work in K–12 settings must include more than linguistic proficiency and interpreting and transliterating competence. Interpreters must also be well equipped to interact socially and professionally with school personnel as well as Deaf and hard of hearing students. They must be able to identify and secure appropriate resources and to be helpful as needs arise. They must be thoroughly prepared to do whatever is necessary for Deaf and hard of hearing students to fully participate socially and academically in school and class activities. K–12 interpreters must also be prepared to optimize Deaf and hard of hearing students' visual access. In addition, students must be afforded abundant opportunities for the development of both sign language skills and English. Educational interpreters must also ensure students' true inclusion in school activities and full access to a quality education. The typical classroom environment, however, makes meeting the unique and fundamental needs of Deaf and hard of hearing students inherently and intensely complex.

CALL TO ACTION: CLARIFYING OUR VISION THROUGH RESEARCH

Without a doubt, years of less than adequate education will result in cumulative deficiencies difficult for even the most capable students to overcome. While hearing students are not only held accountable, they are also provided abundant opportunities for language and content learning in an environment as well as a language that is fully accessible to them. Perhaps more importantly, they are encouraged to be active participants in the learning process throughout their academic careers. There is a crucial and immediate need for research that explores ways in which Deaf and hard of hearing school experiences can truly be equivalent to the school experiences of their hearing peers. After years of insufficient legislative mandates regarding interpreter qualifications, the first step is to make sure the professionals working with these students are well equipped for the demands of the job. Only through extensive, field-based research will we be able to determine the skills and knowledge needed for K–12 interpreters to do their jobs effectively. Without such research, we will remain uncertain about the degree to which interpreter-mediated education can succeed.

In bringing into focus a sharper picture of the skills and knowledge set needed for K–12 interpreters to be effective, this volume is a contribution to this research. However, it has its limitations. My study was limited in scope, duration, and sample size. Although I visited three school sites, observations of each interpreter took place within a single week—moreover, one of the interpreters was a substitute and was only working at that particular school for the week. A long-term study with a larger sample size would greatly enhance understanding. In addition, the time of year (beginning versus the end of the year) limited this study. It is likely that more interaction and negotiation with teachers and students regarding the interpreting process would occur at the beginning of a school year than even a few days later (especially with teachers and students who are working with interpreters for the first time), therefore, the time of year the study was conducted would likely yield different results. By virtue of their willingness to allow video cameras in the classroom, these teachers were also arguably open to collaboration with interpreters. Teachers who are more and less willing to share their space or make adaptations for one Deaf or hard of hearing student would bring to light an additional constellation of interactional factors that could greatly influence interpreters' decisions and actions.

I conducted my observations in fifth and sixth grade classrooms and I did not observe other common types of discourse and activities such as group discussions, student presentations, and overlapping dialogue. Students in higher grades would also be likely to have multiple teachers, each with different teaching styles and ways of interacting with students and interpreters. The topics being studied would also have bearing on the particular sets of factors being considered by K–12 interpreters. For example, one teacher asked that I not observe and set up cameras on days designated for sex education. Other gender issues could surface completely unrelated to class content, such as when one interpreter in this study was asked to assist a student who started her first period while at school.

Individual student factors such as the range of behavioral and non-compliance issues (from minor and predictable to severely disruptive) would shed light on a completely different set of variables than were evidenced in this investigation. Although it would be difficult (if not impossible) to describe every possible constellation of factors that align to inform interpreters' decisions, a larger corpus of data would undoubtedly enhance the quality of this particular investigation. My research illuminated what interpreters do in their endeavors to enhance Deaf and hard of hearing students' school experience in three critical areas: visual access, language and learning, and participation and inclusion; it is likely that other primary motivations informing the practice of interpreters are yet to be identified.

Moreover, this study, by putting interpreters front and center, brings only one perspective into view. Similar studies must be conducted with

Deaf and hard of hearing students in the spotlight. What do students get out of interpreter-mediated education and under what conditions? Future research must also investigate how teachers and Deaf and hard of hearing students themselves impact and are impacted by interactions in interpreted school contexts. In fact, research that examined interactions between teachers and interpreters, or between students and interpreters, would be enlightening. In particular, interpreters would benefit from a solid understanding of the characteristics that enhance the effectiveness of collaborative (teacher–interpreter and student–interpreter) relationships. Successful techniques for improving the quality and frequency of direct interactions between Deaf and hard of hearing students and their teachers or peers are also critical to determine.

Future research will contribute to a sorely needed, well-defined body of knowledge and skills that includes a broad range of strategies for responding effectively to a predictable set of student needs. Educational interpreters must be educated to make decisions that promote conditions in which Deaf or hard of hearing students are more likely to become engaged and active learners. Future research specific to what interpreters and teachers can do to enhance the educational experiences of mainstreamed Deaf and hard of hearing students is unquestionably necessary. Indeed, failing to research factors that perpetuate the status quo of Deaf and hard of hearing students as bystanders (Ramsey, 1997; La Bue, 1998) while continuing to claim inclusion would in itself be ethically negligent.

DEVELOPMENT AND TRAINING: LOOKING TO PRACTITIONERS AND STAKEHOLDERS TO SEE MORE CLEARLY

As I described in Chapter 2, the appropriate roles and responsibilities of K–12 interpreters have been the source of much confusion and controversy. This volume sheds some light on factors and realities contributing to such confusion. Although they are not trained language development experts, interpreters must consider the language realities and communication preferences of the persons for whom they interpret. Interpreters are not trained in pedagogy, especially not that of meeting language needs as unique as those of Deaf and hard of hearing students, but they work with these students day after day and co-construct shared understandings in complex teaching and learning environments. They are not experts in

Deaf education, but they are often the only one in the classroom who understands sign language and are often the primary means through which instruction is conveyed. It is essential to understand the perspectives of those interpreters as they navigate what might appear to be contradictions among their own perceptions of what should be done, what teachers and/or interpreting professionals advocate, and school policies.

In a report of the California Deaf and Hard-of-Hearing Education Advisory Task Force (1999), ASL is listed as one of the communication options that should be made available to Deaf and hard of hearing students. The California Department of Education's guidelines for quality standards for programs for deaf and hard of hearing students (2000) states that each student must be provided with the means to "develop age-appropriate communication skills, in his/her preferred mode of communication . . . which will allow him/her to acquire the academic, social, emotional, and vocational skills needed for the establishment of social relationships, economic self-sufficiency, and the assumption of civic responsibility" (p. 1). Results of my study suggest that interpreters must have a wide range of linguistic skills and strategies for facilitating both language acquisition and academic content. Knowing what should be done and having met minimum qualification standards for working in K–12 settings are not enough. Even highly qualified interpreters are uncertain about what to do in some situations, for example, when printed text is read aloud (as it frequently was in classrooms during my observations).

Certainly, practitioners become more proficient over time. Experts typically have more resources, in that more of the required skills are automatic and more knowledge is ingrained. Interpreters with high levels of linguistic proficiency in both ASL and English, and who have been academically successful themselves, are perhaps better equipped to quickly identify an appropriate response. Expert interpreters are not only likely to interpret more accurately and to possess a broader range of possible strategies for promoting inclusion, they can more rapidly determine a course of action that they predict will be effective within particular sets of circumstances. Camie and Marina both struggled to interpret academic content. Even AJ reported her own difficulty interpreting literature effectively without the opportunity to prepare. As suggested by the description of the interpretation of the lesson on wind and air pressure (pp. 144–45) and Marina's contradicting prompts about where Kristie and Miguel should look, a bachelor's degree in interpreting did not adequately prepare Marina to do what was needed. Although she achieved a 4.2 on the EIPA a year after data collection, this volume illuminates the reality that even a score higher than 4.0 on the EIPA may not be adequate without an understanding of language development and teaching pedagogy, particularly as it applies to meeting the unique academic and social needs of dual language learners. Furthermore, it is not acceptable for Deaf and hard of hearing students to miss out while K–12 interpreters gain experience, improve interpreting accuracy, and learn to efficiently and effectively make decisions. Because of the complexities of educational interpreting, we must ensure that interpreters are thoroughly prepared before they enter the classroom. Obviously, the practice of placing anyone but highly qualified, well-trained, and proficient interpreters in younger grades would be an egregious mistake. In addition, a Deaf or hard of hearing student's consistent exposure to proficient adult language models might provide a benefit that would be difficult to predict and to measure. Given the right set of knowledge and skills, one-to-one highly individualized responsiveness to the student could mirror the effectiveness of other one-to-one learning interactions (Long, 2013). Although Camie had interpreted in K–12 settings for 7 years and worked with Emily for a year and a half, Camie reported that her involvement in training designed for K–12 interpreters was instrumental in helping her to more effectively meet Emily's language and learning needs.

There has been much written about potential barriers to accessing education through interpreters. The placement of Deaf and hard of hearing students in classrooms with interpreters does not ensure that students will be able to participate fully. As is the case with any mediated instruction, it may be more accurate to determine the advantages and disadvantages of an interpreter-mediated education. In mediated instruction, some type of resource is offered for the purpose of learning. For example, in computer-mediated learning, the computer is the point of interaction between the student and the teacher, and students and teachers rarely interact directly. There may be disadvantages to this type of situation. In some ways, the teacher cannot be as responsive to the students' immediate needs. The computer filters out opportunities for dialogue that are the crux of social and constructivist learning theories. However, mediated instruction, when properly designed and used appropriately, has the power to amplify learning. It can be tailored to meet the learner's individual needs and to put the learning process in the learner's hands. Students can decide when they feel ready to be assessed, back up to a previous unit, repeat a lesson multiple times, or skip ahead if so desired.

Deaf and hard of hearing students will both be disadvantaged by and benefit from the interpreter-mediated education they receive. Because of multiple and cumulative timing delays, the use of interpreters reduces opportunities for participation and in many ways creates increased obstacles for Deaf and hard of hearing students. Interpreters make deliberate decisions that result in the loss or distortion of information, and their presence makes Deaf and hard of hearing students very visible to their classmates and teachers. However, interpreters also advocate for the student, filling in the gaps and providing support to even the playing field in an environment that is highly dependent on both sound and English. The benefits of the ability of highly trained interpreters to individualize instruction have not yet been examined, but they are worthy of study. Similarly, continued investigation of potential advantages and disadvantages of interpreter-mediated school experiences would be enlightening, including investigation of the quality of social networks, peer relations, and social status afforded to Deaf and hard of hearing students in mainstream settings.

The range, nature, complexity, and importance of interpreters' decisions (and even their presence) on the educational experience must be determined. Taylor (2004) suggests that when they hire educational interpreters, administrators should assess an interpreter's "skills, expertise, knowledge of the subject matter, and ability to suit the needs of the situation and the individual child. Interpreters must be competent to provide interpretation for the specific teachers and students for whom they are being hired" (p. 179). Interpreters who do not meet high level standards of interpreting proficiency should not even be considered for placement in educational settings, especially with younger children (or language-delayed students of any age) who must rapidly acquire language and knowledge. Simply placing an interpreter in a classroom with one or more Deaf or hard of hearing students (who likely have different language needs and prior knowledge) is not adequate, but individual interpreters cannot solve these problems independently and without adequate professional preparation that takes into account far more than merely linguistic expertise.

Schick (2004) states, "Put simply, educating children with the use of an interpreter is an educational experiment. Although published demographic data documents the number of children who are being educated in classrooms with educational interpreters (Kluwin, Moores, & Gaustad, 1992), no studies have been done to document how well these students are doing" (p. 73).

Researchers have not yet identified the factors and support systems that are necessary to promote student success. Extensive research and ongoing dialogue must take place in order to ensure that Deaf and hard of hearing students do not continue to fall through the cracks. Some students are able to succeed in educational settings, but it seems to be more a matter of chance than any real strategic design based on successful teaching and interpreting practice. In consideration of dismal statistics regarding Deaf and hard of hearing students, this gap in the knowledge base is exceptionally egregious. If "inclusion" is to be more than just a hollow promise that is, in truth, proliferating school experiences that are not separate but certainly not equal, K–12 interpreters must have more highly specialized knowledge and skills than is currently mandated. Ongoing, in-depth research must be conducted to determine how interpreters' decisions and responses to a range of predictable conditions are likely to improve Deaf and hard of hearing students' school experiences and learning outcomes. It is additionally imperative that researchers look at ways in which educational interpreters might help or hinder the development of language and cognition, as well as social development.

Even interpreters who are acutely aware of the importance of making connections between ASL and English to promote the development of students' skills in both languages are not consistently afforded the time in mainstream settings to effectively make those connections. Stakeholders in the education of Deaf and hard of hearing children—researchers, educators, parents, Deaf and hard of hearing students and adults, school personnel, and government officials—must work together to enhance these students' school experiences. They must identify strategies for addressing the pitfalls to and enhancing the possibilities of an interpreter-mediated education. Along with continuing to raise expectations of interpreter qualifications in terms of linguistic expertise and educational preparation, those concerned with the education of Deaf and hard of hearing children must seek to account for and to improve the decision-making processes of interpreters working in K–12 settings. Interpreters' decisions significantly impact the school experiences of the students in mainstream classrooms with whom they work. Simple placement of an interpreter in the classroom does not ensure access to a good education.

All interpreters must be equipped to respond to the complexities of the educational context before they begin to work with Deaf and hard of hearing students in mainstream classrooms. Interpreters need more effective strategies to optimize visual access, facilitate ASL and English language development, promote ample and equitable opportunity for active participation, and encourage social interactions. Before interpreters can be adequately prepared for working effectively with Deaf and hard of hearing students in K–12 schools, stakeholders must reach a consensus regarding what interpreters should know and be able to do—they must determine a set of required knowledge and skills. Identification of recommended best practices in light of universal and predictable student needs will take input from these various stakeholders, as well as from continued, well-designed, longitudinal research.

Just as filmmakers rely extensively on multiple camera angles, telephoto and panoramic views, and the expertise of those involved in the making of the film, this volume seeks to capture a clear and complete picture of the work and decisions of educational interpreters through multiple lenses. The frame-by-frame descriptions and in-depth iterative analyses of educational interpreters' work and decisions presented in this investigation begin to bring into focus the complexities of their decision-making processes. However, much remains to be seen and discovered. There is much more to the work of K–12 interpreters than meets the eye.

Categories and Definitions for Coding Video Data

1. Interpreting—It was often difficult to distinguish when an interpreter stopped interpreting and provided more "fine-tuned, individualized instruction" (perhaps aligned with and essential to achieving instructional objectives). *Interpreting* was eventually operationalized as the interpreter being in place, poised and ready to interpret whenever there was some discourse (usually spoken) to be interpreted. The general expectation would be that if the teacher is talking, the interpreter is interpreting what the teacher is saying (although that was not always the reality).

2. Social interactions—This distinction was also somewhat ambiguous. It was difficult to determine what was social in nature, as opposed to scaffolding learning, promoting participation/inclusion and independence, or enhancing self-esteem. *Social interactions* was eventually operationalized as *any* interaction besides interpreting that occurred between the interpreter and a Deaf or hard of hearing student.

3. Tutor/help—During designated tutoring time or seat work, it was easy to identify tutoring and helping; however, the line of demarcation between interpreting and tutoring/helping was not always distinct. "Social interactions" were easier action to identify.

4. Other tasks—This category was another catch-all for tasks beyond interpreting. The category of other tasks intended to provide a means to examine all the tasks that make up the interpreter's role. These included instances such as when interpreters accessed available resources (e.g., asked the teacher for clarification of objectives, located and obtained handouts/textbooks or other materials, moved furniture to facilitate access to resources or optimize visual access, etc.).

5. DHH student participation—This category was reserved for those instances in which a Deaf or hard of hearing student participated publicly (for the benefit of peers and the teacher) in class activities.

6. Peer/teacher interaction—This category was used to indicate direct interactions between Deaf or hard of hearing students and their peers or teachers (with or without interpretation).

7. Visual access/overlap—This category was selected whenever students were asked to look at one or more sources of visual input while there was discourse to be interpreted (e.g., look at a graphic as the teacher explained what they were seeing).

8. New lesson/transitions—It was important to demarcate transitions between topics and activities for the purpose of finding particular discourse types (e.g., lecture vs. discussion).

9. Different track—This category indicated instances during which the interpreter deliberately chose to stop interpreting (deliberate omission) or in some other way deviate from the interpretation (to varying degrees) in order to respond to a more immediate student need. Examples of more immediate needs include meeting the student where he/she is at the moment (ahead of or behind the rest of the class), scaffolding language/content or general/cultural/social knowledge, troubleshooting problems with assistive listening devices, attempting to redirect off-task students, etc.

10. Timing issues—For this study, timing issues were eventually incorporated into either different track/deliberate omission or visual access/overlap. This coding category would be useful for an in-depth look at group interactions as well as question and answer discussion formats.

11. English or sound-based content—Homophones and other sound-based, English-specific content (e.g., puns and plays on words) proved to be problematic for some interpreters (especially for one who declined participation from the study after being videotaped because of the sound-based nature of the lesson content). I chose to keep this category as a feature of interest for video analysis, but I did not include it as an area of focus for this study.

12. Numbers and spatial orientation—This designation was included because of interviews with and observations of the three interpreters who were excluded in narrowing the study. All three of these interpreters stated that they were taught to flip the number line (breaking rules of ASL) so that Deaf and hard of hearing students' view of the number line would

correspond to the interpreted representation of the number line. Although three interpreters interpreted for the same student, a tremendous degree of variability was observed in actual practice (rhetoric vs. practice inconsistencies). One of these interpreters consistently flipped the orientation of the number line, one of them consistently forgot to flip it, and the third interpreter was inconsistent in her approach. Due to these inconsistencies I had difficulty regarding the interpretation of instructional content, for example, I couldn't tell which direction should be negative and which should be positive on the number line. This was disturbing to me as an educator interested in language acquisition. Given that many Deaf and hard of hearing students (including three of the four I observed) do not have fluent language models at home, I am acutely concerned about interpreters intentionally deteriorating the quality of language output in the name of unsubstantiated claims that it will improve student comprehension of content.

In addition to these, a code button was designated for elicitation, making it easy for me to select excerpts for video elicitation interviews. Two more buttons were subsequently created for outside reviewers to code for the presence of competing demands for Deaf and hard of hearing students' visual attention.

Appendix B

Expanded List and Definitions of What and

Why Categories

1. Assessment	Assess student learning needs (language and prior knowledge) or social and emotional needs, and readiness for independence and participation. Decide which source of visual input is most important. Prioritizing.
2. Beyond interpreting	Get attention, help/tutor/explain, make sure student knows where to look for visual access, make sure student knows who is speaking, chat, build rapport, provide reinforcement/praise/ encouragement, redirect/discipline, consult, teach signs or strategies for using interpreters, and interact with others.
3. Concern re: interpreting text	Consider factors related to interpreting audible text (read-alouds, captions) when interpreting alone all day—mental and physical fatigue, repetitive motion injury, text density and rate of delivery, time to process vs. class timing, visual access, social stigma, reading level, accountability, etc.
4. Consistency	Use knowledge of teacher, student, and course content from previous classes to make decisions appropriate to the context of the classroom. Consistency helps to ensure interpreters' choices are well aligned with teacher norms and student needs in the specified context.
5. Consultation/ collaboration	Inform staff about needs of the deaf and hard of hearing students; collaborate with teacher and brainstorm ideas.

6.	Deliberate omission	Decide NOT to interpret what is being said—often during discussion between the Deaf student and the interpreter, or when students need time to look at something or continue their own work. When discourse is overlapping—interpreter stays with the most prominent or relevant discourse stream, usually the teacher, and omits another.
7.	Discipline, esp. redirecting	Discipline (e.g., awarding or deducting points when students misbehave (hearing and Deaf). Seen as extreme. Most common = redirecting off-task students.
8.	Different track	Decide to be somewhere the teacher is not, often comparable or parallel in nature.
9.	Dilemma/ hidden premise	Express conflict among student needs, teacher desires, and/or what interpreters are supposed to do. Often related to concerns when interpreting various forms of scripted/printed text. Also working ahead with the student vs. staying with the class because teacher seemed to want them together.
10.	Evening the playing field	Attempt to create an even playing field so Deaf students have access to the same knowledge (or amount of confusion) as their hearing peers, can participate fully, are included, can interact socially (with peers, teacher/staff, and interpreter). Juxtaposed with desire for teacher not to give preferential treatment, but to have equally high expectations for Deaf students. Balancing appropriate support/adaptation while avoiding giving the answer (e.g., in spelling activities).
11.	Filling in gaps	Provide background or language-related explanations, especially in terms of what classmates know and can do, while avoiding giving the answer (e.g., in spelling activities).
12.	Fingerspelling or spelling	Make connections between signed lexicon and English print or scaffolding spelling through the use of fingerspelling.

13.	Flow/ efficiency	Maintain momentum and flow of the class and teacher; avoid distracting or disrupting. Equal value for allowing Deaf students to work uninterrupted. Provide and value time for students to work (e.g., answer questions re: information teacher has already given or generally known rather than have student wait in line).
14.	Gender issues	Remain sensitive to gender issues—male interpreters working with female students or vice versa, especially for sex education. A female student asked female interpreter for help when she started her first period (trust, safety, and comfort?).
15.	Helping other kids	Help kids who are not deaf or hard of hearing. Justified as being helpful to an overburdened teacher when Deaf students worked independently, and because they thought it helped Deaf students feel less like they were singled out/different.
16.	Inadequacies of preparation	State that formal training did not adequately prepare them for the job.
17.	Inclusion and participation	Discuss degree to which Deaf students actually participate (or are excused from) class activities/discussions. Express value that students be treated fairly but also offered adaptations for inclusion and active participation in peer and class interactions.
18.	Interacting directly with students	Participate in social conversation, interact about the task at hand (vs. interpreting into spoken English), co-construct meaning (signs/content), praise or reinforce, guide, support learning, redirect (e.g., "you need to put away your art and focus on spelling now").
19.	Job satisfaction	Discuss feelings about their jobs—such as compensation, status, availability of subs, professional development opportunities, vacation, etc.
20.	Language acquisition	Attend to student acquisition of language(s): English and/or sign language.

21.	Limitations— knowledge, skill, and mental or physical	Express lack of confidence in own ability to understand and/or express a concept clearly, e.g., complex or sound-based concepts, printed text. Concern about the effects of mental and physical fatigue on quality of interpretation. Fear of injury.
22.	Number line and spatial orientation	Discuss orientation of the number line and other spatial or numerical concepts. Disagreement among interpreters regarding the spatial structuring of the number line.
23.	Observation of experts	Express lack of opportunity to observe experts; express desire to know what "real" interpreters or I (as an expert) would do.
24.	On the job training	Refer to learning on the job (after being employed).
25.	Other interesting sections	Miscellaneous—things that caught my eye.
26.	Pedagogy	Rely on teaching strategies or learning theory, especially scaffolding and meeting students where they are (whether ahead of or behind their peers at a given time).
27.	Peer interaction	Discuss Deaf and hard of hearing students interacting with hearing peers.
28.	Required skills and knowledge	Discuss competencies necessary to effectively do the job (what they have and what they don't have).
29.	Self-reflection/ monitoring	Reflect on effectiveness of interpretation or strategies used in a particular type of situation.
30.	Student independence	Encourage students to be assertive and take control of their own learning needs depending on readiness.
31.	Teacher as resource	Attempt or express it would be beneficial to know what the teacher wants; wish the teacher would do something differently to meet the students needs.
32.	Teacher comfort and collaboration	Recognize that teachers are more or less comfortable/good at working with interpreters, open to suggestions, willing to adapt teaching style/class activities.

33.	Team/other school personnel	Work with other members of the educational team.
34.	Team interpreting	Mention of team interpreting or lack of opportunity to team and work together to meet student goals, help each other out, or discuss strategies toward approaching their work. This could also include skill development.
35.	Tutoring and helping	Take on task of tutoring or explaining class content, either during designated times or while on deck to interpret (mini-lessons on the side in service of current class activity). Answer questions directly, e.g., when information was already provided.
36.	Uncertainty	Express internal conflict about whether the chosen approach is the correct one, check in with researcher as to whether or not he/she is thinking along the right lines. Especially prevalent re: printed text and spelling.
37.	Visual access/ overlapping discourse	Optimize visual access, lament the fact that they can't interpret everything, especially when students are supposed to look at something else at the same time.
38.	Voicing student discourse: ASL to English	Decide whether or not to interpret what a student signs into spoken English based on discourse cues and appropriateness of comments and/or timing.

Appendix C

Overarching Themes From Interview and Video Data

VISUAL ATTENTION

- Attention-getting
- Directing the student's gaze by pointing or looking at something/someone
- Holding or adjusting the pace/timing (e.g., wait time)
- Identifying the speaker by name or attribute
- Summarizing, paraphrasing, or omitting information; adding visual information
- Consulting, collaborating, negotiating or brainstorming strategies for working more effectively with interpreters and meeting DHH students' visual needs
- Admonishing, directive talk: "Put away your drawing and pay attention; you need to be working on this now."
- *Prioritizing and assessing what is most important for the student to see*[19]

BRIDGING/SCAFFOLDING TO EVEN THE PLAYING FIELD BASED ON DHH STUDENTS' LANGUAGE AND PRIOR KNOWLEDGE

Provide opportunities for DHH students to have access to the same knowledge and opportunity to succeed academically as their hearing peers

- Tutoring, explaining, helping—the interpreter is responsible for or takes on the task of tutoring or explaining class content, especially in relation to what peers know and can do

---

19. Italicized font signifies an implicit feature, not directly observable, reported during interviews.

- Making connections between ASL and English—use fingerspelling and other techniques to promote language acquisition and learning
- Fostering student independence—encouraging or teaching students how to be assertive and take control of their own learning needs and interactions with peers, teachers, etc., such as by prompting them to ask the teacher directly

PARTICIPATION AND SOCIAL AND ACADEMIC INCLUSION

- Evening the playing field by serving as a sounding board, providing general guidance, etc., so that DHH students are more likely to participate actively
  - Adjusting timing or omitting less significant parts of the message to allow student to participate in group discussions
  - Prompting and encouraging students to raise their hands
  - Providing reinforcement/praise/encouragement
- Fostering student independence—Encouraging or teaching students how to take control of their own learning needs in interactions with peers, teachers, etc.
- Building rapport with students by chatting socially and/or about class activities and content; being a partner in communication. Negotiating preferences regarding interpreting and access.
- Collaborating, negotiating or brainstorming strategies to better meet students' language and learning needs and also to facilitate inclusion/full participation
  - Informing other staff about language and learning needs of the deaf and hard of hearing students.
  - Teaching signs to staff and students.
- Helping other kids—Helping kids who are not deaf or hard of hearing so that none of the kids will feel interpreters are "just there for the Deaf kids"

RESOURCES AND LIMITATIONS

- *Consistency—Interpreter indicates that a regular interpreter would have a better understanding of the classroom context, teacher approaches, student needs, etc.*

- *Uncertainty—Interpreter checks in with researcher as to whether or not he/she is thinking along the right lines, e.g., "Is this what we should be doing?" Especially regarding read-alouds, captioned video, spelling and sound-based lessons, and (spoken) recitations.*
- Teacher as resource—Interpreter seeks to discover what the teacher wants or asks the teacher to do something differently to meet the students needs
- Collegiality and teacher comfort—Teacher respects interpreter expertise and accepts or invites collaboration.
  - *Teacher is perceived as being more or less comfortable/good at working with interpreters and sharing space.*
  - *Varied teacher expectations and understanding of interpreter responsibilities; role confusion*
  - Interpreter and teacher develop rapport by chatting and joking
- Collaboration—Interpreter works with other school personnel to glean ideas, materials, and resources to better meet the deaf and hard of hearing students. Collaborating, negotiating or brainstorming strategies to better meet students' language and learning needs and/or to facilitate inclusion/full participation
- *Skill and knowledge—Interpreter discusses that her own limitations in terms of understanding content and ability to deliver an equivalent message puts DHH students at an extreme disadvantage that are in addition to the disadvantages students already encounter, e.g., spelling, phonetics, visual access, common or shared language, timing of interpretation, world views and experiences, etc.*
- *Self-reflection and monitoring—Believes reflection on effectiveness of interpretation is a means to improving professional practice. Concern that students pay the price while interpreters figure out how improvements can be made.*
- *Consulting—Informing other school personnel about the language and learning needs of deaf and hard of hearing students.*
- *Team interpreting—Lack of team interpreter leads to concerns regarding fatigue, the quality of interpreting, and physical injury. Desire to work with colleagues to discuss strategies toward improving their work, better meet the goals of the students, help each other out, and grow professionally.*

- *Preparation and professional development—Belief that preparation for employment was inadequate and employment restricts opportunities to participate in professional development activities (no time off even when teachers have in service days, not paid for in-service days, poorly compensated, distance to quality training opportunities—especially those specific to K–12 interpreting)*

References

Allen, T. E. (1986). Patterns of academic achievement among hearing impaired students: 1974 and 1983. In A. N. Schildroth & M. A. Karchmer (Eds.), *Deaf children in America* (pp. 161–206). Boston, MA: College-Hill Press.

Angelelli, C. (2001). *Deconstructing the invisible interpreter: A study of the interpersonal role of the interpreter in a cross-linguistic/cultural communicative event.* Unpublished doctoral dissertation, Stanford University.

Angelelli, C. (2004). *Revisiting the interpreter's role: A study of conference, court, and medical interpreters in Canada, Mexico, and the United States.* Amsterdam, the Netherlands: John Benjamins.

Antia, S. D., & Kreimeyer, K. H. (2001). The role of interpreters in inclusive classrooms. *American Annals of the Deaf, 146,* 355–365.

Bahan, B. (2004). Memoir upon the formation of a visual variety of the human race. In B. Eldredge & M. M. Wilding-Diaz (Eds.), *Deaf studies today: A kaleidoscope of knowledge, learning, and understanding.* Orem, UT: Utah Valley State College.

Bahan, B. (2008). Upon the formation of a visual variety of the human race. In H-D. L. Bauman (Ed.), *Open your eyes: Deaf studies talking* (pp. 83–99). Minneapolis, MN: University of Minnesota Press.

Bourdieu, P. (1977). Cultural reproduction and social reproduction. In J. Karabel & A. Halsey (Eds.), *Power and ideology in education* (pp. 487–511). New York, NY: Oxford University Press.

Calderon, R., & Greenberg, M. (1997). The effectiveness of early intervention for deaf children and children with hearing loss. In M. J. Guralnick (Ed.), *The effectiveness of early intervention* (pp. 455–482). Baltimore, MD: Brookes.

California Deaf and Hard-of-Hearing Education Advisory Task Force. (1999). *Communication access and quality education for deaf and hard-of-hearing children: The report of the California deaf and hard-of-hearing education advisory task force.* Sacramento, CA: California Department of Education.

California Department of Education. (2000). *Programs for deaf and hard of hearing students: Guidelines for quality standards.* Sacramento, CA: Author.

Cawthon, S. W. (2001). Teaching strategies in inclusive classrooms with deaf students. *Journal of Deaf Studies and Deaf Education, 6,* 212–225.

Cazden, C. (1988). *Classroom discourse: The language of teaching and learning.* Portsmouth, NH: Heinemann.

Cokely, D. (1986). The effects of lag time on interpreter errors. *Sign Language Studies, 53,* 341–376.

Cokely, D. (1990). The effectiveness of three means of communication in the college classroom. *Sign Language Studies, 69*, 415–442.

Commission on Education of the Deaf. (1988). *Toward equality: Education of the deaf.* Washington, DC: U.S. Government Printing Office.

Corwin, K. (2007, January). A perspective regarding educational interpreters. *VIEWS.*

Cuculick, J. A., & Kelly, R. R. (2003). Relating deaf students' reading and language scores at college entry to their degree completion rates. *American Annals of the Deaf, 148*, 279–286.

Cummins, J. (2001). *Negotiating identities: Education for empowerment in a diverse society* (2nd ed.). Los Angeles, CA: California Association for Bilingual Education.

Davis, J. E. (2005). Code choices and consequences: Implications for educational interpreting. In M. Marschark, R. Peterson, and E. A. Winston (Eds.), *Sign language interpreting and interpreter education: Directions for research and practice* (pp. 112–141). New York, NY: Oxford University Press.

Dean, R. K., & Pollard, R. Q. (2001). The application of demand-control theory to sign language interpreting: Implications for stress and interpreter training. *Journal of Deaf Studies and Deaf Education, 6*, 1–14.

Dean, R. K., & Pollard, R. Q (2005). Consumers and service effectiveness in interpreting work: A practice profession perspective. In M. Marschark, R. Peterson, & E. Winston (Eds.), *Interpreting and interpreter education: Directions for research and practice* (pp. 259–282). New York, NY: Oxford University Press.

Dean, R. K., & Pollard, R. Q. (2006). From best practice to best practice process: Shifting ethical thinking and teaching. In E. M. Maroney (Ed.), A new chapter in interpreter education: Accreditation, research and technology. *Proceedings of the 16th national convention of the Conference of Interpreter Trainers (CIT).* Monmouth, OR: Conference of Interpreter Trainers.

EIPA Diagnostic Center. (2004*). Educational Interpreter Performance Assessment evaluation report.* Omaha, NE: Boys Town National Research Hospital.

EIPA Diagnostic Center. (2009). *Educational Interpreter Performance Assessment evaluation report.* Omaha, NE: Boys Town National Research Hospital.

EIPA Diagnostic Center. (2010). *Educational Interpreter Performance Assessment evaluation report.* Omaha, NE: Boys Town National Research Hospital.

Foster, S. (1988). Life in the mainstream: Reflections of deaf college freshmen on their experiences in the mainstreamed high school. *Journal of Rehabilitation of the Deaf, 22*, 27–35.

Gallaudet Research Institute. (2003). *Regional and national summary report of data from the 2001–2002 annual survey of deaf and hard of hearing children and youth.* Washington, DC: Gallaudet University.

Gallaudet Research Institute. (2004). *Regional and national summary report of data from the 2002–2003 annual survey of deaf and hard of hearing children and youth.* Washington, DC: Gallaudet University.

Gallaudet Research Institute. (2008). *Regional and national summary report of data from the 2007–2008 annual survey of deaf and hard of hearing children and youth.* Washington, DC: Gallaudet University.

Glaser, B. G., & Strauss, A. L. (1967). *The discovery of grounded theory: Strategies for qualitative research.* New York, NY: Aldine.

Glickman, N. S. (2003). Culturally affirmative mental health treatment for deaf people: What it looks like and why it is essential. In N. S. Glickman & S. Gulati (Eds.), *Mental health care of deaf people: A culturally affirmative approach* (pp. 1–32). Mahwah, NJ: Erlbaum.

Gustason, G. (1985). Interpreters entering public school employment. *American Annals of the Deaf, 130,* 265–271.

Hatfield, N., Caccamise, F., & Siple, P. (1978). Deaf students' language competency: A bilingual perspective. *American Annals of the Deaf, 123,* 18–47.

Hayes, P. L. (1992). Educational interpreters for deaf students: Their responsibilities, problems, and concerns. *Journal of Interpretation, 5,* 5–24.

Heath, S. B. (1983). *Ways with words: Language, life, and work in communities and classrooms.* Cambridge, UK: Cambridge University Press.

Heath, S. B. (1986). Sociocultural contexts of language development. In *Beyond language: Social and cultural factors in schooling language minority students* (pp. 143–186). Sacramento, CA: California State Department of Education, Sacramento, Bilingual Education Office.

Holt, J. A. (1993). Stanford Achievement Test (8th ed.): Reading comprehension subgroup results. *American Annals of the Deaf Reference Issue, 138,* 172–175.

Hurwitz, T. A. (1991). Educational interpreting: A personal history. *Odyssey, 2,* 28–29.

Jacobs, L. R. (1977). The efficacy of interpreting input for processing lecture information by deaf college students. *Journal of Rehabilitation of the Deaf, 11,* 10–14.

Johnson, K. (1991). Miscommunication in interpreted classroom interaction. *Sign Language Studies, 70,* 1–34.

Johnson, L., Bolster, L., Taylor, M., Sieberlich, A., & Brown, S. (2012). *National research on current patterns of practice in educational interpreting.* [PowerPoint presentation]. Retrieved from http://cit-asl.org/dialogue/conf-schedule/

thursday/national-research-on-current-patterns-of-practice-in-educational -interpreting/.

Jones, B. E. (1993). *Responsibilities of educational sign language interpreters in K–12 public school in Kansas, Missouri, and Nebraska.* Unpublished doctoral dissertation, University of Kansas.

Jones, B. E. (1994). Responsibilities of educational sign language interpreters in K–12 public schools in Kansas, Missouri, and Nebraska. In E. A. Winston, Ed., *Mapping our course: A collaborative venture: Proceedings of the 1994 CIT conference.* Charlotte, NC: Conference of Interpreter Trainers.

Jones, B. E. (2004). Competencies of K–12 educational interpreters: What we need versus what we have. In E. A. Winston (Ed.), *Educational interpreting: How it can succeed* (pp. 132–167). Washington, DC: Gallaudet University Press.

Kluwin, T. N., Moores, D. F., & Gaustad, M. G. (1992). *Toward effective public school programs for deaf students: Context, process and outcomes.* New York, NY: Teachers College Press.

Komesaroff, L. R., & McLean, M. A. (2006). Being there is not enough: Inclusion is both Deaf and hearing. *Deafness & Education International, 8,* 88–100. Retrieved from http://dx.doi.org/10.1002/dei.192.

Kurz, K., & Langer, E. (2004). Student perspectives on educational interpreting: Twenty deaf and hard of hearing students offer insights and suggestions. In E. A. Winston (Ed.), *Educational interpreting: How it can succeed* (pp. 9–47). Washington, DC: Gallaudet University Press.

La Bue, M. (1998). *Interpreted education: A study of deaf students' access to the content and form of literacy instruction in a mainstreamed high school English class.* Unpublished dissertation, Harvard University.

Ladd, P. (2003). *Understanding Deaf culture: In search of Deafhood.* Clevedon, UK: Multilingual Matters.

Lane, H. (1995). The education of deaf children: Drowning in the mainstream and the sidestream. In J. M. Kauffman & D. P. Hallahan (Eds.), *The illusion of full inclusion: A comprehensive critique of a current special education bandwagon.* Austin, TX: Pro-Ed.

Langer, E. (2004). Perspectives on educational interpreting from educational anthropology and an Internet discussion group. In E. A. Winston (Ed.), *Educational interpreting: How it can succeed* (pp. 91–112). Washington, DC: Gallaudet University Press.

Lave, J., & Wenger, E. (1991). *Situated learning: Legitimate peripheral participation.* Cambridge, UK: Cambridge University Press.

Lentz, E. M. (2007). *People of the eye . . . community of vision.* Presentation of the San Diego chapter of the American Sign Language Teachers Association. San Diego, CA.

Long, P. K. (2010). Cultivating the inclination to write. Unpublished doctoral dissertation. University of California, San Diego.

Marschark, M., Lang, H. G., & Albertini, J. A. (2002). *Educating Deaf students: From research to practice*. Oxford, UK: Oxford University Press.

Marschark, M., Pelz, J. B., Convertino, C., Sapere, P., Arndt, M. E., & Seewagen, R. (2005). Classroom interpreting and visual information processing in mainstream education for Deaf Students: Live or Memorex®? *American Educational Research Journal, 42,* 727–761.

Marschark, M., Sapere, P., Convertino, C., & Seewagen, R. (2005a). Educational interpreting: Access and outcomes. In M. Marschark, R. Peterson & E. A. Winston (Eds.), *Sign language interpreting and interpreter education: Directions for research and practice* (pp. 57–83). New York, NY: Oxford University Press.

Marschark, M., Sapere, P., Convertino, C., & Seewagen, R. (2005b). Access to postsecondary education through sign language interpreting. *Journal of Deaf Studies and Deaf Education, 10,* 38–50.

Marschark, M., Sapere, P., Convertino, C., Seewagen, R. & Maltzen, H. (2004). Comprehension of sign language interpreting: Deciphering a complex task situation. *Sign Language Studies, 4,* 345–368.

Marschark, M., Schick, B., & Spencer, P. E. (2006). Understanding sign language development. In B. Schick, M. Marschark, & P. E. Spencer (Eds.), *Advances in the sign language development of deaf children* (pp. 3–19). New York, NY: Oxford University Press.

Mayberry, R. I., & Eichen, E. B. (1991). The long-lasting advantage of learning sign language in childhood: Another look at the critical period for language acquisition. *Journal of Memory and Language, 30,* 486–512.

Mehan, H. (1979). *Learning lessons: Social organization in the classroom.* Cambridge, MA: Harvard University Press.

Mertens, D. M. (1990). Teachers working with interpreters: The Deaf student's educational experience. *American Annals of the Deaf, 136,* 48–52.

Mertens, D. M. (1998). *Research methods in education and psychology: Integrating diversity with quantitative and qualitative approaches.* Thousand Oaks, CA: Sage.

Metzger, M. (1999). *Sign language interpreting: Deconstructing the myth of neutrality.* Washington, DC: Gallaudet University Press.

Metzger, M., & Fleetwood, E. (2004). Educational interpreting: Developing standards of practice. In E. A. Winston (Ed.), *Educational interpreting: How it can succeed* (pp.171–177). Washington, DC: Gallaudet University Press.

Metzger, M., Fleetwood, E., & Collins, S. D. (2004). Discourse genre and linguistic mode: Interpreter influences in visual and tactile interpreted interaction. *Sign Language Studies, 4,* 118–137.

Mitchell, R. E., & Karchmer, M. A. (2004). Chasing the mythical ten percent: Parental hearing status of deaf and hard of hearing students in the United States. *Sign Language Studies, 4,* 138–163.

Moeller, M. P. (2000). Early intervention and language development in children who are deaf and hard of hearing. *Pediatrics, 106,* e43.

Monikowski, C., & Winston, E. A. (2003). Interpreters and interpreter education. In M. Marschark, & P. E. Spencer (Eds.), *Oxford handbook of Deaf studies, language, and education* (pp. xvi, 505). Oxford, UK: Oxford University Press.

Moores, D. F. (1996). *Educating the deaf: Psychology, principles, and practices* (4th ed.). Boston, MA: Houghton Mifflin.

Moores, D. F., & Meadow-Orlans, K. P. (1990). *Educational and developmental aspects of deafness.* Washington, DC: Gallaudet University Press.

Napier, J. (2002a). Omission taxonomy: A new design in interpretation analysis. *Proceedings of the Conference of Interpreter Trainers.* Minneapolis/St. Paul, MN: Conference of Interpreter Trainers.

Napier, J. (2002b). University interpreting: Linguistic issues for consideration. *Journal of Deaf Studies and Deaf Education, 7,* 281–301.

Napier, J. (2005). Linguistic features and strategies of interpreting: From research to education to practice. In M. Marschark, R. Peterson, & E. A. Winston (Eds.), *Sign language interpreting and interpreter education: Directions for research and practice* (pp. 84–111). New York, NY: Oxford University Press.

Napier, J., & Barker, R. (2004). Sign language interpreting: The relationship between metalinguistic awareness and the production of interpreting omissions. *Sign Language Studies, 4,* 369–393.

O, Connell, J. (2007). *Achievement gap for the deaf.* State of education address by Superintendent O'Connell on the status of education in California. Retrieved June 4, 2009, from http://www.cde.ca.gov/eo/in/se/agDeaf.asp.

Patrie, C. J. (1994). The "readiness-to-work gap." In E. A. Winston, Ed., *Mapping our course: A collaborative venture: Proceedings of the 1994 CIT conference.* Charlotte, NC: Conference of Interpreter Trainers.

Peterson, R., & Monikowski, C. (2010). Perceptions of efficacy of sign language interpreters working in K-12 settings. In K. M. Christensen (Ed.), *Ethical considerations in educating children who are deaf or hard of hearing.* Washington, DC: Gallaudet University Press.

Power, D., & Hyde, M. (2002). The characteristics and extent of participation of deaf and hard-of-hearing students in regular classes in Australian schools. *Journal of Deaf Studies and Deaf Education, 7,* 302–311.

Ramsey, C. L. (1997). *Deaf children in public schools: Placement, context, and consequences.* Washington, DC: Gallaudet University Press.

Robinson, W. S. (1951). The logical structure of analytic induction. *American Sociological Review, 16,* 812–818.

Rogoff, B. (1998). Cognition as a collaborative process. In W. Damon, D. Kuhn, & R. S. Siegler (Eds.), *Handbook of child psychology* (2nd ed., pp. 679–729). Toronto, Canada: Wiley.

Roy, C. B. (2000). *Interpreting as a discourse process.* New York, NY: Oxford University Press.

Russell, D. (2006). *Inclusion or the illusion of inclusion: A study of interpreters working with Deaf students in inclusive education settings.* Presentation at Critical Link 5, Sydney, Australia.

Russell, D. (2008). *Getting to skopos in a mediated educational environment: Bridging research and practice.* Paper presented at the National Convention of the Conference of Interpreter Trainers, San Juan, Puerto Rico.

Schein, J. D. (1992). *Communication support for deaf elementary and secondary students: Perspectives of deaf students and their parents.* Edmonton, Alberta, Canada: Western Canadian Centre of Studies in Deafness, University of Alberta.

Schick, B. (2004). How might learning through an interpreter influence cognitive development? In E. A. Winston (Ed.), *Educational interpreting: How it can succeed* (pp. 73–87). Washington, DC: Gallaudet University Press.

Schick, B., & Williams, K. T. (2004). The educational interpreter performance assessment: Current structure and practices. In E. A. Winston (Ed.), *Educational interpreting: How it can succeed* (pp. 186–205). Washington, DC: Gallaudet University Press.

Schick, B., Williams, K., & Bolster, L. (1999). Skill levels of educational interpreters working in public schools. *Journal of Deaf Studies and Deaf Education, 4,* 144–155.

Schick, B., Williams, K., & Kupermintz, H. (2006). Look who's being left behind: Educational interpreters and access to education for deaf and hard-of-hearing students. *Journal of Deaf Studies and Deaf Education, 11,* 3–20.

Schildroth, A. N., & Hotto, S. (1994). Deaf students and full inclusion: Who wants to be excluded? In R. C. Johnson & O. P. Cohen (Eds.), *Implications and complications for Deaf students of the full inclusion movement* (pp. 7–30). Washington, DC: Gallaudet Research Institute.

Seal, B. C. (2004). *Best practices in educational interpreting* (2nd ed.). Boston, MA: Allyn & Bacon.

Smith, M. B. (2004). *Expert educational interpreters in practice: What do they really do?* Poster presented at the National Convention of the Conference of Interpreter Trainers, Washington, DC.

Smith, M. B. (2010). Opening our eyes: The complexity of competing visual demands in interpreted classrooms. In K. M. Christensen (Ed.), *Ethical considerations in educating children who are deaf or hard of hearing* (pp. 154–191). Washington, DC: Gallaudet University Press.

Smith, T. B. (2007, February). EIPA & Us. *VIEWS*.

Sofinski, B. A., Yesbeck, N. A., Gerhold, S. C., & Bach-Hansen, M.C. (2001). Features of sign-to-voice transliteration by educational interpreters. *Journal of Interpretation, 47–59*.

Stack, K. (2004). Language accessibility in a transliterated education: English signing systems. In E. A. Winston, *Educational interpreting: How it can succeed* (pp. 61–72). Washington, DC: Gallaudet University Press.

Stanton-Salazar, R., & Dornbusch, S. M. (1995). Social capital and the reproduction of inequality: Information networks among Mexican-origin high school students. *Sociology of Education, 68*, 116–135.

Stauffer, L. (1994). A response to the "readiness-to-work gap." In E. A. Winston, Ed., *Mapping our course: A collaborative venture: Proceedings of the 1994 CIT conference*. Charlotte: NC: Conference of Interpreter Trainers.

Stewart, D., & Kluwin, T. (1996). The gap between guidelines, practice, and knowledge in interpreting services for Deaf students. *Journal of Deaf Studies and Deaf Education, 1*, 29–39.

Stinson, M., & Lang, H. (1994). The potential impact on deaf students of the full inclusion movement. In R. C. Johnson & O. P. Cohen (Eds.), *Implications and complications for deaf students of the full inclusion movement*. Washington, DC: Gallaudet Research Institute.

Strauss, A., & Corbin, J. (1990). *Basics of qualitative research: Grounded theory procedures and techniques*. Newbury Park, CA: Sage.

Stuckless, R. E., Avery, J., & Hurwitz, A. (1989). *Educational interpreting for deaf students: Report of the national task force on educational interpreting*. Rochester, NY: National Technical Institute of the Deaf.

Taylor, M. M. (1993). *Interpretation skills: English to American Sign Language*. Edmonton, Alberta, Canada: Interpreting Consolidated.

Taylor, M. M. (2004). Assessment and supervision of educational interpreters: What job? Whose job? Is this process necessary? In E. A. Winston (Ed.), *Educational interpreting: How it can succeed* (pp. 178–185). Washington, DC: Gallaudet University Press.

Taylor, C., & Elliott, R. N. (1994). Identifying areas of competence needed by educational interpreters. *Sign Language Studies, 83*, 179–190.

Togioka, P. (1990). Looking at educational interpreting theory: Course content and rationale used during a training program for educational interpreters. In L. Swabey, Ed., *The challenge of the 90s: New standards in interpreter education: Proceedings of the eighth national convention*. Pomona, CA: Conference of Interpreter Trainers.

Traxler, C. B. (2000). The Stanford Achievement Test, 9th edition: National norming and performance standards for deaf and hard-of-hearing students. *Journal of Deaf Studies and Deaf Education, 5*, 337–348.

Turner, G. H. (2005). Toward real interpreting. In M. Marschark, R. Peterson, & E. A. Winston (Eds.), *Sign language interpreting and interpreter education: Directions for research and practice* (pp. 29–56). New York, NY: Oxford University Press.

Veditz, G. (1912). *President's message in Proceedings of the 9th convention of the National Association of the Deaf, 1910.* Philadelphia; PA: Philocophus Press.

Vygotsky, L. S. (1978). *Mind in society: The development of higher psychological processes.* Cambridge, MA, Harvard University Press.

Wadensjö, C. (1998). *Interpreting as interaction.* London, UK: Longman.

Wenger, E. (2006). *Communities of practice.* Retrieved from http://www.ewenger.com/theory/index.htm.

Winston, E. A. (1994). An interpreted education: inclusion or exclusion? In R. C. Johnson & O. P. Cohen (Eds.), *Implications and complications for Deaf students of the full inclusion movement* (pp. 55–62). Washington, DC: Gallaudet Research Institute.

Winston, E. A. (2004). Interpretability and accessibility of mainstream classrooms. In E. A. Winston (Ed.), *Educational interpreting: How it can succeed* (pp. 132–167). Washington, DC: Gallaudet University Press.

Yarger, C. C. (2001). Educational interpreting: Understanding the rural experience. *American Annals of the Deaf, 146*, 16–30.

Yoshinaga-Itano, C., Sedey, A. L., Coulter, D. K., & Mehl, A. L. (1998). Language of early- and later-identified children with hearing loss. *Pediatrics, 102*, 1161–1171.

Zawolkow, E., & DeFiore, S. (1986). Educational interpreting for elementary- and secondary-level hearing-impaired students. *American Annals of the Deaf, 131*, 26–28.

Index

Figures and tables are indicated by f and t following the page numbers.

academic performance, 3–5, 20–21.
  See also schools; students
adjusting timing of interpretations,
  86, 99–103
aide duties of interpreters, 83
AJ (Via Portal interpreter)
  ASL–English connections, 122–23,
    124, 126–28, 145–46
  background and qualifications,
    37–38, 37*n*8, 58–60,
    58*n*15, 59*t*
  on deliberately omitting
    information, 78, 79
  on independence of students,
    77, 78
  interpreting and transliterating
    methods used by, 65
  language and learning needs
    considered by, 116–17, 122–23,
    124, 126–28, 128*f*
  on participation in classroom, 128,
    129*f*, 131, 132–41, 133*f*
  printed text interpretation
    challenges, 151–53, 155
  on redirecting student attention,
    78–79, 161
  reinforcement and praise
    provided by, 79–80
  on re-interpreting answers to
    maintain efficiency, 74
  resource utilization demonstrated
    by, 65–67
  student interactions, 71
  teacher interactions, 68–70,
    95–96, 161
American Sign Language (ASL)
  English language connections,
    121–23, 124–25, 126–28,
    146–48

interpreter efforts to support student
  development of, 123–28
as natural language, 19*n*5
school policies regarding use of,
  5, 19
visual nature of, 1–2
American Sign Language Teachers
  Association (ASLTA), 59
Angelina (Via Portal student)
  conversations with interpreter, 71
  demographic characteristics, 49, 53,
    54*t*, 55
  independent task completion by,
    77, 78
  language and learning needs of,
    116–17, 122–23, 126–28,
    145–46
  participation in class, 80, 131,
    132–38, 139–41
*Annual Survey of Deaf and Hard of
  Hearing Children and Youth*
  (Gallaudet Research Institute),
  2–3
ASL. *See* American Sign Language
ASLTA (American Sign Language
  Teachers Association), 59
axial coding, 36
Azalea Elementary
  data collection at, 30, 31*t*, 32, 33, 34
  demographic characteristics of,
    29, 52
  hearing student interactions with
    interpreters at, 81
  interpreters, 52. *See also* Marina
    (Azalea interpreter)
  students. *See* Kristie (Azalea student);
    Miguel (Azalea student)
  teachers, 52, 53, 54*t*. *See also*
    Kendall, Mrs.

back-channeling cues, 32

beyond interpreting designation, 40, 41

Bourdieu, P., 21

California Department of Education (CDE). *See also* research study on practices and decisions of K–12 interpreters
on failure of schools to meet needs of Deaf students, 165–66
integration of hearing and Deaf students in, 3
on interpreter qualifications, 16, 17, 57–58
on program standards for Deaf students, 170

Camie (Meadowbrook interpreter)
aide duties performed by, 83
ASL and English, making connections between, 124–25, 146–48
background and qualifications, 58, 58*n*15, 59*t,* 60
competing visual demands, methods used in response to, 87–94, 89–90*f,* 94–95*f,* 96–107, 97–98*f,* 105*f,* 142–43
on deliberately omitting information, 79
health concerns expressed by, 107, 143–44, 149, 150
hearing student interactions, 81–82
on interpreting challenging subject matter, 143–44
language and learning needs considered by, 115, 117, 118–21, 124–25
parent interactions, 80–81
on participation in classroom, 130–31, 141
printed text and read-aloud session challenges, 149–50, 154
on redirecting student attention, 76, 78, 79, 161–62
student interactions, 72, 113–14
teacher interactions, 70, 96, 160–61
tutoring process used by, 118–20, 124–25, 155–56

Cazden, C., 156

CDE. *See* California Department of Education

certification requirements, 9, 9*n*4, 16

children. *See* students

class participation. *See* inclusion and participation in classroom activities

classroom interpreters. *See* interpreters

cochlear implants, 53, 53*n*12

coding practices, 36, 37, 39, 43–44, 44*f,* 175–77

collaboration between interpreters and teachers, 22, 68–70, 80–81, 95–96

communication
gestures and facial expressions used to communicate with hearing students, 55, 57
recognizing intent of, 138–39
school policies of, 4–5

communities of practice, 6*n*2

competing visual demands, 42–47, 84–108
classroom scenario involving, 87–92
coding practices for identification of, 43–44, 44*f*
common sources of, 84, 84*t*
defined, 43, 45, 84
frequency and duration of, 43, 45–46*t,* 45–47, 85
interpreter challenges in managing, 142–43
student challenges in managing, 14–15, 85
techniques for responding to presence of, 85–108
adjusting timing of interpretation, 86, 99–103
directing student attention, 86, 96–99

modifying the interpretation,
47–48, 77–78, 79, 86–87,
103–8
physical position adjustments,
86, 92–96
conversations with interpreters,
70–74, 113–14
Cuculick, J. A., 166
cultural capital theory, 21

Decalage, 13
decision-making practices, 20, 22,
23–25, 160–63. *See also*
research study on practices and
decisions of k–12 interpreters
demographic characteristics of study
participants. *See individual
schools*
Department of Education Department,
U.S., 17
discourse cues, 138–39
Dornbusch, S. M., 21
Dorricott, J., 50–51*f*, 50*n*10

Educational Interpreter Performance
Assessment (EIPA), 9, 16, 17,
57–58, 58*n*14
educational interpreters. *See*
interpreters
Educational Sign Skills Evaluation
(ESSE), 17, 57–58
Education Department, U.S., 17
Education for All Handicapped
Children Act (Public Law
94-142, 1975), 2
EIPA. *See* Educational Interpreter
Performance Assessment
Emily (Meadowbrook student)
competing visual demands dealt
with by, 87–94, 96–98,
99–102, 104–7, 142–43
conversations with interpreter,
72, 113–14
demographic characteristics, 53,
54*t*, 55, 56

hearing student interactions, 55, 82
language and learning needs of,
115, 118–21, 124–25, 144,
147–48
participation in class, 130–31
read-aloud sessions, challenges in,
154
English language
ASL connections with, 121–23,
124–25, 126–28, 146–48
interpreter efforts to support
student development of,
121–23, 125–28
signing systems based on, 19*n*5
ESSE (Educational Sign Skills
Evaluation), 17, 57–58

facial expressions for communicating
with hearing students,
55, 57
fatigue, 143–44, 150, 153
fingerspelling, 121–23, 124, 125,
126–28, 145
free and appropriate public education
(FAPE) mandate, 2

Gallaudet Research Institute, 2–3
Gallaudet University, 50
gestures
for communicating with hearing
students, 55, 57
teacher's gestures incorporated
into interpretations, 88, 90,
91, 105–6, 105*f*
grounded theory, 36

Harrison, Mr. (Meadowbrook
teacher), 52, 56, 70, 80–81,
82, 96
health concerns of interpreters, 107,
143–44, 149, 150, 153
hearing student interactions with
interpreters, 81–83
Heath, S. B., 21
HyperRESEARCH software, 37

IDEA (Individuals with Disabilities Education Improvement Act), 2

inclusion and participation in classroom activities, 128–41
  classroom scenarios involving, 132–38, 158–59, 165
  defined, 165
  discourse cues and communicative intent, recognition of, 138–39
  factors affecting, 13–14, 35, 128
  goals of, 5–6
  interpreter challenges in creating opportunities for, 156–60, 165
  responding directly to students as, 139–41
  strategies used for, 129–32

incoming messages, 13

independence, readiness for, 72–74, 77–78, 113–15

Individualized Education Programs (IEPs), 2

Individuals with Disabilities Education Improvement Act (IDEA, 2004), 2

initiation–response–evaluation/feedback (IRE/IRF) pattern, 79–80, 156

injury concerns, 107, 149, 150, 153

institutional review board (IRB) regulations, 28

interactional decision-making, 160–63

interpreters, 1–25. See also schools; students
  author's experience as, 9–12
  Azalea. See Marina (Azalea interpreter)
  certification requirements for, 9, 9n4, 16
  challenges faced by, 141–63
    interactional decision-making, 160–63
    learning of content and language, 143–48
    participation and inclusion, creating opportunities for, 156–60, 165

printed text and read-aloud sessions, 148–55, 157–60
tutoring effectively, 155–56
visual access concerns, 142–43

collaboration with teachers, 22, 68–70, 80–81, 95–96, 160–61

decision-making practices of, 20, 22, 23–25, 160–63. See also research study on practices and decisions of K–12 interpreters

definition of interpreting, 19, 40

development and training needs for, 169–73

health concerns of, 107, 143–44, 149, 150, 153

impact on school experiences of students, 6–7, 12, 35

interpreter-mediated instruction, advantages and disadvantages of, 21–22, 171–72

legislation requiring presence of, 2–3

Meadowbrook. See Camie (Meadowbrook interpreter)

modifying the interpretation, motivations for, 47–48, 77–78, 79, 86–87, 103–8

preparation and professional development, inadequacy of, 7–9, 16, 22, 166–67, 172

qualification standards for, 2, 15–18, 19, 57–58, 58n14

research study participants, 37–38, 57–62, 59t, 61–62t. See also AJ (Via Portal interpreter); Camie (Meadowbrook interpreter); Marina (Azalea interpreter)

roles and responsibilities of, 1, 7, 9, 22–23, 24, 164. See also scope of practice

Via Portal. See AJ (Via Portal interpreter)

IRE/IRF (initiation–response–evaluation/feedback) pattern, 79–80, 156

Jones, B. E., 18, 22

K–12 interpreters. *See* interpreters; research study on practices and decisions of K–12 interpreters
Karchmer, M. A., 3
Kelly, R. R., 166
Kendall, Mrs. (Azalea teacher), 52, 53, 74–75
Kristie (Azalea student)
conversations with interpreter, 71, 73–74
demographic characteristics, 54*t*, 55, 56–57
independence of, 72, 113
language and learning needs of, 109–10, 111, 113, 114–15
read-aloud sessions, challenges in, 158–59
social interactions of, 160
Kurz, K., 14, 18, 165

La Bue, M., 18
lag time, 13
Lang, H., 20
Langer, E., 14, 18, 165
language and learning needs, 108–28
academic stakes and accountability considerations, 112
ASL development, 123–28
assessments by interpreter of, 47, 108, 115–17
classroom scenario involving, 109–11
educational placement and reading proficiencies, 111
English language development, 121–23, 125–28
independence, readiness for, 113–15
interpreter challenges in managing, 143–48
printed text and read-aloud session considerations, 148–55, 157–60

prior knowledge and new learning, formulating connections between, 120–21
socioemotional well-being and, 113
student preferences in, 111, 112
tutoring, helping, and explaining, 117–20, 155–56
Lave, J., 6*n*2
learning. *See also* language and learning needs
scaffolding approach to, 120–21
social nature of, 20, 21
legislation requiring presence of interpreters, 2–3
linguistic capital, 21
literacy skills, 4, 111. *See also* language and learning needs

mainstreamed Deaf students, 2–3, 5–6
Marina (Azalea interpreter)
aide duties performed by, 149
background and qualifications, 58, 58*n*15, 59*t*, 60–61
hearing student interactions involving, 81, 82*f*
on independence of students, 72–74, 113
interpreting and transliterating methods used by, 65
on interpreting challenging subject matter, 144–45
language and learning needs considered by, 109–13, 114–15, 117–18, 118*f*
on participation in classroom, 130, 138
printed text and read-aloud session challenges, 150–51, 153, 158–59
on redirecting student attention, 75, 162
Marschark, M., 5, 19, 20
Meadowbrook School
data collection at, 30, 31*t*, 32, 33, 34
demographic characteristics of, 29

Meadowbrook School (*continued*)
hearing student interactions with
interpreters at, 81, 82
interpreters, 52, 62, 62*t. See also*
Camie (Meadowbrook
interpreter)
students. *See* Emily (Meadowbrook
student)
teachers, 52, 53, 54*t. See also*
Harrison, Mr.
Mehan, H., 156
mental fatigue, 143–44, 150, 153
Miguel (Azalea student)
demographic characteristics, 53,
54*t*, 55, 57
hearing student interactions, 55, 57
language and learning needs of,
109–11, 112–13, 114, 118
social interactions of, 160
teacher interactions involving, 72
Mitchell, R. E., 3
modifying the interpretation, 47–48,
77–78, 79, 86–87, 103–8
Moores, D. F., 20

NAD-RID National Interpreter
Certification, 9*n*4, 17, 57
National Association of the Deaf
(NAD), 1, 9*n*4, 17, 57
National Interpreting Certificate
(NIC), 9*n*4
National Technical Institute for the
Deaf (NTID), 4, 50, 166

Office of Special Education Programs
(OSEP), 17
omitting information when
interpreting, 78–79
open coding, 36

Palomar College interpreting program,
8, 8*n*3
parents
hearing ability, impact on Deaf
students, 3–4

interactions with interpreters, 80–81
participation in classroom activities.
See inclusion and participation
in classroom activities
physical injury concerns, 107, 149,
150, 153
physical position adjustments, 86, 92–96
placement and reading proficiencies,
111
"popcorn reading" activities, 158–59,
165
printed text interpretations, challenges
of, 148–55
prior knowledge, formulating
connections with new
knowledge, 120–21
processing time, 13
Public Law 94-142 (Education for All
Handicapped Children Act,
1975), 2

qualification standards, 2, 15–18, 19,
57–58, 58*n*14

read-aloud sessions, challenges of,
153–55, 157–60
reading proficiencies, 111
Registry of Interpreters for the Deaf
(RID), 8, 9, 9*n*4, 15–16, 57
repetitive motion injuries,
107, 149, 150
research study on practices and decisions
of K–12 interpreters, 26–48
data analysis, 37–42
interview coding, 37
overarching themes from, 41–42,
183–86
video data coding, 39, 175–77
of video elicitation interviews,
38–39
"what and why" category
determination, 39–41, 178–82
framework of study, 34–36
future research needs, 169, 172–73
grounded theory, use of, 36

institutional review board (IRB)
regulations and, 28
interpreter participants, 37–38,
57–62, 59t, 61–62t. *See also* AJ
(Via Portal interpreter); Camie
(Meadowbrook interpreter);
Marina (Azalea interpreter)
limitations of, 167–69
overview, 26–27
primary data collection sources,
29–34, 31t
field observations and
videotaping procedures, 29–33
interview procedures, 30, 33–34
school site and grade level selection,
27–29, 49–53. *See also* Azalea
Elementary; Meadowbrook
School; Via Portal Elementary
scope of practice findings. *See* scope
of practice
student participants, 53–57, 54t.
See also Angelina (Via Portal
student); Emily (Meadowbrook
student); Kristie (Azalea student);
Miguel (Azalea student)
teacher participants, 53, 54t
visual access findings. *See*
competing visual demands
RID. *See* Registry of Interpreters for
the Deaf
RID Views (newsletter), 9
Robinson, W. S., 36
Rochester Institute of Technology
(RIT), 4, 50, 166
roles and responsibilities of
interpreters, 1, 7, 9, 22–23, 24,
164. *See also* scope of practice
Roy, C. B., 35

scaffolding approach to learning,
120–21
Schick, B., 16, 19, 21, 172
schools. *See also* interpreters; students
accessibility of interpreted
educations, 13–15, 35

communication policies within, 4–5
failure to meet needs of Deaf
students, 165–66
interpreter-mediated instruction,
advantages and disadvantages
of, 21–22, 171–72
mainstreaming of Deaf students,
2–3, 5–6
research study sites, 27–29, 49–53.
See also Azalea Elementary;
Meadowbrook School; Via
Portal Elementary
visual access concerns. *See*
competing visual demands
scope of practice, 63–83
aide duties, 83
assessing and responding to
contextual, situational, and
human factors, 64
collaboration with teachers, 22,
68–70, 80–81, 95–96
Deaf student interactions, 70–80
as discourse partner, 73–74
for maintaining efficiency, 74
for promoting independence
and interaction with others,
72–73, 76–78
for redirecting student attention,
74–76, 78–79, 86, 96–99,
161–63
for reinforcement and praise,
79–80
social and personal conversations,
70–72
facilitating language and learning
needs. *See* language and
learning needs
hearing student interactions, 81–83
interpreting and/or transliterating,
64–65
parent and guardian interactions,
80–81
promoting participation. *See*
inclusion and participation in
classroom activities

scope of practice (*continued*)
  resources, obtaining and making
    use of, 65–68
  visual access optimization. *See*
    competing visual demands
Smith, Melissa B., experience as
    elementary school interpreter,
    9–12
social nature of learning, 20, 21
socioemotional well-being, 113
source messages, 13
Spencer, P. E., 19
Stanton-Salazar, R., 21
Stinson, M., 20
students. *See also* interpreters; schools
  academic performance of, 3–5, 20–21
  comprehension level of
    interpretations, 18–20, 22
  cultural and linguistic capital,
    access to, 21
  Deaf student interactions, 70–80
  hearing student interactions with
    interpreters, 81–83
  interpreters, impact on school
    experiences of, 6–7, 12, 35
  language and learning needs. *See*
    language and learning needs
  literacy skills of, 4
  parent's hearing ability, impact on
    development of, 3–4
  participation in class discussions,
    factors influencing, 13–14, 35,
    128. *See also* inclusion and
    participation in classroom
    activities
  research study participants,
    53–57, 54*t*. *See also* Angelina
    (Via Portal student); Emily
    (Meadowbrook student);
    Kristie (Azalea student);
    Miguel (Azalea student)
  social interactions of, 160
  visual access concerns. *See*
    competing visual demands
Studiocode software, 39

Taylor, M. M., 172
teachers. *See also* schools; students
  collaboration with interpreters,
    22, 68–70, 80–81, 95–96,
    160–61
  gestures incorporated into
    interpretations, 88, 90, 91,
    105–6, 105*f*
  research study participants, 53, 54*t*
team interpreters, 149, 152–53
timing delays, 13–14, 86, 99–103,
    106
transliterating
  defined, 5, 19
  scope of practice, 64–65
tutoring, 117–20, 155–56

U.S. Education Department, 17

Veditz, George, 1
Via Portal Elementary
  data collection at, 30, 31*t*, 32,
    33–34
  demographic characteristics of,
    29, 49
  hearing student interactions with
    interpreters at, 81
  interpreters, 49, 51, 61–62, 61*t*.
    See also AJ (Via Portal
    interpreter)
  murals showing opportunities
    for Deaf students at, 49–50,
    50–51*f*
  students. *See* Angelina (Via Portal
    student)
  teachers, 49, 52, 53, 54*t*
video data coding, 39, 175–77
video elicitation interviews, 38–39
videotaping procedures, 29–33
visual access concerns. *See* competing
    visual demands
visual nature of ASL, 1–2

Wenger, E., 6*n*2
Winston, E. A., 13, 14–15, 20, 35